OUT OF THIS WORLD

OUT *of this* WORLD

*Otherworldly Journeys from
Gilgamesh to Albert Einstein*

I. P. COULIANO

Foreword by Lawrence E. Sullivan

SHAMBHALA
Boston & London
1991

Shambhala Publications
Horticultural Hall
300 Massachusetts Avenue
Boston, Massachusetts 02115

Shambhala Publications, Inc.
Random Century House
20 Vauxhall Bridge Road
London SW1V 2SA

9   8   7   6   5   4   3   2   1

First Edition

Printed in the United States of America on acid-free paper
Design by Diane Levy
Distributed in the United States by Random House, Inc.,
in Canada by Random House of Canada Ltd, and
in the United Kingdom by the Random Century Group

Library of Congress Cataloging-in-Publication Data

Culianu, Ioan P.
    Out of this world: otherworldly journeys from Gilgamesh to Albert
Einstein/I. P. Couliano.—1st ed.
        p.   cm.
    Includes index.
    ISBN 0-87773-488-7 (pbk.: alk. paper)
        1. Journeys to the otherworld—History.   2. Astral projection—
History .   3. Altered states of consciousness—History.   I. Title.
BL540.C84   1990   90-52800
291.4'2—dc20   CIP

Contents

      from Plotinus to Marsilio Ficino   188

11   The Apogee of Otherworldly Journeys: *From Muhammad*
      to Dante   212

      Conclusion   232

      Notes   236

      Index   267

Foreword

Let all who enter here know: they are in for a tour of heaven and hell. In fact, here begin many brief, outlandish tours of heavens, hells, paradises, purgatories, limbos, labyrinths, holding stations, inner realms, and outer worlds. Ioan Couliano does not saunter; he moves at the brisk pace of someone familiar with the rooms with their furnishings through which he threads his way. If these other worlds are not his home, they at least prove to be the work places to which he often commutes. He has labored with materials from many periods and cultures in which he is not always a specialist and takes the important risk of presenting these world views in a comparative perspective.

Ioan Couliano does specialize in creating startling juxtapositions. He casts historical materials together in a way that illuminates the nature of their differences and raises questions about the common human capacities for envisioning space-time dimensions and traveling through them. He intentionally conjoins science and literature, ethnography and philosophy, history and system. He examines side by side the normally separate genres of fiction and factual science, and disparate figures like Bohr and Borges, Einstein and Gilgamesh.

This cannot be done seriously without wry wit and irony. Readers will be delighted to discover that Couliano is equal to the task. Some of the matches he makes are as completely fantastic as they are thought provoking. He is not beyond teasing the reader with enigmatic juxtapositions intended to introduce doubts and ambiguities. An ironic treatment of other-world journeys seems to befit a Dutch citizen, born and raised in Romania, a graduate of Italian and French universities, who teaches in the United States.

Ioan Couliano transcends the serial depiction of particular scenarios that stand out in world history. He travels beyond singular descriptions to wonder about them as a whole. In fact, he calls this study "a history of otherworldly journeys." Such a general history and the questions it raises should sharpen subsequent inquiry into specific cases and illumine their meaning.

Couliano brings to light an observation that hides in plain sight: the living, who seldom reside in these other worlds, pay inordinate attention to the details of these places in which they do not precisely belong. Perhaps cultural studies like anthropology, comparative literature, and the history of religions are also examples of this fascination with what is alien; and physics, math, and science fiction are driven by the same desire to fathom the outer, unknown growing-edges beyond the immediate world in which we live. "There will always be a dimension that leads to the unknown," writes Couliano—be it the one of myth, of the fourth dimension, or of the nth dimension. The horizon of the unknown moves outward with the horizon of knowledge.

What role do speculations about other worlds play in the history of culture and in the creative process of the imagination? We the living have come to know and preserve a great deal of information about these worlds, which are complex in design, elaborately outfitted, and densely populated by diverse beings who are "out of this world." Couliano goes so far as to state that "no ancient otherworldly beliefs have been com-

pletely abandoned." If, in the late eighteenth and nineteenth
centuries, physics and mathematics called us to abandon many
otherworldly beliefs as incompatible with the nature of the
material universe, Couliano seems to ask us to think again.

The Irish philosopher, mathematician, and bishop, George
Berkeley, wrote about the way people perceive the world in
his *Essay Towards a New Theory of Vision* (1709). One year later, in
his *Principles of Human Knowledge,* he examined the links among
world-structures, perception, and the nature of being. "Some
truths there are so near and obvious to the mind, that a man
need only open his eyes to see them. Such I take this important
one to be, to wit, that all of the choir of heaven and furniture
of the earth, in a word all those bodies which compose the
mighty frame of the world, have not any substance without a
mind, that their being is to be perceived or known." Thus far,
one could imagine Ioan Couliano agreeing with George
Berkeley.

Berkeley went even further. He denied the existence of
absolute space or time or motion—ideas that were winning a
hearing with the championship of Sir Isaac Newton. On
mathematical and philosophical grounds, Berkeley argued that
all motion is relative. His rejection of Newtonian physics in *De
motu* (1721) prefigures the arguments of Ernst Mach and Albert
Einstein on the one hand, and process philosophy on the
other. Couliano also seems to emphasize relativity in his study
of the perceptions of space. Like Berkeley, he presents materials that throw into question even the primary qualities of
existence, such as solidity and extension. Regarding all possible
spaces and the objects in them, Couliano might find affinities
with Berkeley: their *esse* is *percipi,* their being is to be perceived.
The world of all appearances, then, is the fabric woven on the
loom of perceptions.

Viewed within the debates concerning perceived and apparent worlds, *Out of This World* provides an opportunity to

evaluate Couliano's provocative proposal that historical disciplines should take cognitive transmission as their model for the diffusion of cultural ideas and symbolic behaviors. "We envision cognitive transmission as an active rethinking of tradition out of a simple set of rules. . . . [Such] participation in tradition by every single individual explains very well the tenacity of certain beliefs and practices." Just as Berkeley assured us that there is "no substance without a mind," Couliano fuses tradition and thought in an axiom worthy of Giambattista Vico: *traditio* is *percipi.* "For every individual thinks part of a tradition and therefore is thought by it; and in the process one obtains the cognitive self-assuredness that what is thought is experienced and whatever is experienced feeds back on what is thought. This complex process of interaction among human minds allows us to perceive in some beliefs many of us still share, obscure roots which go back . . . toward the dawn of *homo sapiens.*"

In his own day, Berkeley was forced to conclude that the material world is an illusion and an unnecessary duplication or abstraction that is inconceivable, intangible, and invisible—in short, a world superfluous to the world. In Berkeley's view, there could be no pain that no one feels, no sound that no one hears, no taste that no one savors, no color that no one sees. Perceptions make up the external world. There is no world other than the one that perceptive beings experience.

But Berkeley imagined *one* world imbued from within with *one* set of senses—the human set—and, more importantly, presided over from without by the *unique* set of divine perceptions of God, that infinite perceiver or spectator whose very spectacular character lends cohesion and continuity to the world. Here Couliano differs from Berkeley. Couliano's notion of cognitive transmission seems designed to deal with multifaceted traditions and with the clash of the *many* traditional worlds imagined throughout history.

Drawing concepts of matter from modern physics and math—concepts unavailable to Berkeley—Couliano confronts us anew with decisions about the nature and relationship of matter, space, time, and mind. In this world of ours, unlike the world of Berkeley, matter need not be reasoned away, as Berkeley tried to do. Matter has already been relativized—even evacuated—by subatomic physics, on the one side, and pluridimensional cosmological theory, on the other. From the viewpoint of contemporary science, matter may be largely empty, vacuous; and perception may be a component of its physical state. The world of Albert Einstein, Werner Heisenberg, and Rudy Rucker is not the one of George Berkeley. Today matter gives way to perception without disappearing totally from the scene.

By introducing contemporary and fluid concepts of space and time, Couliano returns us to that moment in the argument before David Hume glossed Berkeley. We are used to reading Berkeley's dissolution of matter and space through intervening lenses. Schopenhauer's dualism ("the world in the head" versus "the world outside the head") recast Berkeley's unity of brain and mind. And where Berkeley had sought to dissolve matter into spirit, David Hume dissolved the spirit into the chaotic labyrinth of time, in which the mind itself became a theater constituted by the temporal succession of perceived appearances on the stage of awareness.

Couliano's presentation of Egyptian afterlife journeys, Chinese ghosts, Iranian ecstasy, Greek medicine, and Jewish mysticism makes us rethink those debates about mind, matter, and appearances that have gone on from the time of Berkeley down to our own time—the time of our own "facts" about physics, math, perception, and the conventions of thought. Couliano's aim is to have us realize—literally to make real—other possibilities. By altering our historically received perceptions of space, time, and matter, we will find ourselves living creatively in an alternate world or, better, in other worlds.

For Couliano, the multiplicity of worlds seems to be an epistemological necessity, a function of the way the mind works in space. The mind functions, after all, within the space created within the mind. The relationship of mind and space is, therefore, inherently paradoxical and open to many ever-unfolding historical solutions. But no solution can be final. However advanced our knowledge of the surrounding world, the space of the inner mind expands beyond it. That is why, in his view, "there is no end to our imagining more space." We imagine more dimensions than the physical universe furnishes. At stake is the nature of imagination, the character of images, and the function of symbols in shaping reality.

Couliano draws freely on the discoveries of cybernetics, physics, literary theory, psychoanalysis, cognitive theory, neurophysiology, mathematics, ethnography, and epistemology. Some of these disciplines are, indeed, "other worlds" for the field of religious studies. Couliano turns to these sciences because he is fascinated with the possible patterned predictability of thought itself—from which texts and historical traditions might emerge. He investigates this possibility in extended case studies. He examines, for instance, the *Purgatory of Saint Patrick,* a twelfth-century work associated with the extraordinary cave at Lough Derg where Christ appeared to Saint Patrick. The cave has inspired visions for a thousand years of recorded history. Couliano analyzes not only the apocalyptic content of these visions but the patterned analogues of the cave's space (e.g., in buildings and cities) as well as of the spaces revealed in the visions suffered out in the cave. He then juxtaposes these accounts with other twelfth and thirteenth-century visions of space, such as *The Vision of Thurkill, The Vision of Tundal,* the vision of the thirteenth-century German peasant Gottschalk, and the *Divine Comedy.*

Using these and other cases, he puts forward a cognitive hypothesis: that cultural traditions are the outcome of a limited set of simple rules, such as "There is another world"; "The other world is located in heaven"; "There is body and soul"; and "The body dies, the soul goes to the other world." Couliano has set forward parts of his case in other writings on gnosticism, flights of ecstasy, and Renaissance magic. He has expanded and embellished his argument in short pieces of fiction. Across a countably infinite period of time, Couliano seems to argue, such rules produce similar results in the minds of human beings. By thus turning historicism on its head, does he imply the existence of a universal system of mind that governs perception and interferes with the physical world? After all, he points out, worlds can be adequately perceived (only?) from dimensions that do not exist within them. For example, it is easier to perceive the properties of a two-dimensional world if one is cognizant of one's own existence in a three-dimensional one.

To make his point, Couliano treats us to some fascinating thought experiments and invites us to inhabit not only the experimental universes of religious visionaries but also those of mathematical puzzles and poetic utopias. What might it be like to live in Flatland, for example, a land of only two dimensions, where the Great Wall of China is composed of the same thin, flat line as the body's skin? We would have to eat and excrete through the same orifice, lest we simply become two disjointed halves.

The worlds of psychoanalysis, apocalyptic prophesy, atomic science, science fiction, and poetic fancy are fused into one narrative in *Out of This World*. From somewhere beyond the text, the reader is asked to look upon journeys into other worlds as examples of a single literary genre or perhaps even a single, multidimensional project of the mind. Moreover, their fusion in the text is presented as having grounds in human history, or at least in the structures of human consciousness: there is a suggestion that none of these worlds would be possible without the historical existence of shamanism. Couliano is betting that, on several grounds, it can be demonstrated that cultural creations have been held unjustifiably distant from one another: the imaginings of pure math and physics, the myths of ancient peoples, and the poetry, utopias, ecstasies, visions, and dreams of historically scattered humankind. The union of these creative traditions may fertilize our own world view.

Readers will be prodded by the general conclusions Couliano draws from time to time throughout the book and by the summary analyses at the end. His interpretations, like the directions of a psychopomp, blaze markings along an uncharted course through the general history of other-world journeys. Couliano sets out to guide the perplexed reader's imagination as it descends through ancient netherworlds, strays through medieval Erewhons, or soars through edenic paradises.

Lawrence E. Sullivan
Director, Center for the Study of World Religions, Harvard University

Acknowledgments

This book comes as a continuation of two others and of a great many articles and reviews published between 1974 and 1986. In these rather specialistic studies I dealt at length with the history of otherworldly journeys in Western religious traditions, without undertaking a serious analysis of other traditions. A few years ago, I realized that a general history of otherworldly journeys should be written, for there is no other way to assess the possible unity in their variety.

Two courses I gave at the University of Chicago in 1988 and 1989 helped me to organize and largely write this book. I would like to thank all the students who attended my classes on "Religion and Science: The Fourth Dimension" and "Otherworldly Journeys in Religion and Literature." During one meeting of the latter, Anthony Yu discussed with us *The Journey to the West*, one of the texts briefly mentioned in the sixth chapter of this book.

Some of the materials collected by me for this book have also served in the redaction of the editorial of the first issue of the journal *Incognita*, published by E. J. Brill in Leiden. I have also lectured on the relation between dimensions of space and otherworldly journeys at the invitation of the Psychology and Religion Group at the University of Chicago; and on Iranian otherworldly journeys at the invitation of Professor Adela

Yarbro Collins of Notre Dame University, Indiana, in her seminar on apocalyptic texts (February 1990).

Over the years, I have received much help from colleagues engaged in research on apocalyptic literature and mysticism. I would like to thank here in particular John Collins and Adela Yarbro Collins, Allan Segal, Florentino Garcia Martinez, Michael Stone, Hans Kippenberg, Ithamar Gruenwald, Carol Zaleski, and Moshe Idel, who disclosed new perspectives in the study of Kabbalah. Lawrence Sullivan's wonderful *Icanchu's Drum* has detailed some shamanistic techniques in South America. All in all, my survey of shamanism remains extremely brief.

None of my works since 1987 could have come into being without the support of Hillary Suzanne Wiesner. She edited this book and helped me revise it on crucial points. All remaining shortcomings are entirely my responsibility.

Introduction

According to a series of Gallup polls, 94 percent of Americans believe in God, 67 percent believe in life after death, 71 percent believe in heaven (as compared to only 53 percent who believe in hell), 29 percent report having had an actual glimpse of heaven, 23 percent believe in reincarnation, 46 percent believe in intelligent life on other planets, 24 percent believe that it is possible to have contact with the dead, over 50 percent believe in extrasensory perception, and 15 percent report having had near-death experiences.[1] The only possible conclusion one can draw is that anyone opening this book falls into one or more of these categories. It is therefore my hope that one would not close it without enriching one's current perspective on these matters. The aim of this book is to provide a short yet comprehensive cross-cultural historical survey of journeys to other worlds (including heaven, hell, other planets, and much more), of otherworldly visions and other altered states of consciousness (ASC), as well as of reports of out-of-body experiences (OBE) and near-death experiences (NDE). And, without fostering the misplaced ambition of giving all these phenomena an "explanation," this book will nonetheless endeavor to assess how people in different temporal and geographical settings would themselves explain their experiences.

The most ancient documents of humankind and the study of its most "primitive" cultures, that is, cultures of hunters and gatherers using rudimentary technologies, both show that visits to other worlds were top priorities on the agendas of early human beings. Faced with the wealth of materials concerning otherworldly journeys and visions from the dawn of civilization until now, both the historian and the epistemologist ask the same question: Where did those people who pretended to travel to another world actually go? Yet the answers expected by each diverge widely.

The historian gathers documentation, written or not, and tries to describe within the cultural setting all other worlds people claim to have explored. Most of this book, with the exception of the first chapter and the conclusions, contains such descriptions.

The epistemologist uses the material gathered by the historian in order to examine the truth of the claims of all these otherworldly explorers. In other words, the question asked by the epistemologist could be rephrased as follows: What is the reality of these worlds that countless people pretend to have visited? Are they parts of our physical universe? Are they parallel universes? Are they mental universes? And, in all these cases, how was access to them obtained?

As will soon become apparent, the widest possible spectrum of ways and modalities of access to other worlds presents itself in the reports, and their interpretations vary greatly. While the witch might claim that she was riding her broomstick and landed at the Sabbath, the observer peeping through the keyhole to ascertain what was going on (such reports exist from the fifteenth century) might see her lying on her bed in an agitated sleep, and the skeptical commissioner of the Inquisition or the representative of natural magic might explain her vision as an ASC resulting from cutaneous absorption of a hallucinogen.[2]

Historically, the most common explanations given by other-world explorers concerning the location of the landscapes they visited were either that those places belong to our physical universe or that they are part of a parallel universe. It was the role of religion to provide full descriptions of such parallel universes. Early philosophy was born from the rationalization of such endeavors. From ancient to present times, dead people and ecstatics have commonly been thought to experience an afterlife. While the dead may return to tell what the afterlife looks like, most often "windows on the afterlife," as George Gallup, Jr., calls them, are obtained by people who live to tell what they have seen as a result of physical accidents, childbirth, surgical operations and other illnesses involving drugs or anaesthesia, sudden illness outside a hospital, criminal assaults, and "religious visions, dreams, premonitions and other spiritual experiences."[3]

The common denominator of the many psychological approaches to the problem of otherworldly journeys and visions is that all of them agree on one fact, and probably on one fact only: that the explored universes are mental universes. In other words, their reality is in the mind of the explorer. Unfortunately, no psychological approach seems able to provide sufficient insight into what the mind really is, and especially into what and where the space of the mind is. Cognitive science, which is young, is striving to obtain some answers to these basic questions. The location and properties of our "mind space" are probably the most challenging riddles human beings have been confronted with since ancient times; and, after two dark centuries of positivism have tried to explain them away as fictitious, they have come back more powerfully than ever before with the dawn of cybernetics and computers.

For more than one reason, as will shortly become apparent in chapter one, we are entitled to believe that our mind space has amazing properties, the most remarkable of which is that it is not limited to three dimensions like the physical universe surrounding us. Obviously, when we go inside our mind space (which is infinite, for there is no end to our imagining more space), we do not really know where we go. Inside our mind there is no place where dreams and ASC could not take us, yet psychologists say that what we experience is intimately connected either with our individual experience, or with what was already present in our mind at the time of our birth. All explanations—be they in terms of repression of personal sexual desires and impulses or in terms of the collective unconscious—are controversial because they are based on untestable hypotheses, and ultimately they are inadequate, for they completely ignore the question of what mind *is*. All the vague talk about "unconscious" and "psyche" that psycho-analysis has given us is the modern equivalent of shamanic performances or the witch's trip through the air on a broom-stick. In all such cases we are dealing with procedures and professional interpretations that are valid only as long as we share the premises of the shaman or the witch. Yet the universal validity of their explanations is highly questionable. We cannot actually understand, for example, what dreams are, if we cannot answer such basic questions as where dreams and visions take place, what dreams are made of, and the like.

Even if we describe our mind space with all its strange "mind stuff" as a complete universe existing in parallel with the world perceived as being outside us, the two of them are still dependent on each other to various degrees: the outside world could not exist without the mental universe that perceives it, and this mental universe in turn borrows its images from perceptions. Thus at least the scenery and script of the mental universe depend on actual structures of percep-tion. The inner world of a bee is completely different from the inner world of a dolphin or from the inner world of a human being, since the perceptive apparatus of each is different, as are the internal impulses of each in response to the perception of the outer world. For example, although snakes can barely see, they scan the outer world through a temperature detector, while frogs have a rudimentary pattern of reaction to stimuli that basically consists of eating whatever is smaller than them, copulating with whatever is the same size, and fleeing from whatever is larger. The inner universe of a snake or a frog is so unfamiliar to us that we scarcely can imagine it, even with the wildest effort. Yet in all these cases a correlation between the inner world and the outer world exists.

Today we take for granted that only mentally ill people (usually those called schizophrenic) and perhaps young children are not able to make a clear distinction between the inner and the outer world. Yet the relation between the two has puzzled all serious Western thinkers not only since Descartes, but even since Plato and Aristotle. Many of them have admitted that the outer world is a construct of our perception, and is thus deprived of "objectivity." What we call the objective universe is in reality a convention created by human mechanisms of perception: the objective world of a snake or a frog looks entirely different from ours. Thus, the world outside us and the world inside us are not truly parallel, for not only do they interfere with each other in many ways, but we cannot even be sure where one of them ceases to be and the other commences. Does this mean that they may actually share space? (Unless we want to raise new mind-boggling questions, we should carefully refrain from defining here what space is believed to be.)

According to the cognitive viewpoint adopted here, the belief of the inhabitants of the Cook Islands that the other world is right under the island and its entrance is a cave (a view substantially shared by many peoples of various cultures who think they can point out the entrance to the netherworld) is less infantile than it appears.[4] Is this belief just a matter of interference between inner and outer world? Psychoanalysts talk about the projection of mental images and assumptions on the outer world. But what then is this outer world if not a convention that varies according to the perception, mood, sex, social position, and even stature of the observer? The optimist and the pessimist see the same glass as either half full or half empty; the philosopher Wittgenstein would say that they do not live in the same world. The same is true of all of us: for each one of us, not only the inner, but also the outer world looks entirely different.

We have now entertained a number of questions that the epistemologist would raise in order to assess the reality of otherworldly journeys and visions. We cannot go further without exceeding the competence of the historian. Yet this survey, however short and inconclusive, has been sufficient to show how complex the whole matter is, and how ill-prepared we still are to fully understand our mind world.

Reverting to the domain of the historian, we should emphasize the universality in time and space of the experience of otherworldly journeys and visions. The word "universal" has been subjected to sharp criticism in anthropology by those who still believe induction to be the only valid method in science. Yet the phenomenon we are dealing with is so widespread that we certainly are entitled to call it universal. After all, it is inherent in the human mind to take trips in its own space, and it is also inherent in our modality of being to have constant interference between the inner and outer worlds. Some of the journeys therefore are reported to take place bodily, some of them "in spirit," and some of them—like the apostle Paul's to heaven (2 Cor. 12: 2–4)—in an unknown way. Some, perhaps most of them, lead to the realm of the dead or to part of it, and some to new worlds, while some disclose overlapping, invisible worlds. Some are in space, some are in time, and some are in both. They can be obtained either by a quest or by a call. The shaman who goes on an otherworldly trip to cure a sick person, the witch who goes to Sabbath, the ecstatic who goes to a famous incubation place in order to have visions, the necromancer who conjures up the realm of the dead, the man or woman who alters his or her state of consciousness by using psychedelic substances or other procedures, the performer of OBE who can control the process of "leaving the body"—all these carry out a quest for their journey or vision and obtain it through means that are within reach. In contrast, the person who is the victim of an accident, or who receives a special yet cumbersome and unexpected ecstatic vocation leading to visions, has a particular call that is by no means the result of a quest, and can even be quite contrary to the world view and the social and mental habits of the recipient.

If on the one hand otherworldly journeys should not be too lightly dismissed as being mere products of imagination, on the other they can undeniably be envisioned as a literary genre. This does not necessarily mean that they belong to the realm of pure fiction. Intertextuality is a widespread phenomenon that can be in part explained by our mental tendency to cast every new experience in old expressive molds. Dreams themselves, or rather what we remember of them, are the product of an interpretive attempt based on known quantities, past dreams, guesses, fears, and hopes. The visions are more complex, in that their recipient is usually acquainted with literary precedents, and if not soon becomes so with the help of others. Here intertextuality can, mostly unconsciously, interfere with the original version to the point that the visionary is convinced that his or her experience falls into an ancient and venerable pattern illustrated by many other visionaries. And indeed, there is a vast mystical literature, Jewish, Christian, and Islamic, in which there are only a few variations on a basic theme.[5] This by no means implies that at least some of the visions are not authentic; it simply shows to what extent intertextuality operates.

Intertextuality means "transmission" in a very complex way. All previous experiences seem to converge and deeply influence what we believe to be a new, fresh experience. This convergence mainly happens below the threshold of consciousness, and it presupposes a mental synthesis of many elements, an active processing of the new occurrence that is not the mere repetition of anything past. In history, transmission is usually viewed as a process in which someone reads and rereads a text and then repeats it to others, often in a distorted way. In reality things are far from being so simple. Sometimes texts never show up in the transmission of ideas, even if they exist; sometimes a general hermeneutical principle is casually or furtively passed on to someone else, who then produces texts according to this rule, and not according to any previous text, which is in fact unknown to him or her. Yet the final result in each case can be very close to texts that circulate in the community of the original transmitters. Historians therefore conclude that transmission is based on texts. They would be surprised to find out that the explanation is a simpler one, unexplored by their methods: people think, and if they have a pattern for their thinking, they produce thoughts predictable from the outset. In many of the cases that form the object of our analysis, transmission took place without actual circulation of texts; "intertextuality" is thus a mental phenomenon, and concerns "texts" sometimes written but usually unwritten.

Yet, with the help of ethnosemiotics, we can establish that human beings had beliefs concerning other worlds long before they could write. Ethnosemiotics analyzes systems of signs without regard to their time setting. It can thus establish— and as a matter of fact it has—that Paleosiberian cave paintings already show all the traits of a developed shamanistic complex as we still find them displayed by some Siberian shamans. To speak about texts under these circumstances would be preposterous. Beliefs about other worlds and patterns of otherworldly journeys were surely transmitted along the lines of cultural tradition. The Italian scholar Carlo Ginzburg (see chapter 2, below), who studied European witchcraft for twenty-five years, came to the conclusion that witchcraft was still practiced in certain zones of eastern Europe at the end of the nineteenth century as a direct derivative of shamanism. Beliefs recorded in Paleosiberian caves around 1000 B.C.E. were still valid less than a hundred years ago. How can we explain such amazing continuity?

Explanations such as genetic transmission or the unhelpfully vague affirmation that some collective unconscious lies behind our individual psyche have no cognitive basis. The best possible explanation remains that of cultural tradition, which is, as we have seen, complex and not dependent on complete transmission of sets of ideas. In other words, the cognitive assumption of this book is that a simple set of rules would generate similar results in the minds of human beings for a virtually infinite period of time. Such rules could be, for example: "There is another world; the other world is located in heaven; there is body and soul; the body dies, and the soul goes to the other world," and so on. Almost all the individual traditions shown in detail in the following chapters are based on such sets of rules, and these sets are similar to each other to a greater or lesser degree. In many cases we can establish that the rules show such dependence upon shamanism that they are probably derivatives thereof.

In some cases, tradition and innovation can be followed very closely. One such case is the Platonic tradition, based both on the transmission of texts (Plato's dialogues) and on popular beliefs. A Middle Platonist like Plutarch of Chaeronea (ca. 50–120 C.E.) adheres to the received data but reinterprets them according to a more sophisticated scientific hermeneutics.

Later, among the late Neoplatonists, we see a new reinterpretation that goes along the lines of a keen interest in mysticism. Accordingly, Neoplatonism tries to establish very precise sets of rules to describe the structure of other worlds and their inhabitants, as well as the way the human soul can gain access to these worlds.

Cognitive transmission is historical; yet it presupposes constant rethinking of old beliefs, and therefore constant failures of memory, deletion, and innovation. In many cases, philosophy is nothing but a systematic attempt to think out the implications of a set of rules. Thus, Platonism for example tries to settle all sorts of controversies that arise from the exploration of a problem. Platonists try to describe all categories of heavenly beings and answer the question of metensomatosis, or the transmigration of the soul from body to body. Obviously, many sets of answers are possible, and the debate can be cut short only by assuming a position of authority. (As in the case of most if not all metaphysical questions, we cannot find hard proof that parts of the human soul can reincarnate in plants or animals, but we have no evidence to the contrary either.)

Recourse to direct experience or encounter authoritatively legitimates a belief. This is why reports of otherworldly journeys abound in many traditions of humankind: confronted with the revelation provided by a venerable character from the past, we tend to accept its truth without question. (For example, the Freudian tradition is based on a set of quite arbitrary and unverifiable assumptions that amount to a revelation about the reasons for the lack of human happiness, and this tradition was vital for a long time, even if it is shaky today.) The quest for legitimacy explains the proliferation of apocryphal apocalypses, or secret revelations, during the Hellenistic period.

To collect all historical documents referring to otherworldly

journeys is a gigantic task, a task that has never been undertaken before. We have chosen to present all traditions geo-
graphically and chronologically, beginning with a chapter that
addresses recent interest in our topic. We leave it to the reader
to assess the profound similarities among different traditions,
as well as the overwhelming importance of shamanism in
shaping the general rules of otherworldly journeys until recent
times. We do not claim to have solved all problems of
transmission, yet we claim that cognitive transmission as it has
been delineated in this introduction is the most flexible model
of diffusion devised so far in historical disciplines. Suffice it to
repeat here that we envision cognitive transmission as an active
rethinking of tradition based on a simple set of rules, and that
such participation in tradition by every single individual explains very well the tenacity of certain beliefs and practices.
For every individual thinks part of a tradition and therefore is
thought by it; and in the process the individual obtains the
cognitive self-assuredness that what is thought is experienced,
and whatever is experienced also has an effect on what is
thought. This complex process of interaction among human
minds allows us to perceive in beliefs that many of us still
share obscure roots going back to the Palaeolithic age and
perhaps even beyond, toward the dawn of *Homo sapiens*. Otherworldly journeys seem to belong to this class of beliefs in
that they are among the most tenacious traditions of
humankind.

1

A Historian's Kit for the Fourth Dimension

For those who believe religious experience to belong to the past, the recent interest in altered states of consciousness (ASC), out-of-body experiences (OBE), and near-death experiences (NDE) remains unexplained. Psychoanalysis has carried out the work of the Enlightenment to the point that the ways of the psyche have seemed to yield all their trivial mysteries; under the scrutiny of psychology, visions and otherworldly trips appear to be shameful infantile dreams and the imaginary fulfillment of desire.

Why have cases of NDE and OBE proliferated? Curiously enough, a confirmation of the possibility—theoretical rather than practical—of otherworldly journeys has come not from psychological disciplines, but from hard science. Physics and mathematics are to be held responsible to a large extent for the return of interest in mystical ways of knowledge. They have opened up new perspectives by asserting that this visible universe is only a convention based on our perception, and that wonderful, unimagined worlds are hidden in tiny particles and perhaps even in the familiar space surrounding us. The history of the discoveries that led to the hypothesis of superior worlds is the topic of this chapter.

"In the first place, we imagine an existence in two-dimensional space. Flat beings with flat implements . . . are free to move in a *plane*. For them nothing exists outside of this plane: that which they observe to happen to themselves and to their flat 'things' is the all-inclusive reality of their plane. . . ."[1]

Written by Albert Einstein in 1916, this attempt to describe verbally the higher dimensions through analogy *(Special and General Relativity, for the General Public)* must certainly have had a different effect among his contemporaries than it has when read now, a relatively long time later.[2] References that were current at the turn of the century are lost today, and the mathematics of hope have changed. For it was a simple mathematical reasoning made toward the middle of the nineteenth century that must be held to a large extent responsible for the most electrifying hopes of humankind in the first decades of the twentieth century. It would be impossible to understand Einstein's general theory of relativity without mentioning its general intellectual context, in which science was inextricably mixed with dream, fiction, and vision. What a few visionaries of the fourth dimension contributed to science still remains to be assessed.[3]

Theirs was an insidious job, which slowly effected a complete change in our views of the universe. No one grasped the profound meaning of the fictitious fourth dimension taking over the earth better than Jorge Luís Borges. The symbolic story of this unclamorous and subtle conquest is masterfully narrated in his "Tlön, Uqbar, Orbis Tertius."[4]

In this story, an article about the unheard-of country of Uqbar appears in the forty-sixth volume of a pirated reprint of *The Anglo-American Cyclopedia,* and in September 1937 Borges, the narrator, inherits from the engineer Herbert Ashe, who has died of an aneurysm in a small hotel in Adrogué, a far more important piece of evidence: the eleventh volume of the *First Encyclopedia of Tlön.* In the story, Ashe was a mathematician, and his main business was to transcribe duodecimal tables into sexagesimal. It is interesting to note that both of his chosen subjects have something in common: they are different from the decimal tables, which are deeply rooted in convention. Transcribing from duodecimals into sexagesimals means playing with new conventions in such a way as to remove the old conventions, or at any rate to reveal their purely conventional character. That is, it dramatically alters ordinary consciousness.

As historical background for this story, it should be mentioned here that during the second decade of the seventeenth century a group of German Protestant gentlemen from the Palatinate headed by Johann Valentin Andreae faked a secret society called the Brotherhood of the Rose Cross, with the intention of leading humankind to incredible spiritual and technological achievements. This invention proved more thought-provoking than anything else; still, several scholars seriously believe that it accelerated if not produced major advances in epistemology credited to the seventeenth century, establishing the goals of scientific endeavor for centuries to come.[5]

To return to Borges' story, the Tlön Uqbar enterprise (whose name was Orbis Tertius) consists of the creation of a fictitious planet, with its own physics, geography, history, races, and languages, by a group of three hundred dedicated visionaries; the project is founded and financed by the ascetic millionaire Ezra Buckley in 1824 and is completed in 1914. In March 1941, the narrator finds a letter in a volume of Charles Howard Hinton that belonged to Herbert Ashe, and this letter reveals the forgery. Yet this is not the end of the story. In 1942, an object inscribed with the alphabet of Tlön shows up in the apartment of the princess of Faucigny Lucinge; some months afterward, a disturbing accident occurs in Brazil—a dying man spills from his belt a cone made of a metal whose density highly exceeds that of any stable element on earth. In 1944, finally, all forty volumes of the *First Encyclopedia of Tlön* are discovered in a library in Memphis, Tennessee. After that, "reality gave ground on more than one point. The truth is that it hankered to give ground." Tlön takes over, and the earth *becomes* Tlön.

In Borges' own view, this fictitious ideological conspiracy, which takes on the traits of an artificial totalitarian takeover, has to do with the negative fascination human beings have with any system which gives the appearance of order, such as dialectical materialism, anti-Semitism, or Nazism. We could also read this story in a different way. It is true that a new world view has in fact surreptitiously taken over, a world view propounded by relativity and quantum physicists, mathematicians, biologists, and even historians. The language spoken by all these people is highly speculative and artificial. Its meaning, if understood, would suffice to bring to despair the most convinced hedonist. It speaks about the universe as the work of an illusionist, and our minds as creating the illusion.

The two conspiracies, the fictitious one imagined by Borges and the actual one that developed naturally, have one key character in common, who is seldom if ever mentioned in histories of Western civilization: Charles Howard Hinton. Born in 1853, Hinton had a rather extraordinary father, the essayist James Hinton, a committed philanthropist, altruist, and feminist. This may explain why the younger Hinton, who possessed the same powerful combination of characteristics, was not content in 1877 simply to marry Mary Boole, one of the daughters of the famous logician Boole, but also in 1885 married a certain Maude Weldon, who bore him twins. Arrested for bigamy, he lost his job as science master at the Uppingham School and started a wandering life that took him to Japan and the United States. He is credited with having invented the automatic baseball pitcher before having been fired as an instructor in mathematics at Princeton. His life ended abruptly in Washington, D.C., in 1907, in the middle of a toast to "female philosophers" at the Society of Philanthropic Inquiry; according to the obituary in the *Washington Post* (May 1), he literally "dropped dead."[6]

Hinton's first article on the fourth dimension was published in 1880. Relevant to the same topic are his nine stories, *Scientific Romances* (1884–86), his basic *A New Era of Thought* (1888), and his mind-boggling *The Fourth Dimension* (1904). This last volume must have been relatively popular, for a second edition was issued in 1906 and it was reprinted in 1912 and 1921.[7] The publisher (Swann Sonnenschein of London) sold *A New Era of Thought* with a set of eighty-one colored cubes that would enable one to think four-dimensionally. Borges (who was born in 1899) played with them as a child in his uncle's house. It is possible that young Albert Einstein (who was born in 1879) learned about Hinton from his erudite friend Max Talmud, who visited him in Munich from 1889 to 1894.[8] Later in his life, Einstein was painfully aware of the mathematician's dilemma about whether every mathematical construct is interpretable in physical terms or not, and he did not hesitate to call himself, to some extent, "a Platonist or a Pythagorean."[9]

The fourth dimension is easily accessed through elementary mathematics, yet its implications are quite extraordinary. If a quantity y is the expression of the size of a one-dimensional line, y^2 is the expression of the surface of a two-dimensional square, and y^3 is the expression of a three-dimensional cube, then what does y^4 stand for? (For that matter, what does any power of y larger than 3 stand for?) Mathematically, y^4 stands for a four-dimensional object, called a hypercube or tesseract. Moreover, it is quite possible, although not easy, to conceive of four-dimensional objects and their mathematical properties. (Mathematically, any n-dimensional world is, algebraically and geometrically, perfectly coherent.) In particular, if in any corner of a room in our three-dimensional space you cannot possibly conceive of more than three perpendiculars at right angles with each other, a four-dimensional room would have, however paradoxical this may sound, not three, but four perpendiculars in each corner. Obviously, dimensions are a property of space. Four-dimensional space, or hyperspace, has different properties than three-dimensional space, and its relationship to three-dimensional space is quite curious. In order to understand this, we must use the Flatland simile.

Flatland was the invention of another four-dimensionalist, the Reverend Edwin Abbott Abbott (1838–1926), a Shakespearean scholar. The first edition of *Flatland* must have been in print by 1883.[10] Although Hinton later devised his own version of it called Astria, which was perhaps more accurately analogous to our universe, Abbott's book remained the most popular attempt to open one's mind to the possibilities of higher dimensions.

Omitting here Abbott's dramatic plot and the details of this strange flat society, with all its antifeminist implications, we will concentrate instead on the essence of his idea. It is easy to imagine a completely flat universe in which two-dimensional beings live. A wall in Flatland is a line, and so is the skin of another individual, behind which are his or her internal organs. These must be somewhat peculiar, since Flatlanders must use the same orifice to eat and excrete; otherwise they would come apart. They can move in two directions (forward and backward, and left and right).[11] While our rooms are approximately cubic, theirs are approximately square. Being three-dimensional beings in three-dimensional space, it is easy for us to have a view of Flatland from a dimension that does not exist in Flatland space. Although rigidly protected in their linear frames from their neighbors' view, Flatlanders have no secrets from us: we can freely look into their locked rooms and drawers, and as strange as this would sound to them we can see their insides at every moment. In relation to them, we can act like gods: we can make objects appear and disappear from the most recondite recesses (such as bank safes), we can take them instantly from one point of their space to another (an experience that they would probably interpret in mystical terms), and we can even flip them around through the third dimension so that their right side becomes left and their left side right. We can observe them at every moment and remain unnoticed. Obviously, the moral of the story is that a being from the fourth dimension would be able to operate in our three-dimensional world in exactly the same way as we could operate in a two-dimensional world. Such a being could be here yet remain unnoticed, could come and go through solid objects, and could reach into a drawer or safe for a valuable without opening it.

If this reasoning can be understood with only a small amount of difficulty, two further questions require more concentration: how would we see a four-dimensional being, and how would a four-dimensional being see us? The first question cannot be properly answered, but imagination can supply some analogies to make it plain; the second can be answered, but to imagine the actual situation is exceedingly complicated. It was Hinton's lifework to supply a satisfactory answer to the second, while his ideas concerning the first, though not supported by any mathematical calculation, were astonishingly revolutionary. Rejected by all scholars for many decades, his ideas were finally fully accepted only in the 1980s.

Essentially, according to his ideas a flat being living on the surface of the soup I am preparing to eat would experience (painfully, I suppose) the spoon crossing his or her space as a simple line whose size varies in time. As astonishing as this may seem, the only way a Flatlander could experience the third dimension of space would be through time. My advantage is that I can figure out what a spoon is by seeing all of its parts at the same time; for the soup creature, the spoon is a crazy and unpredictable transformative two-dimensional (2-D) being that appears and disappears out of nothing and whose shape shows uncanny changes over time.[12] Only a 2-D mathematical genius would be able to make calculations leading to the conclusion that the crazy god is a three-dimensional (3-D) solid object, but obviously no one would understand such a genius, for no plane being, including the genius him- or herself, would really be able to imagine what the 3-D spoon looks like. Even the most open-minded 2-D colleagues would believe the spoon to be a mere mathematical construct. That four-dimensional (4-D) forces are not purely mathematical is today an accepted fact; what we experience as electricity in 3-D space is gravity in the fourth dimension. Analogously, what we experience as time can be conceived of as the fourth dimension of a space-time compound (as Einstein did, although he made clear that time is not just another direction of space).[13]

But how would a 4-D being see us? As plane beings are literally open to us but not to their plane mates, similarly we are completely open to the sight of a 4-D being, even though we could not show the interior of our body to a human being even if we wanted to. Another characteristic of 4-D vision would be that the object of the vision would be visible from all parts at the same time, as if abiding in the middle of the eye of the observer.

It was Hinton's belief that 3-D beings show a "hyperthickness" in the unknown direction of the fourth dimension and that the space of our mind is multidimensional. In order to prove this he devised his famous cubes, memorizing each of their sides and giving each side a color and a name. This permitted him to perform all sorts of mental operations in which he could use the cubes to build objects. He could then see the insides of these objects, having trained himself to visualize all the cubes that composed them. But that was only part of his intention. In *The Fourth Dimension,* a book of uncanny complexity for the untrained reader, the cubes are simply the ancestors of the Rubick's cube, used to perform a number of operations that show how a 3-D object can be rotated through 4-D space. Obviously, the only way to flip an object in such a way as to transform its right side into its left side and vice versa is to move it through a superior dimension of space. Accordingly, to prove that a cube has been moved through the fourth dimension, it is enough to change it into its mirror image. Hinton did this by building a large cube out of sixty-four smaller ones whose sides he knew by color and name; he then devised a complex pattern for rotating the larger cube through the fourth dimension by rotating all the smaller cubes. (By changing a Rubick's cube into its mirror image, you obtain the sequence of the operations that lead to this, but without any 4-D vision involved, since you cannot see the smaller cubes inside.) Although I can clearly understand how Hinton's cubes may allow one to develop something that approximates 4-D vision or to decompose a hypercube, the mathematical significance of the space rotation to which he devotes a whole book is unclear to me, since one cannot change the smaller cubes into their own mirror images.

Devised for the first time in the nineteenth century, the fourth dimension was a fresh hypothesis that conveyed for the first time a simple, attractive, and perhaps even scientifically convincing explanation for many mysterious phenomena usually associated with religion or magic. It does not necessarily validate the possibility that gods could theoretically exist yet be completely invisible to us, for it is rather obvious that, even if we have no organ to experience the fourth dimension itself, we can see in three dimensions things whose explanation can only become clear from a higher perspective. Time is obviously one of these things, although trying to perceive the space-time continuum may be a challenging experience. Yet the sudden mystical journeys and visions that accompany a drastic alteration of consciousness could be interpreted as a mental glimpse into a superior reality, for the fourth dimension compels one to accept that many levels of superior reality may exist. The question is not where to start, but where to end the count of these hypothetical higher dimensions, each one of which behaves toward the previous one as the third does to the second. Physicists today end the count with ten or eleven dimensions, enough to explain the forces operating in our universe; yet, mathematically, dimensions can come in any number.

Hinton firmly believed that the fourth dimension was the conclusive explanation of mysticism, and he therefore believed mystical doctrines to be true, and mystical states and achievements to be real. For unknown reasons, he also believed in a separable (from the body) soul that can experience the fourth dimension, and also in the radical goodness of 4-D beings. Yet it seems to me that a plane being who inferred from our supernormal powers in relation to the plane world that we are ethically perfect would obviously be wrong.

Hinton's *Scientific Romances* are interesting in many respects, one of which is their uniqueness as a genre. As a matter of fact, they are not pure science fiction, like that produced by Edgar Allan Poe or Jules Verne; they are largely mystic-scientific fantasies in which feminine presences, usually in distress, play a crucial role. While Hinton's talent as a writer is debatable, some of his ideas seem to anticipate one of the most pressing questions of this century: how to access other worlds. Obviously, Hinton's advantage is that he knows what the other world is (it is the fourth dimension of space), yet he is not in a position to tell in what direction to search for it. His conjecture is that our mind-space has hyperthickness, and is thus potentially able to open itself up to 4-D vision. What prevents us from educating our mind to be 4-D are the innumerable conventions our mind takes for granted. Only if we eradicate these conventions can we realize hidden potentialities. The character of the Unlearner in "An Unfinished Communication" is typical of this trend of thought. He dispels conventions, thus freeing the mind from their grip. Hinton obviously looms behind the more recent ASC ideology.

In a more than metaphorical way, Hinton was the precursor of Einstein's cosmology as expounded in the general theory of relativity.[14] He also prefigured the physics of the 1980s in his insistence on the interpretation of electricity as a force from the fourth dimension and on the astounding idea (contemptuously rejected not only by all his contemporaries, but by most if not all physicists for many decades) that higher dimensions of space would be wrapped in tiny particles. Today the explanation of electromagnetism as gravity in the fourth dimension is commonly accepted by all Grand Unified Theories (GUTs) of the universe, while most GUTs talk of primordial particles in which no less than seven out of the eleven dimensions of the universe are wrapped.[15]

Seemingly unaffected either by Hinton's speculations on the fourth dimension or by Rev. Abbott's *Flatland* was another clergyman and mathematician, Charles Lutwidge Dodgson (1832–89). Dodgson, a rather fastidious lecturer at Christ Church, Oxford, loved the company of handsome young girls and the new technique of photography. His appreciation of girls made him famous under the penname Lewis Carroll, though this was certainly unexpected and unintended, for Rev. Dodgson's only ambition was to distinguish himself through Christian virtues. *Alice in Wonderland* was first printed in 1865, inspired by and dedicated to Alice Pleasance Liddell, one of the three young daughters of Henry George Liddell. Liddell had been appointed Dean of the Christ Church College in 1855 and is known to all students of classics as the chief author of the Liddell-Scott Greek dictionary. The author of *Alice in Wonderland*, who knew the value of money, would probably have been bitterly surprised to know that the original manuscript, auctioned by Alice in 1928 at the age of seventy-eight through Sotheby's, brought no less than 15,400 pounds sterling. *Through the Looking Glass*, the continuation of *Alice in Wonderland*, was ready in time to be printed before Christmas 1871—over ten years before Abbott's *Flatland* and Hinton's *Scientific Romances*.[16] There are not many instances in it that can be interpreted in terms of 4-D experience, but the basic metaphor itself, that of turning into one's own mirror image, suggests access to the only space where such a phenomenon would be possible: 4-D space.

Hinton's ideas, as *Flatland* shows, readily found enthusiastic supporters. Yet they only became popular in alliance with the spiritualist movement, an alliance which ultimately discredited them. Only their esoteric, mathematical side continued to make progress, becoming one of the undiscussed basics of modern physics.

The spiritualist movement was contemporary with the first speculations on the fourth dimension, and a certain stage in the development of the two coincided. Mediums were used to access the fourth dimension and produce paranormal phenomena that could serve as a confirmation of four-dimensionality. Conversely, the fourth dimension provided an ideal explanation for hidden and powerful presences from higher space. This convergence explains in part why a few quite remarkable physicists adhered to the spiritualist movement.

According to Ruth Brandon, spiritualism began around 1850 with the "Rochester rappings," bizarre knockings allegedly stemming from ghosts but in reality skillfully produced by two teenage girls, Katherine and Margaretta Fox.[17] The phenomenon soon spread from upstate New York to the whole world. Popular séances in Victorian England typically involved a large male audience with a young woman acting as medium. The woman would withdraw behind a screen where she would be tied to an armchair. Her skills consisted in freeing herself quickly, making herself up and changing clothes, after which the "materialized" ghost, scantily dressed, was ready to leave the booth and walk in dim light through the audience. The display was erotic, and it gave men the opportunity to touch the alleged ghost, who felt quite fleshy. Even though mediums were repeatedly exposed as frauds, the audience remained eager to participate in their exhibitions.

Other mediums would produce paradoxical phenomena. The most skillful among them was Daniel Dunglas Home (1833–86), whose audience was select and who was never exposed as a fraud. He would alter the weight of objects, play an accordian closed in a cage at a distance from him, levitate about six inches above the floor, produce luminous phenomena, ring a bell under a table, materialize hands unattached to any arm, and the like.[18] In the debate over psychic phenomena, renowned physicists like William Crookes (1832–1919) and Joseph Zöllner (1834–82) came down in favor of their existence. All this is of direct interest to our topic only because Zöllner, who was professor of physics and astronomy at the University of Leipzig and was known for his work on comets, tried to verify experimentally the existence of the fourth dimension by producing phenomena that could only occur if the fourth dimension were accessed. Unfortunately, Zöllner worked in 1877 and 1878 with an American medium, Henry Slade, whose reputation was far from being unchallenged. His specialty was obtaining spirit messages written on a slate. In London, in September 1876, two scientists had noticed beyond doubt that Slade was actively helping the spirits—on occasion he would switch the slates with others prepared in advance, or would write on the slates using his allegedly tied hands and even feet.[19] Less perceptive than these two scientists, Zöllner was convinced by Slade's supernatural abilities and wrote the book *Transcendental Physics* (1878), which was translated into English two years later by the lawyer Charles Carleton Massey (1838–1905), a member of the British National Association of Spiritualists and one of the founders of the Society for Psychical Research in 1882.[20]

One of Slade's specialties was "the tying of knots in untouched endless cords," a phenomenon which, if performed without tricks, would indeed be possible only by means of the fourth dimension.[21] But he failed several other tests devised by Zöllner. In particular, instead of turning a shell into its mirror image (which would again be possible only by moving it through the fourth dimension), he allegedly made it pass through the top of a table. Zöllner and another witness ascertained that it was "very hot to the touch."[22] In any case, the implication of *Transcendental Physics* was that spirits are beings in the fourth dimension.

This contention was of secondary importance to Piotr Demianovich Ouspensky (1878–1947), a Russian journalist with some scientific training, who found in the fourth dimension a new religion for humankind. Ouspensky undoubtedly understood the mathematical aspects of the question. In two books (*The Fourth Dimension*, 1909, and *Tertium Organum*, 1912) he tried to interpret visions and ecstasies reported by mystics in terms of direct experiences of the fourth dimension, thereby continuing and developing Hinton's view that the fourth dimension is the source of all spirituality. More inspired by theosophy than by the spiritualist movement, Ouspensky was not particularly inclined to fantasize about four-dimensional ghosts.[23]

In 1915 Ouspensky met Gurdjieff, a peculiar spiritual master, in Moscow, and in 1917 he followed him to the Caucasus. In a way, Gurdjieff was the "unlearner" about whom Hinton had written: he insisted on the necessity of ridding oneself of any mechanical conviction that could interfere with the awakening of consciousness and one's mastership over oneself. In his quality as an unlearner, Gurdjieff was more interesting than he was as a teacher—his world system was complicated and unconvincing. But, according to Ouspensky, he had psychic powers and could communicate with his disciple at a distance, without articulated language. Gurdjieff had read Ouspensky's work about the fourth dimension, and he perceptively described the books as definitely wiser than their author.[24]

In 1920, teacher and disciple were in Constantinople. Due to the success of the English translation of his *Tertium Organum,* Ouspensky was invited in 1921 to lecture in London. He subsequently helped Gurdjieff to settle in France and open his Institute of Fontainebleau, attended by rich Parisians. Ouspensky lectured in London, where he could count Aldous Huxley among his audience, until 1940, after which he moved to the United States.

In a chapter of his *New Model of the Universe* (translated in 1931), which is otherwise a pretentious collection of esoterica, Ouspensky shows himself to be ahead of his time in so far as he accepts the idea of superior dimensions (seven of them) in physics. Like *Tertium Organum,* the scientific part of *A New Model* shows genuine understanding of physical questions. Unfortunately, the connection between the physical use of superior dimensions and the occult matters that Ouspensky generously bestows upon us is far from clear.[25] Peculiar to Ouspensky, although not invented by him, is the idea of the state of "cosmic consciousness," with the attainment of which he credits all authentic mystics. His explanation of it is predictably made in terms of the fourth dimension.

In reality, very few descriptions of mystical states correspond to what one would expect from 4-D vision. Two of them are present in *The Autobiography of a Yogi* by Sri Paramahansa Yogananda (1893–1952).[26] Yogananda reports having had the following vision when he was slapped across the chest by a famous saint, Bhaduri Mahasaya, in Calcutta: "As though possessing an omnipresent eye, I beheld the scenes that were behind me, and to each side, as easily as those in front."[27] He experiences "cosmic consciousness," as he calls it, a second time when struck above the heart by his guru, Sri Yukteswar Giri: "My ordinary frontal vision was now changed to a vast spherical sight, simultaneously all-perceptive. Through the back of my head I saw men strolling far down Rai Ghat Lane. . . ."[28] Obviously, intertextuality can not be a priori excluded as an explanation for Yogananda's descriptions, since it is legitimate to assume that Yogananda might have been exposed to Ouspensky's ideas.

What is probably the most clear and famous description of a 4-D vision belongs to the realm of fiction; it was written by a man who, it should be remembered once again, had played with Hinton's cubes in his childhood: Jorge Luís Borges. "The Aleph," which is "one of the points in space that contains all other points" and is visible on a certain step of the cellar stairway in a friend's house, reveals to him the interior of all things as well as their exterior: "I saw the circulation of my own dark blood; . . . I saw the Aleph from every point and angle, and in the Aleph I saw the earth and in the earth the Aleph and in the Aleph the earth; I saw my own face and my own bowels; I saw your face."[29]

Clearly, the fact that the only thing we can say with some certainty about 4-D vision is that it would somehow place the object focused on in its center, that it would contemplate it simultaneously from all sides, and that it would pierce through it as if it were transparent, neither proves nor disproves the interpretation of mystical experiences in terms of the fourth dimension.

Another phenomenon that has a long history behind it and that has been associated with the fourth dimension is the so-called out-of-body experience (OBE). Although journeys out of the body were already performed by the Greek ecstatics before Socrates, much recent interest in them is connected with the case of Robert A. Monroe, a successful businessman from Virginia, who found out in 1958 that he was able to dissociate himself from his physical body.[30] His "second body" was able to visit friends in distant places and report events that occurred there. He was also able to explore two other realms besides the physical, which he called Locale II and Locale III. Locale II seemed to be an intermediate world, populated by unpredictable ghosts, a world we often visit in a dream state. (The closest analogue to it is the limbo world in the movie *Beetlejuice,* or Toontown in the movie *Who Framed Roger Rabbit?.*) Locale III, according to the author's own interpretation, is a world parallel to ours, a universe to some extent similar to the one all of us share, but in which other, less developed technologies exist. There was a Mr. Monroe in that universe too, bearing a different name, doing other things, and involved in other stories than the original on earth.

For those who need an extradimensional explanation of Monroe's space travels, it should suffice to say that according to him his "second body" would become free with a 180-degree rotation, which allowed him to look upon his physical body beneath him. On one such occasion he discovered that his physical body had turned into its own mirror image: right was left and left was right. Obviously, what Monroe suggests here is that, not unlike Alice, he had stepped through the looking glass into a reversed world. Actually, if we look for some reasonable clue, Monroe could certainly not have achieved rotation if not in hyperspace, whereby his "second body," flipped through the fourth dimension, became its own mirror image.

The psychologist Charles Tart tested Monroe's ability to report events while out of the body, with inconclusive results. But Tart found that experiments with other subjects seemed to show that they possessed the extrasensory perceptive skills claimed by Monroe. In conclusion, even if Monroe's own speculations about the three worlds he was visiting turned out to be entirely wrong, his "trips" themselves seem to be authentic, and his reports, published in 1971, although inevitably distorted by his efforts to "translate" them into everyday language, seem to be faithful.

An OBE was reported by Flora Courtois, who claimed an experience of awakening that a Zen master interpreted as "the same sort of satori that Sakyamuni Buddha attained."[31] It happened suddenly: "One day, without knowing why or how, I turned completely around," and in front of her was the "tunnel . . . a long, open window opening directly onto a breathtaking vista."[32]

Yet the most challenging performer of OBEs in the early seventies was widely supposed to be the pseudoanthropologist Carlos Castaneda, that is, before it became clear that he was a novelist, not an anthropologist. Today the interest in the large group of phenomena to which OBE belongs is a common denominator of New Age ideology. Other achievements, like channeling, past-lives regression, and near-death experiences (NDE), seem to be more popular at present. Yet the basis of all of these is to be found in altered states of consciousness (ASC). Obviously, ASC are not a goal in themselves; they are, according to Hinton, the precondition for any 4-D experience. Yet it is perhaps legitimate to advance the theory that an initial cognitive interest in ASC quickly degenerated into a purely hedonistic, anticognitive use of it. As Dr. Louis Lewin noticed in the early twenties, most animals seem also to enjoy drunkenness and drug-induced ASC.

On the other hand, there are many categories of ASC, many of which have nothing to do with external stimulants. The papers on ASC edited by Charles Tart mention the following categories: mystical experience, dreaming and hypnagogic visions, meditation of different kinds, and hypnosis.[33] Obviously, psychotropic and psychedelic drugs receive much attention. To all these, the issue of *Readings from Scientific American* that has an introduction by Timothy J. Tyler and focuses on ASC adds the experimental use of goggles (all of us who use thick glasses know to what extent they alter perception) and the effects on coordination of the brain-splitting operation.[34] In the nineteenth century, in the medical field seriously altered states were collectively called hallucinations, and they were treated as symptoms of insanity. Electroshock therapy, together with cold showers, was already recommended by several physicians by the mid–nineteenth century.[35] Still earlier in history, ASC were associated with demoniacal possession.[36]

The peak of the NDE vogue has only recently passed. It was launched in 1975 by Raymond Moody's influential book *Life after Life,*[37] which was followed and imitated by many other authors who collected NDE reports, usually in hospitals.[38] The main pattern of NDE reports seems to vary largely with the person or persons who collect them. The main scenario includes a buzzing sound, fast motion through a tunnel, the meeting of dead relatives and friends, and a sort of judgment imparted by a being of light who shows the near-dead a panoramic playback of his or her life.[39] Yet sound and the tunnel, which are so crucial in Moody's reports, do not turn up in most of the cases collected by Kenneth Ring.[40] Carol Zaleski's more recent book compares medieval otherworldly journeys and visions with NDE literature. NDE contemporary experience appears to be particularly close to the spiritualist world view.[41]

This short survey of the aftermath of the 4-D revolution would be inconclusive without a brief discussion of the premises of the psychedelic revolution of the sixties and seventies. It seems beyond doubt that psychotropic substances, in so far as they produce ASC, were initially envisioned as a sort of

great "unlearner" (in Hinton's terms), a way to shatter percep-
tual conventions and to gain access to a deeper level of reality.
This is certainly what Richard Alpert, a Harvard assistant
professor of clinical psychology, and his associate Timothy
Leary, must have thought on 27 May 1963, when Harvard
President Pusey decided to fire Alpert for having distributed
drugs to undergraduates. In 1962, Alpert and Leary had
launched a local consciousness-expansion movement based on
the use of mescaline and LSD, and in October they had
founded the International Federation for Internal Freedom
(IFIF). As the two predicted, "restrictions on . . . mind-
liberating research" would indeed become "a major civil
liberties issue in the next decade."[42]

Long before Aldous Huxley and others, Charles Howard
Hinton seems to have been one of the most systematic
advocates of unlearning of conventional modes of perception,
cognition, and training. He certainly favored ASC as both a
technique of unlearning and as a result of obtaining 4-D vision.
Yet Hinton's astonishing insights have proven most fruitful in
the field of modern theoretical physics. To this extent, we can
indeed assume that there are only a few other great ideas of
humankind whose influence can be compared with that of the
fourth dimension, and none of them is closer to us in time
than the fourth dimension itself.

Recent adventures in invisible dimensions inevitably lead us
to the past. As several of the descriptions of utopias provided
by the four-dimensionalists point out, we are three-dimensional beings in a three-dimensional space, yet we are practi-
cally unable to move in more than two dimensions. Indeed,
the up-down direction is only known to us through the
negligible difference between lying (or sitting) and standing.
We penetrate the hard surface of the earth only after death,
and we are unable to fly, except in dreams.

Given all this, it is understandable that the first unknown

and therefore mythical dimension that confronted humankind before the age of aviation and space exploration was in fact the third dimension. Heavenly spheres and netherworlds do not belong only to the deluded fantasies of prescientific people. Experience and science removed such places from the third dimension, but did not supplant them. In a certain sense, there will always be a dimension that leads to the unknown, be it the fourth or the nth. Just as there are vast junkyards where most of the products of our past technologies await destruction, museums where some of the best past technologies are still displayed, and universities, research institutes, and factories where new products are devised, in the same way we can say that cemeteries display symbols attesting to the faith of innumerable people that the dead journey to other worlds; that innumerable accounts of visions are still treasured and commented upon by hordes of scholars; and that new experiences and theories try to adapt the unknown to the exigencies of a science which, to put it in Albert Einstein's words, gives witness to the "subtlety of the Lord. . . ." For the horizon of the unknown moves together with the horizon of science, and is never dispelled by it.

Having assessed the extent to which otherworldly visions still seem to be current in the life of many modern men and women despite society's dominant skeptical attitude toward such experiences, we shall now proceed to a guided tour of past civilizations in which the existence of parallel worlds of spirits was accepted as common fact.

2

Free Spirit
Seeks Free Spirit

An Outline of Shamanism

ETHNOPSYCHOLOGY FOR LAY PEOPLE

According to a recent trend in scholarship, the multitude of interpretations of religion can be reduced to two basic schools: the school of the British anthropologist Edward Burnett Tylor (1832–1917) and the school of the French sociologist Emile Durkheim (1858–1917).[1] The Durkheimian school does not take religion as a phenomenon in itself, but as a symbol for something else, that is, a code for social relationships. The Tylorist school treats religion as a separate product of the human mind, although this view is only partly espoused in the original writings of Tylor and his successors. It correctly describes, however, the view of phenomenologists of religion, up to a certain point. Tylor's own theory was based on an evolution of religious forms from primitive (or animistic) to more complex. In the search for a psychological explanation of religion, the Tylorists devote much attention to ethnopsychology.

Possibly the most famous among the Tylorists, James George Frazer (1854–1941), lectured in 1911 and 1912 on a topic that was also dear to Tylor. In fact, Tylor had based his explanation of the origin of religion on it. Entitled "The Fear and Worship of the Dead," the lectures focused on the Australian aborigines, the Torres Strait islanders, the New Guineans, and the Melanesians. Published in 1913, the lectures were intended to form the first of three volumes called The Belief in Immortality and the Worship of the Dead.[2] Today we have access to far more accurate surveys of the topic in Oceanian religion.[3] Although dated, Frazer's collection of materials still remains impressive, and the overall picture he gives is sharp enough, despite his interpretations. Moreover, unlike the Swedish-German ethnopsychological school that later produced massive works on the concept of the soul among the native inhabitants of North America, Asia, and Oceania, Frazer substantiated his reports with complete descriptions of native beliefs in immortality, and these descriptions, although they may not match the rigorous parameters of present-day anthropology, give us a fair enough impression of the whole. It appears—and this result has been reconfirmed by recent literature—that the inhabitants of Oceania (and likewise those of Asia and North America) make a distinction between a "free" or "separable" soul or spirit, which leaves the body during dream or trance, and a "body" soul (sometimes further categorized into sub-souls), which ensures the primary functions of life.[4]

The other worlds known in Oceania differ widely as to their location and description, as does the fate of the dead in the afterlife. Ghost land (often there are different lands for different categories of the dead) can be distant or close; hidden by natural obstacles like water, rocks, smoke, or fog, or by supernatural obstacles like angry giants; above—in heaven or on a high mountain—or underground; on land or in the middle of the sea; in our universe or in a parallel universe sometimes endowed with strange properties. Souls of chieftains from the Tonga Islands are said to sail to a blissful country on a great northeastern island called Bulotu, with wonderful and immortal flora and fauna. Bulotu must exist in another spacial dimension, for men landing on its shores can walk right through trees and houses. Gods have ghostly bodies that can travel anywhere in the world without need of a canoe.[5]

Ghost land can be blissful or gloomy, and in many places both an enjoyable and a repellent afterlife exist, according to the dead person's status or to his or her conduct in life, which calls for posthumous retribution. Sometimes it is antipodal, meaning that all things there show reversed symmetry: day here is night there, and vice versa. Sometimes the dead speak another tongue and eat food the living cannot swallow. The blissful land can be a place of leisure where only enjoyable occupations are continued, such as sleeping, smoking, dancing, betel chewing, and the like. Yet other people believe that in dead land there is no night and no sleep, for there is no fatigue; nothing unpleasant filters through it, not even boredom. It can be equalitarian and peaceful or, on the contrary, it can be the abode only of aristocrats, with the souls of commoners being destroyed at death. But sometimes aristocrats go up to heaven and commoners go down to a subterranean Hades. When two lands of the dead exist, they can be recognizable by smell: one is fragrant, the other one is foul. In other cases, village life is eternally transposed in the afterlife, and people continue their existence without a change.

In Oceania, fate after death is uncertain. Souls may be reborn or not. Often enough they do not even reach dead land, not being able to withstand the ordeals plentifully distributed throughout the itinerary between the two realms. One's mode of death can work favorably or unfavorably toward one's posthumous fate. Violent death is either bad or good; suicides and women who die in childbirth somtimes share the privileged destiny of the warrior. Yet sometimes one's luck hangs on a trifle: if you are a good dancer you can cross certain tricky bridges; otherwise you go to hell. There are things much worse than death, for instance the second death and even the third. Your soul may be lucklessly destroyed, in which case it either perishes altogether or is reborn as an animal or even an insect. It may turn into a mischievous wood spirit, an ant, or a worm.

If the principle of post-mortem retribution is general, notions of right and wrong can have widely divergent definitions. Thus among Fiji Islanders, only warriors who killed many enemies and fed upon them are entitled to the bliss of paradise. Men who have had the misfortune not to kill anyone during their lifetimes land together with other lost souls in an underwater Hades called Murimuria, where they pound muck with clubs. Other great sinners, such as women who have not been tattooed or men who have not had their ears bored, are tortured and mocked.[6] Men whose wives have not followed them in death (by being strangled) complain bitterly, but their fate cannot be worse than a bachelor's, who may never live enough of his afterlife to see the doubtful splendors of Murimuria. In fact, different monsters try to catch a bachelor's soul, and usually succeed; such monsters include the Great Woman and especially the ferocious goblin Nangganangga, who smashes the soul to pieces on a black rock. A giant appropriately called Killer of Souls, who lies in ambush beyond the town of Nambanaggatai, strikes both married and unmarried, but there are means to get past him. If he catches your soul, however, he cooks and eats it.[7] In the general uncertainty about the fate of the soul, the inhabitants of a Micronesian island draw lots to find out if the soul will be crushed between two stones and deleted from among the living and the dead alike, or if it will continue to exist in a plentiful land. Different terrifying guardians stop, frighten, and torture the soul for no reason at all, or for some reason such as searching the heart for traces of sin.[8]

It is not always necessary to be dead in order to visit ghost land. In eastern Melanesia, living people can go down to the netherworld, Panoi, either in the body or in spirit, and either in dream or in a near-death state. Ghosts advise them not to eat from the food of the dead, for otherwise they cannot come back alive.[9] Yap natives believe that in the past it was relatively easy for living people to go to heaven, but the situation has changed since the secret of ascent was lost. The usual vehicles that can transport one to heaven are clouds or birds.[10] The soul itself can turn into a bird upon death. If it is free from sin, a god leads it to heaven, where it is deified, which essentially means that it will never have to work again.[11]

To understand how complex the problem of the soul is among the Oceanian people, it is enough to read the accurate survey given by Hans Fischer.[12] More recently, Lammert Leertouwer has written a dissertation in which he reviews Western anthropological research on the soul from 1798 to date among only three peoples from the Indonesian island of Sumatra, principally the Batak.[13] His conclusion was that on Sumatra there is opposition between a "life soul" that confers vitality on the body and a "death soul" that comes free at death.[14] Researches similar in scope to Fischer's have been carried out for the northern Eurasian peoples by Ivar Paulson[15] and for North American native peoples by Åke Hultkrantz.[16] And, although there is no comparable survey for Africa or South America (despite enlightening remarks contained in L. E. Sullivan's *Icanchu's Drum: An Orientation to Meaning in South American Religions*[17]), the categories established by the Swedish school (Paulson, Hultkrantz) are sufficient to furnish us with a theoretical framework for the understanding of shamanism.

AN INTRODUCTION TO SHAMANISM

Mircea Eliade defined shamanism not as a religion properly speaking, but as a "technique of ecstasy," a system of ecstatic and therapeutic methods whose purpose is to obtain contact with the parallel universe of the spirits and to win their support in dealing with the affairs of a group or of an individual. Eliade circumscribed the meaning of shamanism so as to exclude phenomena that can be more properly defined as sorcery. According to this definition, shamanism is unknown on the African continent. However, shamanism is in fact identifiable in the religions of all continents and at all levels of culture, its center being Central Asia and northern Asia.

The Tungus word "shaman" means "sorcerer." The common Turkish word that designates the shaman is *kam,* and still other words are used by the Yakut, Kirgiz, Uzbek, Kazak, and Mongols. During the period of the Mongol invasions, the great shaman was called *beki,* from which the old Turkish word *beg,* "lord," derives, becoming *bey* in modern Turkish. Genghis Khan himself, according to Muslim historians, had great shamanic powers.

The languages of the Turks, Mongols, and Tungus-Manchus belong to the Altaic family, which split off from the more ancient Ural-Altaic family to which the languages of the Finns, Hungarians, Estonians, and several other Asian peoples also belong. Most of these peoples later converted to one or more than one universal religions, such as Buddhism, Christianity, Islam, Judaism, Manicheism, or Zoroastrianism. Although as a result the institution of shamanism was often disavowed, it has in fact continued to exist up until the present, surviving even Stalin's persecutions, as the late Hungarian scholar Vilmos Dioszegi ascertained during the short "liberalization" period under Khrushchev.[18]

Ethnosemiotics attributes shamanic origin to ancient Siberian cave paintings (about 1000 B.C.E.) because of common distinctive traits found both in the painted costumes and in shamanist rituals. Ethnosemiotic research finds confirmation in Greek sources from the sixth century B.C.E., which suggest that a local type of shaman who was able to enter a state of trance, travel to the underworld and to a northern paradise, bilocate, and take bird shape, existed in Greece until the fifth century. The presence of local shamans can be inferred from the written evidence of other ancient religions (Iranian, Chinese, Tibetan, and so on). They are well attested by anthropological research among peoples without written records who have lived in conditions of relative isolation, such as the Australian aborigines. New perspectives in the study of shamanism are emerging; in particular, a combination of history of culture and cognitive psychology is slowly but safely moving toward new understandings of shamanism.

In Central Asia and northern Asia, shamanism flourished among the Turkish, Mongolian, Himalayan, Finno-Ugrian, and Arctic peoples and is also attested to in Korea, Japan, Indochina, and North and South America. While diffusionistic theories may explain the existence of American shamanism as an early derivate of Asian shamanism, they do not account for the occurrence of Australian shamanist phenomena.

Present-day scholars distinguish between two Asian shamanist complexes: the Turkic or "cattle-breeder" complex and the Tajik or "agricultural" complex.[19] Among the hunters and fishers of northern Siberia, the shaman has various functions: clanic (Yukagir, Evenki), neighborhood-based (Nganasani), or across society (Chukchee, Koriak). The cattle-breeder complex is defined by the following principal traits: the profession is almost exclusively male; the shaman summons spirits in human or animal shape; upon entering a state of trance, he displays indifference to self-inflicted pain and body injury; and he dances and mimics ascent to heaven (by climbing on the yurt roof) during a healing séance. On the contrary, in the Tajik or agricultural complex, shamans are generally women; they conjure up spirits in human form; their powers are largely explained by the sexual relationship they entertain with a spirit; and they do not dance during the séance.

The two complexes have elements in common, for instance the personal powers of a shaman, which determine his or her status. The shamanic vocation can be directly conferred on someone by the spirits, or it can be a family inheritance. Yet even when it is inherited, Siberian shamans are still supposed to undergo individual initiation in order to obtain knowledge and to acquire supernatural aids. Visited by the spirits, the shaman initially goes through a period of deep psychic depression and illness; these only subside when, having crossed the desert of death, he or she comes back to life and learns to control personal spirits in order to perform ecstatic journeys whose purpose is usually healing through exorcism. During performances, the shaman uses several objects that symbolize supernormal faculties and are supposed to provide help for reaching the land of the spirits. Such objects include a drum made from a tree symbolizing the cosmic tree, a cap, and a costume that associates the wearer with the spirits and recalls at the same time a skeleton—symbol of initiatory death and resurrection. The séance starts with the shaman summoning his auxiliary spirits; then, in a state of trance (which is sometimes obtained through the use of hallucinogenic or intoxicating agents), the shaman travels to spirit land. In central and eastern Siberia—among the Yukagir, Evenki, Yakut, Manchus, Nanay, and Orochi—the shaman is often possessed by the spirits, who speak through his mouth.

The system of shamanism is widespread among all Arctic peoples, no matter the linguistic group to which they belong: Uralic (Saami or Lapps, Komi or Zyrians, Samoyeds or the Finno-Ugrians, Khanty or Ostiak, and Mansi or Vogul), Tungus (Evenki, Eveny), Turkish (Yakut, Dolgan), Yukagir (Yukagir, related to the Finno-Ugrians), Paleosiberian (Chukchee, Koriak, Itelmen), and Inuit (Aleut). Less complex than in southern Siberia, shamanic séances among the Arctic peoples are nonetheless more intense and more spectacular. Sometimes the shaman, like his North American Algonquin colleagues, is tied up with a rope in a closed tent during the shaking-tent ceremony: the tent is violently shaken, allegedly by the spirits, who are also supposed to untie the ropes of the shaman.

Most of the Inuit live in Greenland, Canada, and Alaska. Before obtaining shamanic powers they go through a powerful depression and a shocking near-death experience. During the period of attainment of shamanic powers, the Inuit practice *quamaneq* (skeleton visualization) in order to become indifferent to death and to develop the ability to identify the pathogenic agents that have penetrated the body of a sick person.

The healing séance of a shaman is a dramatic rendering of a trip to heaven or to the underworld (located, in the case of the Inuit, on the sea bottom) whose stages can be followed by the audience. Yet the performance presupposes at least two levels of understanding: one on the part of the spectator and one on the part of the performer. From the performer's viewpoint, the malady is caused by the loss of one of the patient's souls; accordingly, a soul of the shaman must go in search of the lost soul, recover it, and take it back to be installed in the owner's body. According to Ivar Paulson, there are four possible cases of soul pursuit, consisting of different combinations of the two souls or spirits a human being possesses: the free spirit and the body spirit. The classical case of a shamanic healing session can be defined as free soul seeking free soul, that is, the free soul of the shaman goes in search of the free, lost soul of the patient. The other three cases are: free soul seeking body soul, body soul seeking free soul, and body soul seeking body soul.[20]

Women are usually the performers of Korean and Japanese

shamanism. Many of them are blind, as this is supposed to be the sign of a sure vocation. In northern Korea the shaman is chosen by the spirits, but in the south she inherits her function from her parents. She goes through a period of depression and illness, during which she is often visited by a spirit who becomes her permanent lover. After such an experience, marital life often grows intolerable.

Shamanism is also present among the border peoples of Tibet, China, and India (Miau, Na Khi, Naga, Lushei-Kuki, Khasi, and so on), as well as among the peoples of Indochina (Hmong, Khmer, Lao, and so on), Indonesia, and Oceania.

North American shamanism has several traits in common with Arctic shamanism, such as the original lack of hallucinogens and the obtainment of shamanic powers through solitude and suffering. Yet in some geographic areas, shamans form professional associations, and this distinguishes them from most of the peoples acquainted with shamanism. One of these associations is the Great Medicine Society (Midewiwin) of the Great Lakes, whose members initiate a candidate by "killing" him (shooting at him with cowries, quartz crystals, or other symbolic objects supposed to penetrate his body) and then bringing him back to life in the medicine cabin.

As a specialist in spirits, the shaman is supposed to know what the soul looks like. The free soul is often associated with the shadow, being lusterless and gray, but it can also be colored. Among the Paiute in southeast Nevada and among many other North American native people the soul is red or has the color and brightness of fire or light. It sometimes leaves the body in the form of lightning, a spark, a flame, or a ball of fire. The soul is in general a miniature being, in human form or shaped like a winged creature, bird, fly, or butterfly, whose dimensions, though diminutive, can vary in size according to the circumstances. The free soul can change into other animals as well, such as a mouse, a reptile, a mite, a worm, or a grasshopper; it can also look like an object, usually round in shape: a ball of eagle's down, a hailstone, or a bone.[21]

The shaman's deep trance is tantamount to death. Hultkrantz reports, "The medicine-man sunk in ecstatic trance appears to be dead, does not move, shows tendencies to apnoea."[22]

South American shamanism is rich in beliefs and practices that are found in other areas as well, such as initiatory sickness, visualization of the skeleton, marriage with a spirit, healing by suction, and so on. Yet quite peculiar to South American shamanism is the use of hallucinogens such as the *Banisteriopsis caapi* or *yagé*, or intoxicating substances such as tobacco, and the presence of collective ceremonies of initiation. In L. E. Sullivan's words: "South American cultures, perhaps more than those of any other region of the world, make religious use of plants that spark luminous visions. Knowledge of hallucinogenic plants controls the encounter with figures of light. The power of these sacred plants rearranges the shaman's entire sensible being and lifts him or her to another plane of unearthly light."[23] Rattles more often than drums are used to summon the spirits, who are frequently ornithomorphic. One of the most common powers claimed by the shaman is being able to transform himself into a jaguar.

South American shamans are specialists in the recovery of wandering souls. During a séance, the healing shaman of the Shipibo "journeys to the realm of the sun, accompanied by light-colored birds. A great crown of hummingbirds surrounds the shaman as he journeys along the 'way of great light' to the sun."[24] The "good shamans" of the Shipibo use *nishi,* the extract of the liana *Banisteriopsis caapi.*

The Apinayé shaman has the task of recovering a patient's soul from the village of the dead; he visits it in the shape of a black snake that feeds on poisonous snakes. Tobacco is the agent that propels the shaman's soul on its quest for the lost soul.[25]

SHAMANISM BESIDE SHAMANISM

The scholarly attempt to confine original shamanism to Central Asia and northern Asia and to explain the presence of shamanism in other world areas as a phenomenon of diffusion has met with serious difficulties. Australian aborigines, for instance, are fully acquainted with shamanism, which, to make things even more complicated, they do not distinguish from sorcery. In other words, a medicine man can act as a healer in certain circumstances and as a sorcerer in other circumstances.

The "aboriginal man of high-degree," as A. P. Elkin calls his particular character, possesses magical powers, especially the power to fly through space, either in body or—as is more common—in spirit, while the body lies in sleep or trance.[26] The vehicle of the journey is a flame of fire or a magic cord that is received at shamanic initiation and that comes forth from the shaman's body. "This cord becomes a means of performing marvelous feats, such as sending fire from the medicine-man's inside, like an electric wire. But even more interesting is the use made of the cord to travel up to the sky or to the tops of trees and through space."[27] Probably Elkin's and R. M. Berndt's descriptions of the capability of the Australian shaman to project this cord out of his body and to "climb" on it inspired the Peruvian fiction writer Carlos Castaneda to invent the episode of the Yaqui "men of knowledge" Don Juan and Don Genaro moving like Spiderman through space following cords issuing from their abdomens. Other "tricks" of the Australian shaman consist of disappearing and reappearing suddenly from place to place, walking through trees, running fast above the ground, and bilocating.[28]

Although scholars continue to play down the existence of

an African shamanism, African sorcerers are commonly supposed to perform most of the extraordinary feats of their Australian shaman colleagues. Moreover, certain patterns of shamanic initiation are still mentioned in African myth. As we have shown elsewhere,[29] both Australia and Africa are acquainted with the myth of a water serpent, guardian of wells and ponds, often known as the rainbow serpent. The rainbow serpent keeps watch over precious substances connected with heaven and with the origin of the world: pearls, quartz crystal, or simply colored stones. These substances have magical powers. One who obtains them can become rich, beautiful, and even immortal.

In Australia, this myth is related to an initiatory ritual in which the rainbow serpent uses magical substances to "kill" and restore to life a candidate shaman. This type of ritual, in which quartz or rock crystal, pearls, stones, cowries, or rice are used, is very widespread, at least in North America, South America, and Japan.[30]

Is Shamanism Witchcraft?

In the most typical shamanist areas a distinction is made between "white" and "black" shamans, that is, between shamans acting as healers and shamans acting as sorcerers. Moreover, the very same shaman may act as a healer within his own ethnic or regional group and as a sorcerer toward outsiders. Similarly, in areas where sorcerers are active, "good" and "bad" types may both be represented, and sorcerers may specialize in healing or witchcraft.

In the early 1970s, the Scottish functionalist anthropologist Ioan M. Lewis tried to establish permanent distinctions among "shamanism," "witchcraft," and "possession cults," based on the relationship of the spirit operator toward the spirits.[31] According to Lewis, all three phenomena are based on the existence of a world of spirits, but they differ in the attitude of the spirits toward the human participant. In possession cults such as the North African *zar,* ancient Dionysiac cults, or Afro-Caribbean and Afro-Surinamese cults, the participant is unwillingly possessed by the spirits. On the other hand, the shaman, after being so possessed, heals him- or herself and becomes master of spirits: he or she is like the "wounded surgeon" of T. S. Eliot. The sorcerer or witch is a master of spirits and directs the spirit's action toward an unknowing subject, who becomes possessed.

Obviously, none of these distinctions holds true. Possession cults are commonly associated with acts of witchcraft, and possession trance is induced at will by specialized mediums who therefore do not differ much from shamans; moreover, the characteristic of "unwillingness" of possession is quite debatable, for obtaining trance follows certain preestablished patterns. These patterns fall into two main categories, defined by anthropologists as "sensory deprivation" or "hypoaroused state," and "sensory bombardment" or "hyperaroused state."[32] During preinitiatory possession the shaman avoids human contact and seeks solitude and quiet. In contrast, the practicing shaman has recourse to sensory bombardment obtained in general through powerful drumming or rattling, ecstatic dances, and hallucinogenic or intoxicating agents. Similar techniques are used in possession cults, in which collective ceremonies take place but trance occurs individually. On the other hand, shamanic initiation in South America is often collective, and consists of ceremonies in which hypoarousal is succeeded by hyperarousal. Therefore, although the three main types devised by Lewis may have some heuristic use, they seldom if ever occur in a pure state. A close relationship with the world of spirits can manifest itself in all these guises in a single individual, who may act successively as a possessed person, a witch, or a shaman.

Is Witchcraft Shamanism?

A far more interesting question has recently been raised by the Italian historian Carlo Ginzburg, who has been working with materials on the phenomenon of witchcraft in Friuli in the fifteenth and sixteenth century. He has ascertained that the Friuli *benandanti* were a group of beneficent sorcerers whose spirits fought nocturnal battles against evil witches, the outcome of which determined the quality of the crops.[33] After collecting information on European witchcraft for twenty-five years, Ginzburg recently has come up with a revolutionary reassessment of the phenomenon.[34]

Like most historians, Ginzburg holds that western European society at the beginning of the fourteenth century persecuted minorities such as lepers, Jews, and witches.[35] Yet, unlike many of his colleagues, Ginzburg believes witchcraft to have been much more than a mere invention of a "persecuting society." The phenomenon he describes was basically the encounter of two cultures, a popular culture and a "high" culture that imposed its interpretive network on all reality. Since the intellectual categories of the representatives of high culture—mainly Catholic theologians—were inadequate, the result was bad anthropology. Yet in the beginning the Christian authorities were not alarmed by popular witchcraft; they were only embarrassed by what they took for sheer superstition. Starting in the eleventh century, reports started accumulating about women who flew to attend nocturnal meetings in the company of fairies or in groups led by goddesses such as Diana, Holda, Perchta, Domina Abundia, and Herodias. This happened west of the Rhine River. East of it, nocturnal meetings were attended by both sexes, and they turned into battles that would determine the quality of the harvests. Wicked witches were fought by good witches—called *benandanti* in Friuli and werewolves in the Slavic regions of eastern Europe. In south-eastern Europe the battle did not take place in a swoon or in a dream, but was ceremonially enacted by groups of young people. Ginzburg shows with absolute certainty that *benandanti,* "werewolves," and young dancers and fighters existed, and that they believed in the harmful return of the spirits of the dead, whose presence could have compromised the welfare of the living. In presenting this view and in arguing that the people of Europe had their own culture, whose origins were ancient and prestigious, Ginzburg dissociates himself from many of his colleagues. The literate interpreted this ancient culture according to their morbid and fanatic intellectual categories and according to their restricted vision of infernal fires and the pestiferous anus of Satan.

Yet this is not the conclusion of Ginzburg's book; it is only the beginning. He courageously argues that the common explanations for this ancient, popular heritage are too vague. Talking about "palaeolithic roots" of such beliefs and practices does not explain much. Yet Ginzburg is equally reluctant to accept the structuralist explanation that we are dealing here with constant structures of the human mind. He reverts to a historical, diffusionistic hypothesis.

Asiatic shamans go to ecstatic group meetings that turn into witchcraft performances. They too defend the interests of their community, although publicly and not privately like the werewolves or the *benandanti.* This difference aside, the isomorphism between shamanism and ancient European witchcraft is complete.

Thus, according to Ginzburg, European witchcraft is nothing but shamanism. And not only typologically so. Ginzburg believes that shamanism was disseminated in Europe through the Scythians, Indo-European tribes who practiced shamanic ecstasy with the help of marijuana and perhaps mushrooms like the fly agaric *(Amanita muscaria).* Another hallucinogen the witches might have used is the *Claviceps purpurea,* a parasite growing on rye, from which Hoffmann extracted lysergic acid some thirty years ago and which already in the eighteenth century was known to produce religious epidemics in Holland.[36] They were rather heirs to a long shamanic tradition, which was mistaken by our inquisitors and Puritans for diabolic knowledge.

Ginzburg's revolutionary research opens up a wholly new perspective in the study of the relationship between shamanism and other religious phenomena. In the study of each particular tradition of otherworldly journeys, we will keep in mind the multifarious aspects under which shamanism passes through the ages and the tenaciousness of the most ancient religious inheritance of humankind.

↶ 3

Dark Treasures

Otherworldly Journeys in Mesopotamian Religion

Sumerian written records are available from 3500 B.C.E. Does this make it easier to understand the treasures of a past immersed in the darkness of faded millennia? No, if we believe the famous Assyriologist A. Leo Oppenheim, who gave more than one reason "why a 'Mesopotamian religion' should not be written";[1] yes, if we rely on the admirable reconstruction, *Treasures of Darkness,* by Thorkild Jacobsen.[2] For the purpose of our survey, the answer is certainly yes: Sumer yields the most ancient written reports of otherworldly journeys, and even if we may miss the point of a few episodes or misunderstand the psychology of the characters, in general the story can be followed by a modern reader. In this respect the wealth of Egyptian tomb inscriptions we will meet in the next chapter are far more enigmatic, for they are not woven into a coherent narrative.

Around 4000 B.C.E. the Sumerians built an advanced civilization around the cities of Ur, Uruk, and Kish, with their mysterious ziggurat temples. Their Semitic conquerors, the Akkadians, showed high respect for Sumerian culture and

translated many records into their own language. Between
2100 and 1600 B.C.E. an Amorite dynasty flourished in Babylon;
around 1600 B.C.E. another Semitic people, the Assyrians,
established their empire in northern Mesopotamia. The millen-
nial struggle for power between Assyria and Babylonia seemed
to end when Assyria conquered Babylonia in the eighth
century B.C.E. Yet Babylonia helped its new allies, the eastern
Medes, to capture Nineveh, the capital of Assyria, at the end
of the seventh century B.C.E., and in 539 Babylon opened its
gates to the emerging power in the region, the Persians. The
multilayered Sumerian-Akkadian-Assyrian-Babylonian civilization, with its many languages and dialects, was thus engulfed
by another world power; its remains, trodden underfoot, were
preserved for the eye of the modern scholar who can afford
the leisure of studying history.

However diverse Mesopotamian culture may have been for
three millennia, its mythology shows remarkable continuity.
The first stories of otherworldly journeys come from Sumer:
"Gilgamesh and the Land of the Living," "The Death of
Gilgamesh," and "Inanna's Descent to the Nether World."[3]
The elaborate Akkadian epic of Gilgamesh evolved around 1600
B.C.E. from an ancient Sumerian tradition (around 2100 B.C.E.).

THE PRICE OF IMMORTALITY

Alarming rumors that human life can be doubled, and even
that immortality may be within reach, are a current fact of the
biological revolution. Immortality could after all have a price,
and that price could be too high (at least in terms of Social
Security). Gilgamesh is the first human being on record to
have settled for nothing less than immortality. (Innumerable
shamans must have done it before him, but they disappeared
without a trace.) For reasons beyond grasping, his quest was a
failure; like Faust, Gilgamesh consoled himself by erecting

durable buildings in his native city of Uruk. Scholars seem to agree that this wild, uncommon man was a historical king of Uruk around 2600 B.C.E.; his feats must have been impressive, yet they may not have had much in common with the stories that began to circulate about five hundred years later. The contours of the later epic had been established around 1600 B.C.E., but the form in which it has reached us is the work of a certain Sin-liqi-unninni (end of the second millennium B.C.E.), copied for the library of Ashurbanipal in Nineveh about 600 B.C.E.[4] It is extant in twelve tablets, the last of which, a translation from Sumerian, contains a variant of the story that contradicts the previous eleven.

There are no indications that the epic was read as a part of the religious cult. Like the *Odyssey,* but more explicitly stated, it was the report of an otherworldly journey ascribed to a highly gifted mortal; it was "religious" in its topic, but not in its use. It spread the word about an authentic religious quest undertaken outside the boundaries and the scope of an official cult; as such, it must have enjoyed great popularity and set on fire the imagination of many people whose enterprising spirit could not be content with the pursuit of any mundane goal. Its conclusion, however, was cautious: Gilgamesh, whom the title of the poem defines as "he who saw everything" (*sha nagba imuru*), gained experience but failed in the quest. One could venture to assert that something strange occurred in Mesopotamia: Gilgamesh, otherwise a typical hero of high civilization, was not a successful but rather an unsuccessful shaman. His deeds would not have gone on record among the Inuit, the Tungus, or the Algonquins. Yet they fit very well into the Faustian spirit of Western civilization, and deep within ourselves there is more understanding for Gilgamesh than for a shaman who conquers immortality. We will follow here his voyage to Hades according to the Nineveh tablets, mentioning the Sumerian variants when available.

A Hittite fragment informs us that the gods themselves helped to fashion the oversized Gilgamesh, who is thus two-thirds a god and only one-third mortal. His sexual lust equals his strength, and after he becomes ruler of Uruk, angry citizens start complaining about his continuous seductions and revels. (Apparently he was exerting the *jus primae noctis* and sleeping with brides before their legitimate spouses did.) The gods decide to create the undaunted giant Enkidu to challenge him, but when Gilgamesh sends a harlot to him, after six days and seven nights of mating the wild man loses his innocence and the animals once friendly now shun him. The woman, who "was not bashful as she welcomed his ardor,"[5] finds that he is ripe to be taken to the city, and there he meets mighty Gilgamesh. Like bulls they fight each other; Gilgamesh seems to yield, but Enkidu is impressed with his strength and the two become inseparable friends. Enkidu's company inspires Gilgamesh to higher enterprises than the taming of all maidens of Uruk, and the city is saved when its ruler and his friend move against the monster Huwawa who lives in the cedar forest. The Sumerian poem "Gilgamesh and the Land of the Living" makes this episode into a part of the conquest of immortality: Huwawa is the last peril Gilgamesh confronts after crossing the seven mountains between Uruk and the land of the living. The Akkadian version makes this into a prelude to higher exploits: after having slain Huwawa and the bull of heaven sent to him by the goddess Ishtar, whose advances he had rejected, Gilgamesh meets the mystery of death, which due to the curse of the god Enlil takes away his valiant friend Enkidu. After bewailing his motionless corpse, Gilgamesh stumbles upon the unexpected revelation that he too will die: "When I die, shall I not be like Enkidu?"[6]

This revelation requires immediate action; Gilgamesh sets out for the distant and hypothetical land of his ancestor Utnapishtim, who became immortal. Smiting lions in ambush, he comes to the formidable cosmic mountain Mashu, "whose peaks reach to the vault of heaven and whose breasts reach to the nether world below."[7] Awful scorpion-people guard the gate of the sun, but they let Gilgamesh pass on account of the divine part in him, and he crosses twelve leagues of dense darkness, coming eventually to the deep sea that surrounds the earth. There he chats with the barmaid Siduri, who tries to dissuade him from attempting to cross the endless waters of the cosmic ocean, deadly to anyone but to Shamash, the sun. "Let full be thy belly, make thou merry by day and by night" is her philosophy,[8] for he cannot conquer immortality anyway; yet she shows him to the ferryman Urshanabi. The following episodes are obscure: to cross the waters of death, Urshanabi apparently needs stone figurines and the *urnu* snakes that sailors love; yet Gilgamesh has smashed the stones and done away with the *urnu,* and he is therefore obliged to use brute force to propel the ferry. Eventually they come in sight of Utnapishtim Atrahasis ("the exceedingly wise"), the Babylonian Noah who fled from the destruction brought by the flood of Enlil upon the city of Shuruppak on the ark he built on divine instruction. The gods have made him and his wife immortal; he could perhaps speak a word for Gilgamesh in the assembly of gods, if Gilgamesh can stay awake for six days and seven nights. But he falls asleep and does not awake before the seventh day. Even if he cannot obtain immortality, Gilgamesh receives from Utnapishtim the secret of the thorny plant of rejuvenation that grows in the depth of the ocean, and Gilgamesh picks it and saves it for later, when he will be old in Uruk. Yet this is not to be, for while Gilgamesh is bathing in a well, a serpent smells the odor of the plant and carries it away; hence serpents shed their old skins and are rejuvenated. Gilgamesh weeps bitterly; he finds consolation only in the solid walls of Uruk, in the perfect construction of which he takes pride. His circumvented frustration sounds like an ancient variant of Goethe's Faust who becomes a philanthropist before he dies in order to escape Mephistopheles.

INANNA-ISHTAR MAKES FOR HELL

We do not know what the Sumerian Venus Inanna, predecessor of the Akkadian Ishtar, had to seek in hell, the realm of her sister Ereshkigal; it appears that she was foolish enough to wish to dethrone her. Therefore, descending from heaven, she took on the seven symbols of her power, which differ in the Sumerian and Akkadian versions: a crown, a measuring rod (or earrings), a necklace (of lapis lazuli), a breast ornament (of sparkling stones), a gold ring (or loin girdle), a breastplate (or bracelets), and a cloak. Clever enough to leave her maidservant Ninshubur at the gate of hell and to instruct her to seek the help of gods if she does not come back, Inanna enters the road of no return. The gatekeeper announces her to Ereshkigal, who is obviously unhappy with the visit. But she lets her sister in, and Inanna is stripped of her seven attributes one by one at the seven gates of hell. When she comes before Ereshkigal and pushes her off her throne, Inanna is actually devoid of any power; the seven dreadful Anunnaki, the judges of Hades, coldly condemn her to death. Inanna "turns into a side of meat hung on a peg in the wall; she is not even fresh, but green and tainted."[9]

After three days and three nights, Ninshubur goes to alert the gods, but her plea fails with Enlil and Nanna. Only Enki stands by and devises a plan: out of dirt he makes two zombies, the *kurgarru* and the *kalaturru,* great experts in mourning, and entrusts the two with the grass of life and the water of life, instructing them to sprinkle the side of meat with them sixty times so that Inanna will rise up. The plan is based on Ereshkigal's main business, which is to lament the dead, especially young children, assuming the attitude of a grieving mother. When the two specialists join her in her laments, she is obviously pleased and ready to grant them a boon. The mourners ask for the moldy side of meat on the peg; they sprinkle it sixty times with the grass and the water of life, and Inanna is restored to life. Yet the Anunnaki are unwilling to let her go unless a substitute takes her place in hell, and an army of deputies from the netherworld must ensure that this will happen. Inanna cannot resolve to hand over to them people who have mourned over her disappearance, but she gets irritated when she notices that her husband, the shepherd Dumuzi, seems to be enjoying himself. Looking at him "with a look of death," she yells to the messengers of death: "Take this one along!"[10] Another text contains the denouement of the drama: Dumuzi's sister Geshtinanna is willing to sacrifice herself for him, and Inanna lets her replace him in hell half of each year.

Other descents to Hades are known from Sumero-Akkadian texts, such as the rather enigmatic encounter of Ur-Nammu, king of Ur toward the end of the third millennium B.C.E., with the Anunnaki, who assign him a post-mortem residence.[11] Two are particularly interesting.

One is tablet 12 of the Gilgamesh epic, directly translated from Sumerian. It is a shamanist story, whose first part, uncovered by S. N. Kramer, expands on the destiny of a tree that has grown since the creation of the universe, when it was planted by Ishtar in her garden in Uruk to be used for her bed—an important accessory for the goddess of love—and her chair. This tree is threatened by enemies but is recovered by Gilgamesh. To reward the hero, Inanna makes a drum (pukku) from the base of the tree and a drumstick (mikkû) from the crown, and gives them to him. But one day the objects fall into the nether world, and Gilgamesh laments bitterly over their loss,[12] something any shaman would certainly do. Enkidu offers to descend and bring them back, and Gilgamesh gives him precious advice, saying he should slip in surreptitiously, stripped of every attribute; Enkidu, however, does the opposite and is detained in hell. Gilgamesh seeks the help of Enlil and Sin without success; only Ea of Eridu orders Nergal (a heavenly god who has become Ereshkigal's husband) to open a hole in the earth. Scarcely has he opened it "when the spirit of Enkidu, like a wind-puff, [issues] forth from the nether-world."[13] We are not told if the shamanic drum and drumstick come out as well. Furthermore, the text of this Sumerian *Divine Comedy,* which was supposed to tell us who is who in hell, is badly mutilated.

Far more detailed is the description of hell in the dream of the Assyrian prince Kummâ, who was presumptuous enough to ask for such a vision. He cannot believe his eyes: Namtaru, the mistress of the major-domo Namtar, is a sort of sphinx, while other monsters are serpent-headed, bird-footed, lion-headed, bird-headed and -winged, ox-headed, goat-headed, provided with two heads of different kinds or with three feet, and the like. The gloomy, majestic Nergal, surrounded by the awesome Anunnaki, throws his scepter like a viper to kill the intruder; the prince escapes death in this hellish dream due to the intervention of Ishum, the compassionate counselor of Nergal. Thus Kummâ awakes, his mouth filled with other-worldly dirt.

ASCENTS TO HEAVEN

The Mesopotamian gods lived in heaven. Only two cases are known of human beings who joined them.

One is the wise Adapa, the blameless first human being and priest of Eridu, who provides daily bread, water, and fish for his city god. One day when he is fishing, the south wind capsizes his ship; in his anger, Adapa curses the wind and breaks his wings. The god Anu is furious and orders his vizier

Ilabrat to bring Adapa before him. Ea instructs his servant, Adapa, to wear mourning attire, to tell the two gods at the heavenly gate that he is mourning for Tammuz and Gizida, and not to eat or drink of the stuff of death that Anu will put before him. Adapa does as advised. The gods at the gate, who are in fact Tammuz and Gizida, are happy to find out that someone is still mourning after them on earth, and they put in a good word for him with Anu. Anu listens to his story and is embarrassed: good manners oblige him to serve Adapa the bread and water of life, which will make him immortal. Fortunately for the gods, Adapa refuses to eat or drink, as the cunning Ea has advised him. For Ea does not want to confer immortality on this human being any more than Anu does.

Etana, king of Kish after the world flood, is credited with another ascent to heaven, which he undertakes in order to bring down the plant of birth as a remedy for his childlessness. This ascent is more spectacular than Adapa's, for it occurs with the aid of an eagle that Etana has saved from a pit. The eagle was trapped there by his former friend, the serpent. On the other hand, the eagle is certainly not innocent: he betrayed his friend's confidence by eating up his offspring and has thereby offended both Shamash, the sun god, and the gloomy Anunnaki, with their impersonal justice. Along with Etana we move from heaven to heaven and see the land underneath becoming smaller and smaller, "and the wide sea just like a tub."[14] The text, badly mutilated, seems to end with a crash, for Etana is too heavy a burden for the eagle. Yet it seems that the two must eventually obtain the plant of birth, which apparently belongs to the goddess Ishtar, for a son and heir of Etana is recorded among the kings of Kish.

Fastidious as they may have been in their divination records, the ancient inhabitants of Mesopotamia were obviously no experts in otherworldly journeys like their Egyptian neighbors.

They left us only a few fragmentary myths to dwell on, myths with a moral that sounds familiar: human beings are doomed to mortality and, as such, they are not entitled to glimpses of other worlds.

4

Puppets, Playhouses, and Gods

Journeys through Other Worlds in Ancient Egypt

In the evening, after closing time, when visitors leave the Egyptian Museum in Cairo, what do all those statues, reliefs, and images do when unobserved? Do they come to life, some to eat and others to be eaten, some to enjoy the possession of servants and others to serve? Obviously, for us the answer is no. In the darkness of the museum, statues and images remain still. Yet an inhabitant of ancient Egypt would not have shared our skepticism, nor would the Egyptian fellahs who not long ago mutilated many statues, breaking at least their thumbs, out of the belief that while unbroken the statues could do harm. The Greek lexicon of Suidas informs us that specialists were able to tell if a statue was "charged" or not, that is, if it had undergone the rite of "opening the mouth." This rite was performed by other specialists, who could also charge the small Egyptian tomb figurines that represented various workers by reciting over them a powerful magic verse from chapter 6 of the *Book of the Dead*. In the silence of the tomb those statues were supposed literally to come to life and to perform the work for which they had been created. The tomb was a complete universe, active as long as no observer disturbed it, for the sight of an untrained observer could freeze this frantic activity, reducing it to nothingness.

For this reason, only a few specialists were allowed to share the intimacy of the god or goddess of the temple. The most accurate description of a Near Eastern temple, also valid in the case of Mesopotamia, is a playhouse with gods. These gods were mere statues only to the untrained observer; not so for the hordes of shaven-headed priests who attended them, fed them, bathed them, and took them out for strolls.

A prime function of the gods was oracular. Gods and goddesses were taken out in procession fairly often and installed on boats, whose dimensions varied according to a number of criteria. Specialized porters were present, but common people from the crowd were eager to join them, for carrying a god, invisible in his or her wooden booth, was a meritorious deed. On such occasions, people could address the god with yes-or-no questions. Some of the inquirers wished to obtain confirmation of their innocence of a crime; usually the plaintiff was also present, seeking confirmation of his suspicions. Due to the conflict of interests, questions were asked more than once, and to different gods, until everyone obtained a satisfactory answer. The god spoke through his carriers: an affirmative answer would result in an increase of the weight in the front of the boat, so that the front carriers would stumble, kneel, or rush forward, while a negative answer would be translated into a backward movement of the carriers. In a study of oracles among the Azande of eastern Africa, the anthropologist Evans-Pritchard found that, of three available methods of divination, people thought only one was truly dependable, although this one was unaffordable under normal circumstances. For reasons too obvious to be mentioned, the Egyptian divine oracles were not very dependable either;

therefore, two written answers were in later times presented for the gods to choose between.

Priests did not rely on the gods only for delivering oracles. In the sanctuary of Deir el-Bahari at Luxor, where the local god would talk to sick pilgrims at night and prescribe medication for each of them, his voice was actually produced by a priest through a masked opening in the vault. Subtler devices were used in the temple of Karanis at Fayyum, where the divine statues were hollow and a priest could make them talk through a pipe.

The Egyptians were famous in the ancient world for their capacity to "charge" inanimate objects through magical formulas and to make them work for them. In his *Philopseudes* (a title meaning "lover of lies," in itself a poor recommendation of credibility), the Greek satirical author Lucian describes Egyptian household robots of a kind now familiar to us from Walt Disney's cartoons. Using a powerful formula, the magician Pancrates ("almighty") was able to animate broomsticks, pillars, and door bolts and have them perform zombie labor. Eucrates, who tells the story, was able to do the same: he got a cane to fetch water for him, but he did not know the formula for stopping it. When all his efforts were to no avail, he split the cane in two, but then the two sticks continued fetching water until the whole house was flooded.

Animating objects or images is a common magic operation, documented all over the world. The Chinese sorcerer Ke-yü, who lived in the Shang dynasty (twelfth century B.C.E.), was famous for the wooden goats he sold. They were not ordinary goats, for they came alive. Another Chinese sorcerer did the opposite: he sold actual horses, which turned into clay as soon as the customer got home. Examples can be multiplied. A book published in 1926 by the Belgian Egyptologist Weynants-Ronday, under the influence of Tylorist animistic theories that were passé by then and are even more so today, lists many such examples from China, West Africa, Finland, and so on.[1]

The best of what the Egyptians did was not for this life, but for the afterlife, which was conceived of as a continuation of one's occupational patterns. When the physical body was gone, the *ka* (double) was released. In order that it would never be deprived of a body to carry out ordinary activities like eating and drinking, the *ka* was supplied with a large number of statues animated by specialists through the ritual of opening the mouth. As we will see, that so many efforts should be devoted to ensuring the double's surrogates a proper physical survival is unique among the religions of the world. The Chinese, it is true, installed the ghost of a deceased male in an inscribed tablet that was kept at home to endow the household with his protection. In more ancient times, the function of the tablet was fulfilled by a wooden statue, tended and fed like a Near Eastern god or a dead Egyptian king. Statues and tablets were supposed to last forever, as was the memory of those they represented. Other societies commemorated their dead less: in Santa Cruz, a dead person was first replaced by a stick, which was presented with offerings for some time. But eventually the family would forget to whom the stick referred; they would eat up the offerings and throw the stick away.

Yet beyond the posthumous mirroring of this earthly existence, the Egyptians had distinct and elaborate conceptions of other worlds. To these we will devote our attention in this chapter.

FROM PYRAMIDS TO COFFINS

During the dynasties of the Old Kingdom, all hopes for eternity were focused on the king, who would spend his afterlife in heaven. Through the king, eternity was vicariously enjoyed by the builders of those vast funerary complexes, the pyramids. These were "staircases for the king's ascent to heaven,"[2] and the further adventures of the king were hinted at in carved inscriptions on the pyramid walls from the late fifth and the sixth dynasties. These are known as the pyramid texts.[3]

An afterlife in heaven remained the exclusive privilege of the king, but the nobles built tombs so that they might continue their earthly existence after death, and they often borrowed some of the immortality of the monarch. During the first intermediate period and the Middle Kingdom (about 2100 B.C.E. to about 1700 B.C.E.), many aristocrats wished to be proclaimed "righteous" and to obtain divine glorification in the realm of the dead; for this purpose, they used texts and formulae on the inner part of their coffins. The collection of 1,185 such "spells" has been appropriately called the coffin texts.[4]

In the Middle Kingdom, funerary beliefs became increasingly democratic: even the poor could enjoy post-mortem existence in the Field of Reeds, where they would be allotted a piece of land to till. The bliss of the attainment of the Field of Reeds is the topic of a collection of funerary papyri, often based on precedents among the coffin texts and even among the pyramid texts, and conventionally called the *Book of the Dead*.[5] The earliest extant papyri forming the *Book of the Dead* have been dated to the fifteenth century B.C.E., yet the beliefs they reflect are more ancient.

Pyramid texts, coffin texts, *Book of the Dead*—these three stages in Egyptian conceptions of the otherworld each deserve separate examination.

THE PYRAMID TEXTS

In the pyramid texts, the heavenly destiny of the pharaoh is to be transformed into Osiris: "Osiris the King," son of Nut, brother of Isis. His son Horus would "open his mouth," that is, revive him in the afterlife. The pharaoh is sometimes identified with Horus himself or with the sun god. He is crowned and enthroned, becoming ruler of the beyond and supreme deity.

To us, the spells seem to contain innumerable metaphors of ascent and rebirth. In reality, they were precise references to situations in the afterlife that the king was supposed to meet. Thematically, one can distinguish the ascent spells from the spells that presuppose heaven as their background. Both categories are spectacular.

The privileged ways of ascent to heaven are two: by means of a ladder made by Re, the sun god, or through transformation into a bird, either the falcon of Horus or a composite creature that is half falcon, half duck.[6] Sometimes this transformation seems to be only metaphorical. "I have soared in the sky as a heron, I have kissed the sky as a falcon, I have reached the sky as a locust," declares the king.[7] Ascent often takes place "in a blast of fire" or in an earthquake; the pharaoh is said to become "a flash of lightning" in the beyond. One text magnificently combines several themes: "The sky thunders, the earth quakes, Geb [the earth god] quivers, the two domains of the god roar, the earth is hacked up. . . . I ascend to the sky, I cross over the iron (firmament) . . . I ascend to the sky, my wing-feathers are those of a great bird."[8] During his ascension, the dead pharaoh undergoes transformation into a cosmic being whose head is a vulture, whose temples are the starry sky, and whose face, eyes, nose, teeth, and so on are each gods.[9]

Usually the gate of heaven opens before the pharaoh, but sometimes he finds it locked, the door bolt the phallus of the god Babi. When somehow the gate is unlocked, the pharaoh reaches the beyond and is transformed into the crocodile god Sobk.[10] Several actions accomplished in the beyond have magical purposes. The king is reborn from a vulture, or from the great wild cow. He bathes in the scented sweat of Osiris or in the Field of Rushes. He becomes imperishable, his bones turning into iron. He becomes a spirit or a star. In order to appropriate for himself as much magical power as he can, he chases the gods and eats them. "He eats their magic and gulps down their spirits," and he "swallows the intelligence of every god."[11]

A whole category of texts, some of which are called ferryman texts,[12] describe the way the pharaoh crosses the river of death, ferries over the sky, travels to Re on the reed float of the sky, or becomes Re's ferryman. "I go down to my seat, I take my oar, I row Re when traversing the sky (even I) a star of gold. . . ."[13]

THE COFFIN TEXTS

Texts from the Middle Kingdom show aristocrats feeling entitled to share in royal immortality and have spells inscribed inside their coffins. The coffin represents the universe: its ceiling is the sky, its floor the earth, its sides the four directions of space.[14] In the coffin, the dead become Osiris, as the pharaoh does in the pyramid texts. The magic eyes (oudjat) painted outside at the level of the dead person's eyes allow him to see the world of the living.

The picture of the beyond that emerges from the coffin texts is more complex than that of the pyramid texts. Many popular beliefs barred from the more restricted pyramid texts seem to find their way into the new conceptions of the afterlife. They show striking analogies with the Oceanian material briefly examined in chapter 2, above.

In the texts, the deceased can only reach heaven if he escapes a number of ordeals and ambushes. A fishnet stretched between earth and heaven has the purpose of intercepting all rising souls. The dead must show determination and knowledge of the names of the parts of the net and boat of the soul fishers in order to escape. "O you fishers of the dead, O you children of your fathers who catch the dead, you may trap those who are all over the land, but you shall not catch me in your nets in which you catch the dead; trap (only) those who are all over the land, because I know your names. . . ."[15]

Escape is accompanied by transformation into the crocodile god Sobk or a bird.

> See me, you fishermen of the gods; look at me, you fishermen of men. You shall not seize me, you shall not grasp me, you shall not work your will against me, because I have gone up from its heart, I have escaped from its clutch as a falcon of seven cubits along its back, I eat with my mouth, I defecate with my anus. Those who exist see me, those who do not exist worship me, those who are yonder give me praise. . . . I have escaped from its clutch as Sobk and Horus the Northerner. . . . I have escaped from its clutch as the great heron, the lotus-bird which catches fish.[16]

Other dangers lie in ambush in the form of animals and evil demons, such as Gebga the Black Bird or Rerek the Slayer of the *ka* (double).[17] Tbtt and 'Isttt, the two "noble companions of Re," who enjoy pleasures, threaten to physically exhaust the dead person, at which the latter has to discard all impure thoughts and declare, "I have brought away my soul, I have rescued my magic, I will not give away my powers, for I am a pure one who has discarded his body, I am a child and I am inert."[18] Knife in hand, the deceased is ready to stab the "two sisterly companions who put the love of them in the hearts of the spirits."[19]

Ascent to heaven takes place as the bird *ba* (soul). Transformation into a bird (falcon, heron, ibis, vulture, and so on) is one of the most frequent motifs of the coffin texts. The dead person may also change into a flame of fire or into a god.

Judgment of the dead person by a tribunal of gods was a later development in Egyptian mortuary beliefs. Yet, even at the point when the deceased has been admitted to heaven and has become identified with Osiris, his destiny may still be in jeopardy because of the plottings of Osiris's brother Seth, who tries to kill him. If Seth succeeds, the dead person dies a second, definitive death.[20]

The Book of the Two Ways is usually found written on the coffin floor. It describes two routes of the dead—a water route and a land route—leading to the glorious domains of Horus the Elder. These routes are surrounded by an insurmountable circle of fire, which the soul can only cross by showing knowledge of the proper spells. Many dangers await the dead person: lakes of fire, aggressive knife wielders, people who shout, destroyers, and the big Dog-face, as well as many other gatekeepers, such as He-who-is-driven-off-with-two-faces-in-dung, High-of-winds, Lord-of-striking-power, One-who-spits-out-the-Nile, He-who-cuts-them-down, He-who-eats-the-droppings-of-his-hinder-parts, He-who-glowers, He-whose-face-is-inverted, He-who-lives-on-maggots, and so on.[21]

The Book of the Two Ways can be properly described as a guide to the different gates of the beyond; it introduces the secret names of their formidable keepers and gives spells meant to ensure the dead harmless passage.

> Guide to the double doors of the horizon when they closed on account of the gods. This is the name of their keepers which is in writing and this is their entire nature. As for anyone who does not know what they speak, he shall fall into the nets of those who net there. . . . As for anyone who shall know what they speak, he shall pass by, and he shall sit beside the Great God wherever he may be, and he shall give respect to him, for he is one wholly equipped and spiritualized. As for a man who shall know, he will never perish, and their seal shall be on him like any god for whom they do it among all the gods.[22]

At every step the deceased is threatened to be burned out by fire: "This is its path which is the Mansion of Incense; you should not walk on it. My flesh is afire. He should not go back on it. This name of his is Aggressor. He and his power have gone down. This name of his is Dreadful-of-fire."[23]

THE BOOK OF THE DEAD

During the Middle Kingdom, the Egyptian beyond opened its gates to everyone, rich and poor. This stage in mortuary beliefs is expressed by *The Book of the Dead,* which is actually a condensation of ancient funerary motifs compiled during the New Kingdom.

The Field of Reeds and the Field of Offerings—two conceptions of the Egyptian paradise—are as old as the pyramid texts.[24] The western Field of Offerings is guarded by the Heavenly Bull of Re, which Raymond Weill identifies with the constellation Orion.[25] The Field of Reeds is located in the eastern quarter of heaven. It was originally a place of ablution, purification, and rebirth that allowed the dead to follow the sun westward and to reach paradise, that is, the Field of Offerings. Yet at some point the distinct functions of the fields merged, and both fields were depicted as Osirian abodes of the dead who continued to exist happily and to till their pieces of land. *The Book of the Dead* illustrates a further phase of this belief. Now the dead person is unwilling to perform any menial work in the afterlife, so he is buried with miniature images of workers *(shabti),* who come to life under the power of spell 6, "making arable the fields, . . . flooding the banks or . . . conveying sand from east to west."

Two major innovations in Egyptian afterlife beliefs found in *The Book of the Dead* are the description of the trial of the dead in spells 30b and 125b, which consists of the famous "psychostasy," or weighing of the soul on the scales of the keeper of the balance, and the no less famous "negative confession of sin" by the deceased in spell 125a. Although in general an Egyptian was supposed to do good and shun evil, his list of wrong actions may strike us as odd, especially when it comes to overwork, which is considered to be one of the worst transgressions: "I have done no evil, I have not daily made labor in excess of what was due . . . my name has not reached the offices of those who control slaves, I have not deprived the orphan of his property . . . I have not killed . . . etc."

To the same series of wrong actions belonged making off with food offerings for the gods and the spirits, cheating, and any ecological devastation such as building illicit dams in flowing water, diverting watercourses, or catching fish in marshland, where they lay their roe. The first "negative confession" is followed by a more elaborate one, in which the deceased names each member of the tribunal and denies any participation in the sin that a particular member is supposed to punish. (For example, the Eater-of-entrails punishes perjury, and The-one-whose-face-is-behind-him punishes copulation with a boy.)

Then the deceased delivers a discourse before the jury, after which the gods interview him; questions and answers are enigmatic. To go further, the deceased must be able to identify correctly by their names the living parts of each gate he finds in front of him (for example, the name of the doorposts is Plummet of Truth, and the name of the door bolt is Toe of His Mother), as well as to identify every gatekeeper.

Egyptian mortuary beliefs continued to exert a powerful influence on Hellenistic religion, especially on the mystery cult of Isis and on some of the late Coptic Gnostic texts that emerged in the nineteenth century.

🖎 5

Crane Riding, Soul Raising, and Ghost Brides in Taoist China

LIVING ON AIR

Weightlessness is a Taoist specialty, as is immortality. From the most ancient times, the two were closely related, for it is by lightening one's body, either by esoteric means or by special contrivances, that one can ascend to heaven where the immortals dwell. The tractate *Pao-p'u-tzu* written by Ke Hung before 317 C.E. describes the Taoist immortal *(hsien)* as a being who can walk equally well on fire, water, and air, "carried by the wind in a chariot of clouds."[1] He is a "walking corpse," and although he conceals his true nature, he can be identified by the square pupils of his eyes, by the tops of the ears, which reach the top of his head, and by the feathers covering his body. Weightlessness is promised to the adept of Taoism: "He will have a garment of feathers, will ride on a lightbeam or saddle a star, will float in emptiness. . . . His bones will shine like jade, his face will glow, a halo will surround his head, all his body will emit supernatural light and will be as incandescent as the sun and the moon."[2] He is a master of the "art of ascending to heaven in full daylight," he can change himself in seven different ways, becoming light or a cloud, and he can hide in the sun, in the moon, or in the stars.[3]

An-ch'i Sheng, an inhabitant of the isles of the blessed in the eastern ocean, obtained the power of invisibility and ascended to heaven after having lived in the Lo-fu Mountains of Kwangtung province eating only water-rush stalks. This frugal Taoist diet is called "living on air," and many are those who tried it. Straying is impermissible. Chang Liang, who died in 187 B.C.E., failed because he ate a bit of rice offered to him by the empress. Li Pi (722–789 C.E.) attained immortality under the appropriate nickname of "Collar-bone Immortal of Ye"; after living only on wild fruit and berries, he was reduced to a skeleton.

If diet for some reason would not do, one could resort to an elixir invented by the physician T'ao Hung-ching (452–536 C.E.). It was made of gold, cinnabar, azurite, and sulfur, had the color of "hoarfrost and snow," and tasted bitter. The emperor tasted it and must have flown, for he rewarded its manufacturer.[4] The alchemist Shao-kun, under the Han emperor Wu Ti (141–87 B.C.E.), was already in possession of a similar elixir, for he boasted: "I can rein the flying dragon and visit the extremities of the earth. I can bestride the hoary crane and soar above the nine degrees of heaven."[5] And the second-century B.C.E. alchemist Liu An was renowned for having prepared an elixir that allowed not only him to ascend to heaven, but also his poultry and dogs when they licked the vial he dropped into the courtyard upon his sudden takeoff.[6]

Some plants, like *huang-ching,* are reported to produce immortality, which comes together with weightlessness. Traditions about the immortals have it that chrysanthemum on rare occasions produces a red seed with miraculous properties.

A young woman of sixteen ate one "and suddenly flew away borne by the wind." After a while, she "vanished in the blue firmament, her head disappearing first, and her legs last."[7]

Taoists generally, however, preferred airborne vehicles for travel to heaven. First in order of importance was the crane, white or black, but wild ducks and even tigers would do on occasion, and even special shoes like the cloud-raising shoes made by Sun Pin from fish skin were thought to be efficacious.[8] The famous emperor Chi reached the heavenly immortals by ascending to them on a winged horse, or according to another version on the back of a long-bearded dragon capable of carrying seventy people at once. The low-ranking imperial officers who were unable to find a seat on the dragon's back clung to his beard hairs, which unfortunately gave way. In the process, the emperor's bow was dropped as well; both bow and hairs were reverently collected by people on the ground.[9]

Humanlike, befeathered, red-eyed, white-headed, long-jawed beings born from eggs and appropriately called Yü-min or "bird people" were said to live on the peaks near the seashore on an island in the southeastern ocean. They had bird beaks and could fly short distances.[10]

In ancient times, dragons were the best airborne vehicles. Emperor Shun, who lived according to tradition in the twenty-third century B.C.E., learned from the two daughters of Emperor Yao, Nü Ying and O Huang, how to fly and creep like a dragon. K'u Yüan (332–295 B.C.E.) wrote an allegorical poem about flying over the Kun-lun Mountains in a chariot carried by dragons and preceded by Wang-shu, the charioteer of the moon.[11]

Flying mechanical contrivances also enjoyed a venerable tradition. A certain Chi-kung is credited with the invention of a flying chariot *(fei-ch'e)* during the reign of the emperor Ch'eng T'ang (eighteenth century B.C.E.). According to another source, the chariot was built instead by the tribe of the Chi-kung, known from other testimonies to consist of single-armed, three-eyed people riding striped horses.[12] Kung-shu Tzu (Lu Pan), a contemporary of Confucius, was known for his skill at flying kites. Yet it is not clear from the contradictory sources that concern him whether he could fly for three days in one of them, or rather if, after working for three years on it, the kite was smashed upon the first flying attempt. Kung-shu was worshipped as the patron of Chinese carpenters until recent times, much in the same way as the seventeenth-century levitating saint Giuseppe Desa of Coppertino is held by the Catholic Church to be the patron of aviation. According to ancient informers, Lu Pan was clever enough to volunteer his father and mother to first test his inventions; he lost both of them.[13]

These bodily experiences of flying seem to single out China in the prehistory of modern aviation; yet Taoist and popular beliefs are also extremely rich in soul travels to other worlds.

THE TWO SOULS OF CHINA

Between 1901 and 1910, the Sinologist J. J. M. de Groot published a book (comparable to Frazer's forthcoming *The Belief in Immortality* in length, method, and approach) concerning ancient and modern Chinese beliefs in a separable soul.[14] De Groot's evolutionary conception of "animism" and religion in general may seem crude by modern standards, and his generalizations questionable; yet the materials he collected are invaluable.

According to de Groot, the existence of two souls is a widespread belief in ancient and modern China. In Confucianism they are *shen,* the yang soul or breath *(ch'i)* soul, which becomes after death a refulgent spirit *(ming);* and *kuei,* the yin soul, which operates in the living body as *p'o* and after death returns to earth. The meaning of *shen* is not confined to animal breath, but extends to natural movements like the "breath" of the wind, of a stream, or of thunder. In its turn, *kuei* is a link to past life: the ancestors, to whom sacrifices are offered in temples, are *kuei*. All elements have *shen* and *kuei,* and so do "the invisible beings that abide in the World of Darkness" and the statues made by man.[15]

The relationship between *shen* and *kuei* is complex. It can be expressed in a series of oppositions: yang and yin, dilation and contraction, deployment and contraction, sun and moon, day and night, morning and afternoon, the waxing and waning of the moon, flood and ebb, spring and winter, and so on. As we may expect, the more we investigate it, the more complex Chinese psychology appears to be. Different notions like *ching* (vital spirit) and *ling* (the manifest activity of the *ching*) play a crucial role. They are part of a vast and mutable system of classification based on homologies between the micro- and the macrocosm. Like their earlier colleagues the Greek Pythagoreans (see chapter 8, below), scholars of the late Sung dynasty (tenth to twelfth century C.E.) saw innumerable legions of *shen* and *kuei* floating about between heaven and earth.

Taoist nomenclature is more complex. The two souls are multipartite: *hun* has three parts, *p'o* has seven. Besides, there are no less than five *shen* in the five main viscera of the body: liver, lungs, heart, spleen, and kidneys. They are depicted as five spiritual animals—dragon, tiger, red bird, phoenix, and stag—to which a sixth one, a composite turtle-snake, is added for the gall bladder. Sometimes the five *shen* are externalized in the form of five kings. However, the number of internal *shen* can be multiplied ad libitum: a Taoist treatise of the tenth or eleventh century lists three dozen *shen,* and medical treatises generously ascribe to every human being "a hundred *shen*" (in Chinese, "a hundred" can mean "a large number"), whose location moreover varies with age. In ancient times, the heart was supposed to be the main seat of the *shen*.

The *shen* or *hun* soul was generally considered to be separable. Certain death ceremonies installed it in a tablet, in an image of the deceased, and in a banner to be placed in the grave. Upon burial, the *hun* was deposited in a permanent tablet, thereafter kept at home as a powerful protective object. Buddhist priests sometimes piloted the *hun* soul of the deceased to the western paradise of Amitabha.

Yet death is not the only occasion when the free soul can exit the body. Many such occurrences were collected in the *Record of Researches after Spirits (Shen-shen chi)* by a certain Yu Pao, whose brother experienced temporary death for several days, during which he "had witnessed all sorts of things relating to *kuei* and *shen* in the heavens and on earth."[16] A *Posterior Record of Researches on Spirits (Shen-shen hou-chi),* attributed to a certain T'ao Ch'ien (365–427 C.E.) but in reality reporting events that allegedly took place centuries later, explains one case of bilocation by describing the free soul of a person as a perfect duplicate thereof. Skillful magicians are said to be able to extract the souls of others from their bodies. They usually do this with the souls of beautiful women, who then have no recollection of the occurrence, as if it happened in a dream.[17] People can dispatch "their soul out of themselves on purpose, especially with the aim to see hidden things."[18] A twelfth-century story reports that a young man called Chien-pu and also Shun-yu was "able to emit his own *shen*" and thus to obtain information on things going on elsewhere. One day a person frightened him, and thus Chien-pu lost his gift and died shortly thereafter.[19]

The art of leaving the body was also known to Buddhist monks, who explored the western paradise of Amitabha even before going there to abide after death. This seems to be a shamanistic interpretation of Buddhist *dhyana* (meditation) in terms of an otherworldly journey. An eighteenth-century story ascribes to a notorious criminal the unusual talent of hiding his soul in a vase right before any imprisonment or execution. Obviously, he comes back to life many times, to the amazement and despair of the police. But he does not treat his mother well; out of exasperation, she delivers the vase to the authorities, and thus the man dies.[20] In general, trances were used from ancient times for visiting heaven. Mu of Chin (658– 620 B.C.E.) and Chien-tse of Chao (498 B.C.E.) are said to have visited the Emperor of Heaven, and a record of Chien-tse's visit was preserved by Ssu-ma Ch'ien.

Catalepsy, or apparent death, is known as *chüeh* and is attributed to different causes, among which the loss of *hun*. Different charms and drugs are supposed to bring back the *hun*, which is entirely transferable and which can even enter an animal (just as Lucius ended up in an ass in Apuleius's *Metamorphoses*). A case of metempsychosis, or animation of the body of a deceased by the soul of a different person, is reported by Chang Tu, a ninth century C.E. officer, in his *Records of the Manifesto Apartment (Sun-shih chi)*. The *General Description of Strange Things (I-wen tsung lu)*, a tractate of either the Yüan or the Ming dynasty, ascribes to a *kuei* the capacity of sneaking into a fresh corpse in order to come back to life. The *Marvels Recorded in My Private Closet (Liao-chai chi i)*, a collection of 430 narratives of ghosts written under the Manchurian dynasty by a certain Pu Sung-ling, a native of Shantung Province, describes the case of a dead Buddhist monk who took the place of the *hun* of a nobleman; the latter then went back to the monastery and lived among the former's disciples.[21] Belief in metensomatosis (reincarnation), and especially zoanthropy, or reincarnation in animals, were-beasts, and plant-spirits was widespread.

Where spirits were believed to be involved with the living in so many ways, one would expect to find a powerful group of specialists able to deal with them. In China those were the *wu*, belonging to the most ancient official priesthood. Initially *wu* priests were mainly women, but when Confucianism became the state religion women were expelled from the performance of imperial sacrifices. In ancient times they were so famous for their journeys to heaven that King Chao of Ch'u (515–488 B.C.E.) required an explanation of their strange feats from his minister Kuan She-fu; he explained that the *wu* priests did not ascend bodily to heaven, but only their *ching,* which was "in a bright and shining condition," could "rise to higher spheres and descend into the lower," thus being able to forecast the future and to know the past. The *wu* could also be possessed by the *shen* of others, which again explained their extraordinary qualities.[22]

In the following pages we will see the shamanic *wu* priests at work in recent times.

SOUL RAISING IN SINGAPORE

Alan J. A. Elliott studied shamanist possession in the Shenism of Singapore in the late 1940s.[23] During that period, most Chinese in Singapore still described themselves as *pai shen,* worshippers of the *shen,* and Chinese psychology was based on the existence of a threefold *hun* and a sevenfold *p'o.* Shen was the positive influence related to *hun,* and its opposite was *kuei,* the negative influence related to *p'o.* Both *shen* and *kuei* were said to survive death, but *shen* did so in a more consistent way.

The soul specialist in Singapore, man or woman, was referred to as the *tang-chi* (divining youth) independently of his or her real age. Most *tang-chi* performed in temples and needed a whole arsenal of instruments, especially weapons, to display the power of trance over pain and self-inflicted bodily injuries. The most common utensils were swords, skewers, knife beds, and painful "prick balls" that lacerated the flesh.

The *tang-chi* were thought to be possessed by *shen.* There were hordes of *shen,* but two were considered most important.

The first was a male, Ch'i-t'ien Ta-sheng ("the great saint equal with heaven"), that is, the Monkey God, main character of the novel *Journey to the West,* whom we will meet again in the next chapter; the second was female, the Buddhist goddess Kuan-yin.

In Singapore, female *tang-chi* specialized in otherworldly journeys for "soul raising" *(khan-bông)* or necromancy. Soul raisers sought out the help of Kuan-yin to guide them through the spirit world. During every séance they reenacted a sort of new *Divine Comedy,* talking with spirits in hell, imitating their voices, and describing their atrocious mutilations and tortures, continuing until they found the ghost they were looking for. "When all business is finished Kuan-yin emerges from the gates of hell, chanting as she goes. The soul raiser stands up with her hands crossed and falls back into the chair behind her. Assistants come forward to revive her with charm water. After a few seconds she regains consciousness and makes ready to leave the house."[24]

TAIWANESE GHOST BRIDES

Between 1966 and 1968, David K. Jordan performed field research in a village north of Tainan city, in Hokkien-speaking southwestern Taiwan. The beliefs he reports are but a variant of those described by de Groot or by Elliott in Singapore. The Hokkien Taiwanese acknowledge two souls. The *phek (p'o)* is associated with earth, femaleness, darkness, and yin; it is necessary to life yet transitory, for after lingering in coffins and around graves for a while it eventually expires. The *hwen (hun)* or *ling (leng),* popularly called *linghwen (leng-hun)* is immortal and yang; it can be sent to hell, reincarnate, or live in a ghostly world, or it can become a wandering ghost, *goei (kuei).* If a *hwen* is good, it can become a *shern (shen),* a heavenly spirit or a god, after death. The will of the innumerable spirits is revealed by specialists called *tang-chi,* who inflict injuries upon their own bodies by means of five instruments: the prick ball, the sword, the saw, the spiked club, and the axe.

The permanent interaction between this world and the invisible world of spirits is exemplified in the phenomenon of "hell marriage," which is invariably the marriage between a ghost bride and a human groom. A special female *tang-chi* is in charge of the oracle of the Little God in Chiali. She "specializes in spirit marriages and has a stock of equipment for her performance which can be rented by the day."[25] The bride-to-be, the ghost of a girl who has died in childhood, requests a wedding either by appearing in the dream of someone in her family, or by inflicting sickness or bad luck on someone close to them. It is the job of the medium to determine the will of the spirit and to assist the family in the marriage. The groom once used to be chosen randomly—the first man to pick up a red envelope left in the street was selected—but, according to Jordan, in recent times the marriage is increasingly kept in the family by wedding the ghost to one of her sisters' husbands. As an explanation for this, Jordan suggests possible exhaustion of all ghost brides-to-be in some village communities; but economic factors cannot be discarded, since the ghost bride receives a rather substantial dowry. Thus keeping it in the family must please everyone involved. The wedding actually takes place and looks like a real wedding, except for the fact that, when she appears from the taxi, the bride is a dummy two and a half feet high, dressed like a dead person in three layers of clothing; her face, instead of being pale and preoccupied like that of a real bride, wears the perfect smile of a Japanese calendar model.

The ghost bride is a threat to her husband. Moreover, she cannot be fooled: if the husband tries to avoid this otherworldly presence and does not honor the marital contract, she can take vengeance on the living by bothering them as before. She lives in two worlds, as does the man who agrees to marry her.

MASTERS OF CRANE RIDING

The ancient goal of immortality was still pursued in Taoist circles until not long ago.[26] Taoist priests still perform the most impressive journeys between worlds. In his book *The Teachings of Taoist Master Chuang,* Michael Saso describes the eclectic techniques of Master Chuang-ch'en Teng-yün of Hsin-chu City in Taiwan, who died in 1976.[27] Not unlike the early sixteenth-century German magician Cornelius Agrippa of Net-tesheim, Master Chuang could conjure the spirits of the stars, of which he knew the names and aspects. This practice is one of the standard Taoist operations concerning stars, which include conjuration, installation of stars in one's body, and walking on stars. The last one, as described in relatively ancient sources, is particularly interesting: the stars of the constellation of the Dipper take the adept through the three gates of the nine heavens, where he shows each keeper a talisman and says the keeper's name; the keeper then lets him enter. The adept comes to the golden gate, the gate of paradise, where his talisman is checked by the guardians of the four poles, who let him pass after consultation with the emperor of the golden gate. Having reached the heaven Yu Ch'ing, where there is no spatial direction, he eventually enters a paradise, in the middle of which grows a jade tree with golden branches, surrounded by dragons.[28] The closest Western analogue to this practice is the so-called "Mithra liturgy," a magical Hellenistic text in which the stars help the adept in his heavenly ascent (see chapter 10, below).

Like Michael Saso, John Lagerwey worked with an extraor-dinary informant, the Taoist priest Ch'en Jung-sheng of Taitung in present-day Taiwan. More ambitious than Saso, Lagerwey undertook research on *wu* priesthood starting at the point at which it had been abandoned by de Groot in 1910, and he came up with spectacular results.[29]

Taoist liturgy appears to be the enactment of a heavenly journey, strongly reminiscent of a shamanistic performance. Lagerwey describes in detail a ritual of consecrating a temple that took place in November 1980 in Taitung, with Ch'en Jung-sheng as *kao-kung* (priest of high merit).[30] The ritual, which lasted three days (altogether twenty-five hours), included nineteen main sequences of great complexity. On the eve of the first day, all the paraphernalia to be used were purified by fire, followed by a short but powerful drum concert, the announcement, the flag-raising, the noon offering, and the division of lamps. The second day was taken up with the "land of the Way."[31] On the third day, the orthodox offering and the universal salvation concluded the sequence, and like other sequences they were highly symbolic of communication between worlds.

Posted on the outside wall of the temple was a placard describing the purport of the ritual. According to this, when the drums beat, evil is expelled by an oil-fed fire. Documents are sent to the three realms of heaven, water, and earth to invite the notables to a "fragrant banquet." These communications with otherworldly presences, redacted in the fastidious style of Confucianist bureaucracy, are dispatched to the secretaries of the celestial kings and dignitaries: the golden gate in the jade capital of heaven, the gate of the four bureaus of the three realms, the bureau of the great sovereign of the office of heaven, the court of the celestial pivot in the highest purity, the office of the eastern peak Tai, and so on. No gods or celestial clerks of high rank in heaven and hell are omitted. To extend the invitations, the high priest relies on messenger gods.

Let the mounted gods gallop each in his own direction and give (his documents) to the right office, penetrating on high to the Golden Gate of the Jade Capital and below into the bright waters and dark earth. . . . The above is announced to the jade lasses of the Three Heavens charged with transmission, the messengers of the roads through the clouds of the Nine Heavens, the officers of merit of Orthodox Unity, the great generals of the molten metal and fiery bells, the potent officers in charge of memorializing on this day, the clerks mounted on the flying dragons—all the gods of transmission.[32]

The ritual of announcement that follows was devised by a Taoist movement of the tenth century C.E. called the orthodox method of the heart of heaven *(t'ien-hsin cheng-fa)*. By the end of the twelfth century, the practise of *fa-piao* (dispatching the memorial) had become the norm.[33] It survives today in a simplified form. It starts with a long sequence of purification; the priest is transformed into a cosmic being whose head is a cloud of ink, whose hair is scattered stars, whose nose is a mountain, and whose teeth are like a forest of swords. This giant hides behind the Big Dipper, summons his celestial and terrestrial souls, and then starts walking on the stars of the Dipper in order to reach the golden gate and be received in audience by the Emperor of Heaven. At the same time he is purified by "the nine phoenixes that destroy filth" and incorporates energies from the stars.

In front of the altar, the priest offers incense to the six masters and four saints, who leave the golden gate behind them and descend to earth in a chariot of cloud carried by a team of cranes.[34] When the guests have invisibly arrived at their thrones, they are offered wine. Sprinkling the altar with a flower dipped in water, the priest enjoins the demons to leave, and he is accompanied by furious percussion sounds. Incense is then offered again; its fragrance ascends to heaven, taking the form of celestial seals and drawing to the altar the immortals sitting on colored clouds, "all the generals and marshals of outer space."[35] The summoning of heavenly guests continues, as the priest proclaims how hard it is "to go up there without a phoenix-team or a crane-mount; no way to get there unless you ride the mists and clouds." Yet the priest seems to succeed, and the invitation is dispatched to "the Three Pure Ones, the Jade Emperor, the nine categories of saints and immortals, the sun, the moon, and the Dipper. . . . the immortals of the five peaks and ten caves, the three islands and nine isles, and all the ghosts and gods of the nine springs and the six caves, all gods, from the rulers of the Nine Heavens down to the most humble earth god. . . ."[36] Two documents written in red ink assure that the gate of heaven is open and the "stellar winds" are favorable. The priest prepares for the "unicorn walk," announcing that his assistants have opened the gate of heaven and have prepared his way so that he can meet the potentates of heaven. Then, pronouncing the name of each of the seven stars of the Big Dipper, he "walks" on them. The esoteric meaning of the ritual is that the priest is sending to heaven the "red infant," an energy from his lower abdomen, through the stars of the Dipper to a "silent audience before the Supreme Emperor."[37] Taken at their face value, however, the gestures of the performer of the Taoist liturgy are a simulation of a heavenly ascent, and as such are strongly reminiscent of a shamanistic séance. After several other sequences, the guests are dismissed. They mount the cloud chariot, and the team of cranes takes off.[38]

Part of the otherworldly journey of the announcement is more elaborately repeated in the ritual called land of the Way (tao ch'ang), which is the central episode of an offering ritual. The six masters and four saints come again upon invitation in their cloud chariot. A message is taken to the Emperor of Heaven by means of smoke "of the five colors"; accompanied by powerful gonging and drumming, the potentates of the four winds are summoned through a "sword dance"; wine and incense are offered; tea is presented to the Master of Jade Purity by the priest, who bows and genuflects; and the final tea offerings are repeated two more times, concluded by hymns.

The performance can be understood from at least three perspectives: first, the audience can follow the main episodes of the heavenly journey; second, the priest executes complicated visualizations; and third, the priest describes what "really" happens in terms of subtle energies of the body and events in what we may call his "anthropocosmic organism." As a matter of fact, a double hermeneutics of space voyage is possible: one reading is external, theatrical, and macrocosmic; the other one is microcosmic and has to do with actual "descents" and "ascents" in the interior palaces of the body, carefully constructed and furnished in the mind according to ancient Taoist procedures. It is instructive to follow the priest's visualizations during an ascent to heaven as recommended by a thirteenth-century text:

> Visualize the red inkstone and the dish of water as the sun and the moon respectively, the paper as golden strips, the brush as a green dragon, and the smoke of the incense as white clouds. The clerks of the symbol are atop these clouds, and the lads and lasses, officers and generals of the symbolic method are arrayed to the right and left. When this is accomplished, form in your hand the sign of the Big Dipper, and visualize the dippers of the five directions enveloping the body. Walk the *huo-lo* Dipper, press the point of the Emperor on High in your hand, and visualize yourself entering the Three Terraces and the Big Dipper.[39]

Like the shaman, the Taoist priest also goes to the nether world in search of the soul of a deceased person, accompanied by heavy drumming; by means of cranes he ascends to heaven to mediate on the soul's behalf so that it may be admitted in the celestial world.[40] In another ritual, a writ of pardon is obtained from heaven; it is issued by the chief of the teaching of the Green Heaven, otherwise known as the savior from distress, and it is carried by a participant who mimes riding a horse. Symbols of ascent abound: hymns are, for example, sung on increasingly higher tones;[41] the priest wears platform shoes, and so on. The descent to hell in order to release a departed soul (part of the ritual called attack on hell) is particularly theatrical. After the deafening sound of drums and gongs has indicated that the hour on stage is midnight, the officiant, who is often a medium, comes before the gate of hell and summons the gatekeeper (represented by the drummer or another actor) to let him enter the gloomy kingdom of Yama. In an elaborate scene, the gatekeeper asks for money, that is, real copper money, not paper money. Since the officiant has none, he is let in after he sings from the scriptures. He continues singing, but his song is about the inferno, describing what he witnesses beyond the gate of powerful Yama, in the kingdom of darkness. There, at the center of hell, he performs a powerful exorcism to release the soul of the deceased and, summoning the "divine soldiers of the Five Camps," he smashes the abode of the dead symbolized by a paper fortress. The family of the deceased help in the destruction.[42]

At every step of Taoist ritual the various levels of understanding suggest that an external, shamanist performance has been adapted to internal Taoist exegesis.

6

Journeys through the Mind

Buddhism and Otherworldly Journeys

THE FREE SOUL IN HINDUISM

Rightly or wrongly, Vedic India is commonly regarded as having been the homeland of ecstasy. Three times a day, Vedic priests drank the inebriating and probably hallucinogenic freshly squeezed juice of a mountain plant called *soma*. The identity of the plant has been lost since early times. Several substitutes were used by the Brahmans in its stead, but their properties were surely not equal to those described in Vedic hymns. In the 1960s, R. Gordon Wasson, a retired banker, and Wendy Doniger, a scholar of Indology, assembled a great wealth of data in order to show that the *soma* plant was fly agaric *(Amanita muscaria)*, a widespread Eurasian mushroom possibly used in the past by Siberian shamans in order to enter a state of trance. According to Wasson's theory, fly agaric was used by the Indo-Iranians in their Asian homeland during a period in which active linguistic exchange took place between them and the Finno-Ugrians. When they moved on to the conquest of Iran and India they lost touch with the fly-agaric mushroom, which does not grow in any of those regions. This is why substitutes had to be found.[1]

Vedic afterlife was spent in the underground abode of Yama,

who had been the first to die and the first to journey to dead land. The soul had to find its way past two frightening dogs whose four powerful eyes watched over the entrance (*Rigveda* 10.14.11)—meager versions of the Greek Cerberus. In the lusterless realm of Yama, the soul was not supposed to expect any particular glamor; it was simply the abode of the ancestors, the *pituh* (from *pitr-,* "father"). Yet other Vedic hymns speak of a heavenly judgment of the dead and of posthumous retribution for deeds committed in life. The picture becomes clearer during the post-Vedic period,[2] when a distinction is made between heavenly immortality for the good, and punishment in one of the twenty-one underground hells for the wicked. The Upanishads refer to the soul as rising from the fire of cremation and going either the way of the gods *(devayana)* without return, or the way of the fathers *(pitriyana),* which leads back to the earth through rebirth.[3]

The conception of a free dream soul called *atma* is at home in the Upanishads (see *Chandogya Upanishad* 8.10.1). A dreamer is supposed to visit the gods, for in deep sleep man and god are identical (*Brhadaranyaka Upanishad* 4.3.20), and heaven is already in one's own heart (*Chandogya Upanishad* 8.3.1–3). A person should not be suddenly awakened, for the soul may be in danger of not finding its way back to the body (*Brhadaranyaka Up.* 4.3.14).[4] The Upanishads also make mention of other-worldly journeys.[5]

Reference to the freedom of the dream soul explains the special magical powers *(siddhi)* obtained by ascetics and yogins. One of these *siddhi* is the faculty of flying through the air, already mentioned by the *Rigveda* (10.136.3–4), which is an outgrowth of weightlessness, such as we already encountered in ancient Taoism. According to Hemacandra, the Jaina ascetics could make their body lighter than air,[6] and Patanjali's *Yogasutra* lists *laghiman,* or the achievement of weightlessness, among the eight major magical powers *(mahasiddhi)* of the yogin.[7]

Innumerable stories of levitation and journeys to other worlds are part of the multifarious Hindu tradition. They belong to the transformations of an ancient shamanic folklore that deeply penetrated yogic mysticism. Legends of miraculous powers abound in connection with the names of the yogin Nagarjuna, or Gorakhnath. He lived sometime between the ninth and the twelfth century C.E. and is reported to have gone to the underground world of the Nagas (serpent beings) in order to obtain magical incense to save the life of a woman. According to another tradition, he went to the underworld, threatened Yama with destruction, shook the foundations of the realm of the dead, and then modified the records in order to change the destiny of his guru Matsyendranath, who had too pronounced an inclination toward sex.[8] Having studied a number of instances of Chinese "soul raising," we are better equipped to understand the shamanistic background of these stories.

Without neglecting otherworldly journeys, the Hindu tradition evolved in two ways, which seemed to be separate but were actually not always distinct: ecstatic rapture and yogic mysticism. The two overlap in that yogic mysticism culminates in ecstasy similar to ecstatic rapture. Mircea Eliade distinguished shamanic ecstasy from yogic "enstasy," but the distinction is problematic. Yoga presupposes interiorization of ecstatic practices and of a vertical hierarchy of being, and in this respect is very similar to Western mysticism, be it Platonic or Christian. To the extent that we call ecstasy the Plotinian union of the soul with the One, or the Bonaventuran union of the mind with God, then we are certainly entitled to apply the word ecstasy to the yogin's supreme achievement.

The psychoanalyst J. Moussaieff Masson[9] has reapplied the Freudian expression "oceanic feeling" *(ozeanisches Gefühl* or *Einigkeitsgefühl)* to the Indian context from which Freud originally derived it. Freud based his term on Romain Rolland's *Life*

of Ramakrishna, and more precisely on an ecstatic experience
(samadhi) reported by Ramakrishna: "In whatever direction I
looked great luminous waves were rising." A recent analysis of
"divine madness" among Bengali mystics shows that *bhava*
(ecstasy), though similar in content and oftentimes based on
the "oceanic feeling," can be obtained through various methods. The best example of multiplicity of methods and unity of
results remains Ramakrishna (Gadadhara Chatterji, 1836–86)
himself, who "include[d] both the singular dedication of
devotion to a deity and the universalism of Vedanta, combined
with yoga and tantra."[10] As a child, Ramakrishna was possessed
by the gods. At nineteen he was appointed priest of the
goddess Kali near Calcutta. There he practiced asceticism and
meditation, and had visions of fire and light, but the vision of
the Mother was denied him until he attempted suicide. It was
in that instant that the Goddess revealed herself to him as an
ocean of consciousness.[11] For a time, he alternated between
blissful ecstatic union with the Mother and painful awakening;
in the eyes of others he was incurably mad, until a holy woman
who visited him declared that his was not a state of ordinary
madness, but of divine madness. Others then equally recognized in him an avatar of Vishnu, and he began practicing
Vaishnava mysticism according to more formal methods, later
learning yogic meditation and entering a state of *samadhi* for
six months (ordinarily such ecstatic states last only a short
time). Even when practicing yoga, he had personal visions of
quite particular tones. For example, one time he saw a young
man licking his seven subtle centers *(cakra)* up to the last, the
thousand-petaled lotus *(sahasrara)* at the top of the head, and
the lotus blossomed.[12]

In these examples of Hindu *samadhi,* neither yogin nor saint
experienced otherworldly journeys. On the other hand, afterlife geography and visits to the other world became increasingly a specialty of Buddhism.

THE FREE SOUL AND OTHER
WORLDS IN BUDDHISM

At least in theory, the existence of a "free soul" in Buddhism is problematic. Indeed, the Buddha ("awakened one") strongly opposed the brahmanic *atman* theory. Developing his famous negative logic, the Buddha taught that there is nothing permanent, and therefore no such thing as a stable soul *(atman):* "No phenomena are *atman,*" declares the Pali *Majjhima Nikaya* (1.230). When Vacchagotta asks him what he thinks about *atman,* the Buddha gives no reply at all, for anything he could say would be misinterpreted *(Samyutta Nikaya* 400f.).

On the other hand, primitive Buddhism strongly affirmed the freedom of the dream soul, a freedom on which all the great *iddhi* (Pali for *siddhi)* were based.

> From one person he becomes many, and from many he becomes one again. Now he shows up, and now he hides again. Unhindered he goes through walls and through mountains as if they were empty space. He dives into the depth of the earth and comes back again as if out of water. He walks on water without sinking, as if on earth. He floats cross-legged on air like a winged bird. He takes the great and powerful luminaries, the sun and the moon, in his hand, and pets them. He even reaches the world of brahman (i.e. the universal soul) while in his body.[13]

According to Pali texts, the main *iddhi* of the Tathagata (Buddha) is levitation *(Samyutta Nikaya* 5.283). Shortly after his enlightenment, the Awakened One flew over the water of the river Ganges, "vanishing from one side of the river and standing on the further bank in company of the brethren."[14] Another source reports that the boatmen asked the Buddha the fee for crossing. "My good men," the Buddha replied, "I do not have the fee for crossing"; and in the same instant he flew over the water to the opposite bank.[15] Yet, on the other hand, we know that the Buddha dissuaded an ascetic from walking over water if he could use a boat. As John S. Strong noticed, magical powers, and especially the power of levitation, are treated in quite a contradictory manner in Buddhism: on the one hand they are discouraged by the Buddha, but on the other hand they are actively practiced by both the Buddha and his disciples.[16]

Similarly, although one would expect from Buddhism opposition to the multiplication of parallel worlds where Buddhas, gods, demons, and the dead live, the idea of an intermediate condition between this world and extinction in *nirvana* is constitutive of ancient Buddhism. Thus parallel worlds proliferated in Buddhist circles, including paradises of the buddhas and of the luminous, asexual, and perishable gods, and hells populated by ancestors and demons.[17]

Combined with genuine yogic practices adapted to a new purpose, Tibetan Lamaism became a paradigm for otherworldly journeys.

THE FUNERAL LITURGY OF
TIBETAN BUDDHISM

The *Bar-do'i-thos-grol* (The book of the dead; read *Bardo thödöl*) is a *gter-ma* (hidden treasure), that is, an apocryphal work of uncertain date, allegedly authored by the eighth-century apostle of Tantric Buddhism in Tibet, Padmasambhava, and hidden during his lifetime, to be exhumed centuries later. From the main biography of Padmasambhava, written by his disciple the princess Yeshe Tsogyel, we discover that the guru of Tibet was an incarnation of Buddha Amitabha, that he received his yogic instruction directly from heaven, and that he could fly like a bird.[18]

The *Bardo thödöl* is a Lamaistic funeral liturgy whose aim is to provide guidance for the soul of the dead, thus fulfilling the function of a shamanistic manual for "soul raisers," adapted to the highly sophisticated exigencies of Lamaistic doctrines and ritual. The purpose of reading the *Bardo thödöl* beside the deceased for forty-nine days is to "close the door" of the gaping womb ready to catch the soul in order to trap it in a body, and to ensure the soul a good posthumous fate.[19]

Bardo actually means any "intermediate state" and is not necessarily limited to the state after death. The text therefore speaks of six *bardo:* "the bardo of birth, the bardo of dreams, the bardo of samadhi-meditation, the bardo of the moment before death, the bardo of dharmata and the bardo of becoming."[20] In death, one can experience only the last three *bardo.*

Reciting the *Bardo thödöl* for the deceased is only necessary in the case of those unfamiliar with the special yogic practices that permit direct liberation after death. In ordinary cases, the *Bardo thödöl* should be read beside the dead, and since the *bardo* state cannot exceed forty-nine days, that is how long recitation can last. The text does not explain how the reciting priest knows if he has succeeded in installing the roaming soul in one of the heavenly mansions (described below). Theoretically, recitation should cease on cessation of the *bardo* state.

The first *bardo*, which occurs before death, is a unique but brief occasion on which one can be absorbed into Buddhahood. The sign of this state is a clear light; if followed, it leads to immediate liberation. The *bardo* priest urgently repeats this to the person crossing the threshold of death.

The second *bardo,* entered by the many who are not absorbed into the light of the first, begins with a new opportunity to disappear into Buddhahood. The light of pure consciousness flashes before one's mind. If followed, it leads to liberation; if not, the consciousness of the deceased enters the confusing *bardo* of karmic illusions, during which it is very important that professional guidance be provided, since the deceased's mind is in a state of shock.

At this time his relatives are crying and weeping, his share of food is stopped, his clothes are removed, his bed is taken to pieces, and so on. He can see them but they cannot see him, and he can hear them calling him but they cannot hear him calling them, so he goes away in despair. Three phenomena will appear at this time: sounds, colored lights and rays of light, and he will grow faint with fear, terror and bewilderment, so at this moment the great showing of the Bardo of dharmata should be read.[21]

Bardo experience is actually a simple but persuasive trick played by one's own mind. If one recognizes its emptiness from the outset, then one can avoid it by being absorbed in the colorless light. If not, new insubstantial phantoms appear, all wrapped in light, some good but too bright and some bad but inviting. It is therefore essential that the anguished consciousness in this *bardo* be instructed that whatever appears before it is pure illusion of the mind. With this, in a roar of thunder, the show commences and the deceased dives into a glamorous and mysterious Disneyland of apparitions, starting with the five meditation Buddhas (that is, mental Buddhas created for meditative purposes). They occupy the center and the four directions of space. Each of the five realms is assigned a color, a Buddha with a particular female consort, two bodhisattvas with their consorts, an element, and a *loka* (inferior world) that the dead must avoid.

From the radiant blue center first appears the blessed Vairocana seated on a lion throne; his element is ether, and his inferior world is the *devaloka* (paradise of the gods), emitting a dull white light. If the deceased misses the blue light, then the *bardo* continues with the rising, from the east, of a bright white light, corresponding to Buddha Vajrasattva with his consort Mamaki and two bodhisattvas with their consorts. This realm is connected with the element water and with the inferior world of hell, announced by a "soft smoky light." The consciousness of the dead, terrified by the intensity of the white light, may be attracted by the light of hell, from which it should by all means stay away.

If the dead person's consciousness is not absorbed into Buddhahood on the second day, the *bardo* continues on the third day with a yellow light rising from the south, corresponding to Buddha Ratnasambhava with his consort and two bodhisattvas with their consorts, to the element earth, and to the soft bluish light of the human world.

Similarly, if during the fourth day the deceased is still indecisive, from the west dawns the intense red light of Buddha Amitabha with his consort and his retinue of bodhisattvas. The element is fire, and the *loka* is *pretaloka,* announced by a soft yellow light.

The text does not devote much attention to the pretas, a special category of ghosts called "hungry ghosts." Their mouths are as small as the point of a needle and are located in the middle of the head, making it hard for them to eat. They are among the most picturesque creatures of the Indian tradition. They are burning, morose, miserable demons, continuously fighting with and maiming one another.[22]

Eventually, if the deceased misses the opportunities offered by the fourth day, the green radiance of the fifth day dawns from the north, featuring Buddha Amoghasiddhi with consorts and retinue, the element air, and the soft red light of the *loka* of the warlike asura demons. Like actors at the end of a show, if the dead is still there all five realms fill the sky during the sixth day, together with forty-two deities, and on the seventh day the encore continues, along with two other worlds, paradise and the animal realm.

From the eighth to the fourteenth day the show is a repetition of the first seven days, but in a monstrous and terrifying key. The five meditation Buddhas with their retinues, although remaining substantially the same in that they are mental projections, appear as wrathful, blood-drinking deities who generate fear and confusion. Recognition now becomes extremely difficult, for these heruka Buddhas with their consorts are not meant to be pleasant. This is Vairocana in his scary guise. "His red-gold hair flies upward blazing, his (three) heads are crowned with dried skulls and the sun and the moon, his body is garlanded with black serpents and fresh skulls."[23] The final recapitulation, when all of the deities congregate on stage, is memorable. "With teeth biting the lower lip, glassy-eyed, their hair tied on top of their heads, with huge bellies and thin necks, holding the records of karma in their hands, shouting 'Strike!' and 'Kill!', licking up brains, tearing heads from bodies, pulling out internal organs: in this way they will come, filling the whole universe."[24] The bardo priest must now do his best to persuade the deceased that this nightmare is nothing but his own mind at work, that is, that it is pure emptiness and illusion. "When projections appear like this do not be afraid. You have a mental body of unconscious tendencies, so even if you are killed and cut into pieces you cannot die. . . . The Lords of Death too arise out of your own radiant mind, they have no solid substance. Emptiness cannot be harmed by emptiness."[25]

Starting around the tenth day, the deceased can learn some important things about the bardo body, which is actually a free soul or dream soul, endowed with all the miraculous siddhi one could wish for. This is particularly important for the deceased to know after finally realizing that he or she is dead, in order to make an end to the frightening illusions of karma that can torment the consciousness in a thousand ways. The deceased now has the opportunity to see friends and relatives, although his or her presence remains unknown. The thought then arises that it would be good to have a body again. The unpleasant episode of the judgment of the dead then intervenes. The good genius and the bad genius count the deceased's good and bad actions, the lord of death verifies the count by looking in the all-knowing mirror of karma. He then administers capital punishment to the soul, but yet this capital punishment produces pain without killing. "Then the Lord of Death will drag you by a rope tied around your neck, and cut off your head, tear out your heart, pull out your entrails, lick your brains, drink your blood, eat your flesh and gnaw your bones; but you cannot die, so even though your body is cut into pieces you will recover."[26] At this point it is especially good to know that the *bardo* body is made only of dream stuff and that nothing can affect it in any way; pain is an illusion. The reader understands here that the logic of the *Bardo thödöl* is not to displace popular representations of the world of the dead, but to reinterpret them as sheer mental states that create powerful illusions. It is ultimately you who write the script for your own death, and it depends on only you whether you turn it into an endless horror show, a divine comedy, or nothing at all. This realization brings recognition of the *bardo* state, and its recognition brings immediate liberation.

Nevertheless, recognition may not come. In this case, the deceased is doomed to be reborn in one of the six realms ready to receive the soul: the realm of the devas, hell, the human world, the realm of the pretas, the realm of the asuras, and the animal world. All of them now send visible signals in the guise of colored light, as we already saw above. At this point, the *bardo* priests must perform a ritual intended to sway the dead from incarnation in low and painful worlds, and they concentrate equally on deterring the soul from entering any world at all. For this they have recourse to a set of methods for "closing the door of the womb." Indeed, by that time, innumerable copulating couples appear, and wombs of all sorts are arrayed to receive the soul. The mechanism of rebirth is desire for the opposite sex: one enters the womb and becomes a daughter if one is attracted to the father, and one becomes a son if attracted to the mother. In each case, one experiences strong jealousy toward the parent of the opposite sex who is copulating with one's favorite.

The implications of this text are numerous. First, it is easy to see that it gives the Oedipus complex a transcendental explanation. This is clearly one version of the Oedipus myth, a version in which the Freudian reading is already included. Second, it shows that it is children who choose their parents, a decision they may live to regret bitterly. At the same time, this explanation gives children a sort of uncanny superiority over their parents.

During all this time, the *bardo* priests actively try to dissuade the dead person's consciousness by all means from entering a womb. Should this not work, they try at least to provide the roaming soul with the most suitable womb to enter, according to criteria of geographical location, wealth, and social position. The choice is difficult, for bad wombs can look good, and vice versa.

The text alludes to yogic techniques that one should perform during one's lifetime in order to pass unharmed through the *bardo* and then make the right choice. These techniques are intensely advertised among monks: we read several times that, no matter how high one's religious merits, one may still be confronted with all the unpleasant aspects of the *bardo* if proper attention has not been devoted to yogic preparation for the *bardo*. W. Y. Evans-Wentz, who brought the *Bardo thödöl* to Europe, also brought the remedy, the yoga of consciousness transference.[27]

YOGA FOR THE DEAD

The 1935 English translations of Tibetan yogic texts by Lama Kawa Dazi Samdup, edited and introduced by his disciple W. Y. Evans-Wentz, contain two tractates dealing with yoga

exercises intended to bring about recognition of the *bardo* state
and prevention of rebirth: "The Epitome of the Six Doctrines,
Which Are the Psychic-Heat, the Illusory Body, the Dream-
State, the Clear Light, the After-Death State, and the Transfer-
ence of the Consciousness"; and "The Transference of the
Consciousness."

Preliminary exercises consist of meditation and visualization
intended to show that all phenomena are illusory. The adept
must especially work on dreams and the dream state, reaching
a state in which dream contents can be manipulated, thereby
showing that any illusion is created by one's own mind and
can be arranged into new patterns by mind itself.

The nature of the dream state can be comprehended
through resolution, breathing, or visualization. Resolution refers to the continuity of consciousness. If the state in which
there is no break between sleep and awakening is attained, all
phenomena are shown to be continuous and illusory, like
dream stuff. This method demonstrates that the substance of
"reality" is as insubstantial as dreams are. Breathing refers to
a particular technique that enhances the vividness of dreams,
whereby dreams are shown to be as convincing as daylight
reality. This method is thus the opposite of the first.

The text describes four visualization methods whose purpose is to circumscribe dreaming and to initiate a further state
of recognition of the dream state and manipulation of the
content of dreams. The dreamer should assume an active
posture in dreams, reacting strongly toward whatever may
cause emotions. For example, if a fire is threatening to burn
and consume him, the dreamer should say: "What fear can
there be of fire which occurs in a dream?" This should suffice
to dispel the power of illusion. More elaborate instructions for
dream manipulation follow: dream fire should be turned into
water, minute dream objects should be turned into large
objects, single things into many, many into one, and so on.[28]

The rest of the tractate is about the art of dying and teaches preparation for the *bardo* state. The adept is taught how to recognize the clear light dawning on the mind at death and how to avoid the illusions of the *bardo* by being absorbed into this nirvanic light. Even if recognition of the clear light fails, the adept is taught to recognize the subsequent sequences of the *bardo,* and, if rebirth cannot be prevented, how to choose an appropriate womb. It is clear that, in this case, the yogin undergoes an imaginary otherworldly journey in anticipation of the *bardo.* The stages of learning can be summarized thus:

1. Dream is "mind stuff";
2. The surrounding world is dream, and therefore is mind stuff;
3. The *bardo* is also dream, and therefore mind stuff.
   Mind stuff is illusion. Mind itself can abstain from producing illusion and withdraw into its own emptiness, which is nirvana.

POPULAR BUDDHISM

Popular Buddhism has produced countless stories of other-worldly journeys. The most impressive among them, both quantitatively and qualitatively, found their way into Chinese literature. One recurring theme is voyage to the underworld by various characters of Buddhist legend, such as Devadatta or by the bodhisattva Kuan-yin.[29]

One such story, unexceptional other than in its fastidious-ness was inserted at the end of a 1597 collection authored by Lo Mou-teng. It is the fictitious account of a 1405 to 1432 expedition to Mecca led by the chief eunuch Cheng Ho, accompanied by the Taoist master of heaven and by the Buddhist state master. The setting is ecumenical and puzzling. When the sailors get lost, the officer Wang Ming sets out to explore a dark shore. He lands at a city whose population is a genetic mixture of human beings and animals in bizarre proportions. Among them, Wang finds his deceased wife, who is now wife of one of the deputies of Yama, the lord of the dead. Wang realizes that he has landed in the underworld. He passes for his ex-wife's brother and is given a tour of hell by her new husband. Noteworthy are a river of blood with two bridges that can be crossed only by relatively good people (the best go to heaven, but there are not many of them), while the wicked must muddle through the blood, fighting against brass serpents and iron dogs. All this is Chinese Buddhist scenery, at times grotesquely transformed: Dame Meng is supposed to mix the potion of oblivion for the dead, which is a sort of water of Lethe that allows them to reincarnate, but here she becomes an old prostitute mixing a tea that produces confusion of mind.[30]

Along a dam where a nasty wind throws water in the faces of the people, making them despondent, walk ten categories of ghosts, who are thus expiating past sins: wine ghosts, poverty ghosts, pestilence ghosts, reckless ghosts, ghosts with irregular teeth, ghosts struggling for their lives, begging ghosts, ghosts of suicide by strangling, spendthrifts, and misers.[31] Crossing the gate of the Palace of Spiritual Radiance, Wang visits ten royal residences bearing the Chinese names of the ten Buddhist hells, and these are divided into purgatories for people whose conduct was honorable and hells for those who sinned against the eight Confucian virtues. In the rear are another eighteen hells where frightening punishments befall the sinners. Fortunately, the visit ends with the eighth hell, since Wing Ming's host is "called away on urgent business."[32]

Another sixteenth-century Chinese text, which has been compared with Dante's *Divine Comedy,* is one of the masterpieces of world literature. *The Journey to the West (Hsi-yu chi)* is attributed (perhaps falsely) to the writer Wu Cheng-en and is now available to Western readers in the masterful English translation by Anthony C. Yu.[33] Like Dante's *Comedy,* writes Yu, "the *Journey* is at once a magnificent tale of fiction and a complex allegory, in which the central drama of its protagonist's 'approach to God' unfolds within the interplay of the literal and figurative dimensions of the work."[34] This certainly applies to the part of *The Journey to the West* that is based on the pilgrimage of the Buddhist monk Hsüang-tsang (596–664) to India in search of Buddhist scriptures. This part of the novel has been defined as a "Buddhist allegory,"[35] and it is based on a pilgrimage, not an otherworldly journey.

Otherworldly journeys abound in the other, eminently comical part of the novel, devoted to the adventures of a very unusual Taoist sage and immortal who eventually converts to Buddhism, the Monkey God or "great sage equal to heaven."

The Monkey God is in a privileged position that allows him to visit other worlds; in fact, he is an inhabitant of other worlds, having been born from a miraculous stone on top of the cosmic mountain in which were concentrated the essences of the cosmic principles of heaven and earth. This noble origin makes him into a divine being endowed with supernatural powers that exceed the powers of the Taoist deities. With his phallic weapon, which grows as large as a mountain or shrinks to the dimension of a needle, and with his boundless capacities for transformation, the Monkey God plays havoc with the mansions of the Taoist heavens, and all attempts to civilize him fail. After he eats the peaches of immortality and drinks all heavenly elixir reserves, heaven declares war on him.

It is impossible to relate here all of Monkey's adventures in heaven and on earth. Turned into the character Pilgrim, he becomes the ambiguous ally of the monk Hsüang-tsang, alias Tripitaka, in his journey to the west.

Monkey is an almighty shaman, more ancient than the gods, even than the Taoist gods. Yet, on the other hand, in Buddhist meditation "monkey" stands for the mind, which is as old as heaven and earth and is almighty and transformative. Read according to this key, the novel becomes a Buddhist allegory of the process of taming one's own mind, according to the Mahayana principle that the world is merely the illusory web of mind.

Complex and subtle, *The Journey to the West* has a multiplicity of messages for every category of reader, from those who enjoy Monkey's scurrilous jokes to those who take delight in the covert Buddhist allegorical meaning.

7

From Furor to Spiritual Vision

Ancient Iranian Ecstatics

IRANIAN SHAMANISM?

Even more than India, ancient Iran has been regarded by an influential German school of history of religions (*religionsges-chichtliche Schule*) as the homeland of otherworldly journeys. This theory, now entirely obsolete, should not detain us here; it has been dismissed in a previous book and series of articles that Philippe Gignoux, one of the leading specialists in Iranian otherworldly journeys, found convincing.[1]

More interesting, a book by the great Swedish Iranologist Hendrik Samuel Nyberg, which became famous in a 1938 German translation by H. H. Schaeder, claims that pre-Zoroastrian Iranian religion was dominated by communities of ecstatic warriors who performed shamanic ecstasies and other-worldly journeys to a heavenly place of ritual singing.[2] Intoxi-cated with *haoma*, these warriors would reach a dangerous state of murderous furor (*aeshma*). Zarathustra's reform was directed against these male shamanistic, warlike brotherhoods.

We already know that the Indo-Iranian prototype of *haoma,* called *soma* by the Indians, must have been a powerful drug, possibly—if we believe R. Gordon Wasson—dried fly agaric mushroom.[3] Yet when the Iranians migrated to their eventual homeland, the plant was lacking and substitutes were sought. The Avestan drug *bangha,* probably henbane (*Hyoscyamus niger*) was one such substitute. Later the Middle Persian word *bang* came primarily to mean hemp (*Cannabis indica*).[4]

The Greek historian Herodotus (fifth century B.C.E.) reports that the Scythians, an Indo-European population living north of the Black Sea who were related to the Iranians, would gather in a tent and breathe the smoke of roasted hemp seeds.[5] That marijuana (*Cannabis sativa*) was used in such a way by Altaic shamans in ancient times is demonstrated by the discovery of roasted hemp seeds in a second-century B.C.E. eastern Altaic tomb beside a drum and a stringed instrument similar to those used by Siberian shamans two thousand years later.[6]

Studying the Avesta, such scholars as Philippe Gignoux and Gherardo Gnoli have reached the conclusion that Iranian religion was indeed based on a shamanistic ideology. Gnoli deduces this from the "state of *maga*" mentioned in the *Gâthâ,* or Zarathustra's hymns, the most ancient parts of the Avesta. According to Gnoli, the Gâthic *maga* refers to an ecstatic experience, to a state of visionary union with the Zoroastrian archangels, the *amesha spentas* (beneficent immortals). This state is defined as a special illumination (*cisti*), a form of transcendental knowledge beyond language and perception. The Middle Persian tradition also speaks of a spiritual vision, an incorporeal psychic (*mênôg*) vision as opposed to physical (*gêtîg*) vision.[7]

Gignoux makes a different case for Iranian shamanism, preferring to rely not on information concerning the use of hallucinogens, but on Zoroastrian psychology. Like Gnoli,[8] Gignoux analyzes the Avestan terminology used to refer to a seer, who is usually described as "righteous" (*ashavan* and *ardây*) in the sense that, like the righteous dead, he can have a glimpse of the afterlife while still on earth. Furthermore, Gignoux believes that shamanistic elements in Zoroastrianism are connected with the Iranian concept of the free soul, called bony soul (*astvand ruvân*) in Avestan.[9]

Although the problem of ancient Iranian shamanism is speculative, later Persian tradition, from the Sassanians (226–640 C.E.) to the tenth century, contains a few interesting descriptions of otherworldly journeys.

THE VISION OF THE PRIEST KIRDÎR

Kirdîr, chief *môbad* (priest) under a series of Sassanian rulers, was an influential man at court and a persecutor of heretics—he was responsible for the disgrace of Mani, who died in prison in 276. He also left a few inscriptions on stone. One of them, at Sar Mashhad in Fars, reports an otherworldly journey granted to him by the gods in order for him to test the truth of Zoroastrian belief. The inscription has many lacunae, and some characters of the story are difficult to identify. On the bright road of heaven, Kirdîr is met by a young woman of indescribable beauty coming from the east, who must be his *daêna* (the celestial image of his faith). In giving this information, Kirdîr implicitly declares that he is one of the righteous, for otherwise his *daêna* would be old and ugly. The maiden takes his double—which is, according to Gignoux, his bony soul—toward the gods. One of the gods, who must be Rashnu, is seated on a golden throne and has a balance in front of him. Another character, a knight or a commander, accompanies both Kirdîr's double and his *daêna* toward the east. They encounter a throne of gold, a hell full of vermin, a bridge "more wide than long" (which must be the bridge Cinvat), and eventually paradise, where Kirdîr stops to eat bread and meat.[10]

According to Gignoux, the appearance of Kirdîr's double is the key to this story, which he defines as shamanistic. Indeed, the double is none other than Kirdîr's free soul, his bony soul that can be projected out of the body.

THE JOURNEY OF THE
RIGHTEOUS VIRÂZ

Kirdîr's otherworldly journey can perhaps be better understood in the light of much later reports, redacted in the Middle Persian language in the tenth century C.E. but based on more ancient material. This material concerns a vision of Vishtasp (the prince who protected Zarathustra) and a vision of a certain Virâz. Among the two visions, that of Virâz is certainly not only more extensive but also more authentic.[11]

In both cases, emphasis is given to the potion that releases the soul from the body, traditionally known as "*mang* of Vishtasp." Its composition is sometimes described as a mixture of *hôm* and *mang*, where *mang* is synonymous with *bang*, (henbane); in both of the visions, *mang* is a mixture of wine and henbane.[12] For three days and three nights Vishtasp goes through a near-death experience, while his soul travels to the upper paradise, Garôdmân, and visits the place where he will receive retribution after death. Here he will spend the time after death and before the judgment of the world by final conflagration.[13] This episode occurs during Vishtasp's conversion to Zoroastrianism, and a Middle Persian source adds that the mixture of *hôm* and henbane is brought to him by the Archangel Ashvahisht (Asha Vahishta).[14] According to Zoroastrian belief, anyone who had undergone the initiation rite called Nawzôd between the ages of seven and fifteen would go to Vishtasp's upper paradise, Garôdman.[15]

The journey of the soul of the righteous Virâz is more elaborate. The *Book of Ardâ Virâz* has been traditionally dated to the late sixth century C.E.,[16] although its Middle Persian redaction is no earlier than the tenth century. Still, there is no compelling reason to contest the traditional dating. The narrative is set in a period of decadence followed by a revival of the ancient faith led by the high priest Adurbâd î Mahraspandân who lived under Shapur II, 309–79 (C.E.) and compiled the Avesta. Fereydun Vahman, the most recent commentator on this Iranian *Divine Comedy,* suggests that the narrative wishes to establish a link between the otherworldly journey of Virâz, meant to be a confirmation of the Zoroastrian faith, and the subsequent reform initiated by Adurbâd.[17] Indeed, in another Persian text, Adurbâd is said to have undergone an ordeal in order to verify the truth of the revelation of Virâz.[18] In this case, if the character of Virâz has any historicity at all, he has to be placed in the first half of the fourth century C.E.

Elected by the assembly to test the veracity of Zoroastrianism, Virâz is reluctant to take the potion of wine and henbane, especially since, as a faithful Mazdaean (Zoroastrian), he is married to his sisters, and there are no less than seven of them who protest, weeping and shouting. The numerous allusions to the virtues of consanguineous marriage (*xvêdôdah*) in this text refer to Sassanian practice.[19] This is again a recently developed trait of Sassanian Mazdaeanism (probably introduced by the western Iranian priests called Magi), and its presence seems to recommend the sixth to tenth centuries C.E. as the most plausible date for the composition of the *Book of Ardâ Virâz.*

The priests reassure Virâz's sister-wives: nothing will go amiss, and in seven days he will be back. Yet Virâz himself makes preparations for a one-way voyage: he makes a will and performs the rites of the dead for himself. Eventually in a fire temple he perfumes himself, puts on new garments, takes three cups of *mang,* and sleeps on a couch, where he is watched for seven days by the Mazdaean priests and by his seven sister-wives. On the seventh day, Virâz's soul comes back to him, and the righteous one awakens "cheerful and joyous," bringing the assembly greetings from Ohrmazd, from the archangels, from Zarathustra (the religion's founder), and from the gods of the dead. He then dictates to a scribe the report of his otherworldly journey, and this represents the main body of the *Book of Ardâ Virâz*.

In his account, the gods Srosh and Adur receive his soul as soon as it leaves the body. Together they take off in three steps, corresponding to *humat* (good thought), *hûxt* (good words), and *huwarsht* (good deeds), the three pillars of the Mazdaean faith. Thus they arrive at the Cinvat Bridge. There the soul of Virâz remains until the third day. The explanation for this delay is found in another text, the *Hadôkht,* which deals with the fate of the dead. The soul of a righteous one, delivered from the body, spends the first three nights by the body rejoicing in its liberation and singing Avestan hymns of praise to Ohrmazd. At the end of the third night, at dawn, "the soul of the Righteous has the feeling of abiding in the middle of plants and breathing fragrances. It feels an intensely fragrant wind blowing from the south. The soul of the Righteous breathes this wind through its nostrils."[20]

As the *Book of Ardâ Virâz* continues, it shows many parallels to the narrative of the *Hadôkht* and to other Middle Persian writings such as the *Mênôk-i Khrat,* the *Dâdestân-i Dênîg* by the priest Mânushchihr, and the *Selections* by his brother Zât-spram.[21] On the third day a scented breeze rises from the southern region of Ohrmazd, and the *daêna* of the righteous one, the image of "his own religion and his own deeds," comes before him in the form of a young girl with large breasts, long fingers, and radiant skin, more beautiful than any mortal woman. The *daêna* explains to him that she is such because of his own "good thoughts, good words, good deeds, and good religion." She tells him, "It is because of your will and deeds that I am thus great, good, well scented, victorious and without blemish."

Because of Virâz's merits, when he advances on the Cinvat Bridge it becomes nine lances wide. The righteous one passes, the souls of the heavenly righteous ones bow to him, and the god Rashn, who holds in his hand a golden balance to weigh the deeds of the deceased, appears in front of him.

Then Srosh and Adur take him on a tour of paradise and hell, but first they visit *hammestagân* (purgatory), where people whose good and bad deeds are equal await resurrection, punished by an alternation of cold and heat. Then they take three steps to heaven, coming first to the level of the stars corresponding to *humat* (good thoughts). There on shining thrones are righteous ones who were good and pious in their earthly lives, but who did not recite Mazdaean prayers, observe kin marriage, or practice "lordship, rulership, and leadership."

The second step leads them to the level of the moon, corresponding to *hûxt* (good words), where they find righteous ones who did everything except reciting prayers and marrying their sisters. The third step leads to the level of the sun, corresponding to *huvarsht* (good deeds), where even more perfect righteous ones dwell. Beyond the three heavens there is a fourth level, the endless light (*anagra raoça*), where the paradise of Ohrmazd is located. In it a place is already prepared for the righteous Virâz.

The great Archangel Vahman takes Virâz's hand and introduces him to the courtiers of the sovereign god, who are the bony souls of Zarathustra, Vishtasp, and other religious leaders and major supporters. Eventually he is introduced to Ohrmazd himself, who greets him graciously and then orders the gods Srosh and Adur to show him the rewards of the good and the punishments of the wicked. A hierarchy of good souls is established. The criteria according to which Zoroastrians grant posthumous retribution may appear no less strange to us than some that are met with in Oceania (see chapter 2, above). For example, according to Zoroastrian belief women can reach the highest abodes if they have "satisfied their husbands and lords, and were submissive, respectful and obedient to them";[22] another meritorious deed that opens the gates of paradise is to kill many reptiles, because they are created by Ahriman, Ohrmazd's opponent.[23] Also, according to Mazdaean religion it is not good to shed tears for the departed because those tears contribute to a large afterlife river, and the souls of the dead have great difficulty crossing it.

The second part of the story is more interesting, and it also reveals the basic oppositions on which the beyond is based: Ohrmazd as opposed to Ahriman is like being as opposed to nonbeing, paradise as opposed to hell, good as opposed to evil, and south as opposed to north. At the level of human sensations, it appears clearly that Zoroastrianism translates this entire series of binary oppositions into olfactory terms, that is, fragrant as opposed to foul.

Thus, when Virâz is led back to the Cinvat Bridge to witness the fate of the wicked, the first thing that he notices is that a bad soul is met by "a cold stinking wind" rising from the north, the direction of the demons of Ahriman. "And in that wind he saw his own religion (*daêna*) and deeds in the form of a naked whore, rotten, filthy, with crooked knees, with projecting buttocks."[24] The structure of hell is symmetrical with the structure of heaven; it has four underground levels. Hell is pitch dark, narrow, "and in such stench that anyone getting that wind into his nose would struggle and tremble and fall."[25] The main sins seem to be sexual, but not all are. Thus, we find in hell Sodomites; women who touched water and fire while menstruating; men who copulated with women during their menstrual period; adulterous women; people who urinated while standing; women who quarreled with their lords and husbands; thieves; evil rulers; slaughterers of cattle;

witches; heretics; people who did not take a ritual bath after polluting water and fire; false witnesses; apostates; and so on.

It is impressive how frequently crimes derive from pollution and to what extent punishment is olfactory. Most of these unfortunate inmates of hell, in fact, gorge themselves with excrement. At the bottom of hell, diametrically opposed to Ohrmazd's paradise, is Ahriman's hell, looking like a "dangerous, fearful, terrible, painful, harmful, stinking, very dark" place; among the extreme punishments of this abode of wickedness we again find stench.[26] This part of the story is repetitive: the categories of transgressors overlap with those already mentioned in the other layers of hell. The motivation for such insertions must be to emphasize the most abominable of sins. Thus, we find a woman who continuously cuts her breasts with an iron comb (and the breasts presumably grow back), because she was evil with her lord and husband and "she beautified herself and she whored with the husbands of others"; another one licks a red-hot oven she holds on the palm of her hand for having been sharp-tongued and having quarreled with her lord and husband. Moreover, she "was disobedient and did not consent to copulation whenever he wished."[27] As if this were not enough, elsewhere we find women hung upside down, with "the semen of all kinds of demons," stench, and filth poured continuously into their mouths and noses, for having denied their husbands intercourse.[28] This hell abounds in adulterous women, many of whom had abortions, and others of whom committed the abominable crime of wearing make-up.

After leaving the dark, stinking abode of Ahriman, Virâz is led again before Ohrmazd, who is made only of light, and who does not have a body. This episode must have originated due to pressure from the Muslim rejection of the anthropomorphism of God. The Muslim legends of the mi'râj (ascent of the Prophet Muhammad to heaven) may also have had some influence on this episode, since the legends are about an otherworldly journey. As such, they must have certainly intrigued the tenth-century redactors of the *Book of Ardâ Virâz,* and they may even have stimulated them to fulfill their literary task.

8
Greek Medicine Men

SAILING AMONG GODDESSES

In the Western literary tradition, the blind storyteller Homer (whom legend and conjecture place about the eighth century B.C.E.) kicked off the genre that the Latin Middle Ages would later call *peregrinatio,* meaning vagrancy or wandering around, rather than pilgrimage. Various traditions know of this type of journey by sea, usually leading to miraculous and often other-worldly territories. Suffice it to mention here the Celtic *imrama* (navigation narratives), which certainly predate the voyages of Sinbad the Sailor, for the Arabs were reluctant to sail or build fleets. (According to the reasoning of the shrewd general Amr ibn al-As, the conqueror of Egypt, one can hold a land by taking all enemy strongholds, but how can one conquer the sea, where there is nothing but waves?)

Homer's hero Odysseus, a warlike Achaean from the island of Ithaca, is returning from the Trojan War with his black ships to his homeland and his faithful wife Penelope. The gods, however, decide that he cannot reach the end of his journey before undergoing many adventures. He brings death to the Cicones and Ismanes; he visits the lotus eaters, who feed on the highly addictive "honey-sweet fruit of the lotus," which makes one forget the past and live only to eat more; and by cunning he escapes the evil fate that awaits him in the cave of the giant Cyclops, the one-eyed Polyphemus. All these territories are not strictly this-worldly, and Odysseus's voyage can be—and has been—interpreted as simply symbolic.

After such a male, warlike inception, his adventures take an unpredictable turn: Odysseus visits the Mothers. First comes "Circe with the braided tresses," daughter of the sun and sister of the wizard Aietes. With the aid of a potion and a magic wand, Circe changes Odysseus's companions into swine. Yet the god Hermes gives Odysseus the herb of virtue, the mysterious plant *moly,* "black at the root" but with a milky flower, and thus Odysseus remains sober. At his command, the sorceress Circe changes his companions back into human beings, younger and handsomer than before. Albeit reluctantly, they all leave Circe's enchanted land.

Odysseus is further detained, however, by the fair and crafty nymph Calypso on the enchanted island Ogygia, where he becomes an "unwilling lover by a willing lady."[1] Parting from her is not easy after they have spent seven years together. On his way home once again, Odysseus is shipwrecked at the country of the Phaeacians, where Nausicaa "of the white arms," daughter of King Alcinous, takes him in.

Although at least Circe and Calypso are goddesses, and Nausicaa shares with them beauty and fairness, these episodes should not necessarily be interpreted as otherworldly. The "goddesses" were, very probably, representatives of the matrifocal society that preceded the coming of the Indo-European invaders of whom Odysseus was a successor.

If we believe Marija Aleskaité Gimbutas, a great Estonian-American archaeologist now living in San Francisco, Europe prior to the Indo-European invasions (which she calls "Old Europe") had "a culture matrifocal and probably matrilinear, agricultural [or preagricultural] and sedentary, egalitarian and peaceful," and this culture lasted for twenty thousand years, from the Palaeolithic to the Neolithic.[2] Artifacts show that from the eastern shore of the Black and Mediterranean seas to the Aegean and Adriatic seas a goddess was worshipped, and her stylized corpulence, inherited from the steatopygic (having an extreme accumulation of fat on or about the buttocks) Palaeolithic "Venuses," emphasized the attributes of fertility. Between about 7000 and 3500 B.C.E., the inhabitants of old Europe developed a complex civilization. They formed small towns, worked copper and gold for ornaments and tools, and even used a rudimentary script. Sometimes they represented the goddess as a water bird or a snake-woman. Her animal companions were many: bull, dog, bear, deer, male goat, bee, butterfly, turtle, hare, and hedgehog. Her figurines were sometimes strangely shaped, looking at once like a steatopygic woman with a long, birdlike neck, and at the same time like a phallus, with the buttocks representing the testicles.

During the third millennium B.C.E., the old European goddess culture was brutally replaced by the patriarchal Indo-European culture of seminomadic herdsmen, whose values were destruction, war, and violence based on a male code of behavior. The Indo-Europeans came in waves and overcame Greece about 2000 B.C.E. Open cities were replaced by walled ones. Native goddesses became consorts, were transformed into males, or were recast as monsters.

The Trojan War epitomizes Indo-European culture and habits. In his island wanderings, Odysseus was likely to meet survivors of the fair "goddesses" of old European civilization. These meetings bear witness to the clash of two diametrically opposed systems of values, and Homeric poetry, which obviously belongs to Odysseus's own conquering culture, preserves biased reports of those occurrences. To my knowledge, Elémire Zolla is the first to have rectified Homer's perspective, which he has done in a recent essay.[3]

From the viewpoint of the old European culture, Odysseus, the killer with his black ships, plundering and bringing death by cunning to all the places he visits, was obviously a criminal.

If Homer gives us a fair idea of how Odysseus saw the "goddesses," how did the goddesses see him?

Zolla asks this legitimate question and seeks an answer in other cultures. Why listen only to the views of intruders and rapists like Odysseus and his men, and not consider the attitude of a religious woman toward her intruders and rapists? Such a viewpoint is found in the legendary autobiography of Lady Yeshe Tsogyel,[4] one of the first disciples of the Buddhist apostle of Tibet, Padmasambhava.[5] Yeshe was a beautiful Tibetan princess who underwent all possible austerities and mortifications in order to reach Buddhist perfection. Yet because of her beauty and ornaments she was assailed by suitors, rapists, and thieves; and because of her asceticism, she was assailed by demons.

In her autobiography, her father, angry at her determination not to marry, sends her away and tells the hordes of suitors that "whoever lays hands on her first can have her."[6] One catches her by the breast and attempts to carry her away, but she braces her legs "against a boulder so that [her] feet [sink] into it like mud."[7] Then the suitors strip her naked and whip her with a lash of iron thorns. When she tries to explain her viewpoint, she receives an answer that might have come from Homer as well: "Girl, you have a beautiful body that is rotten within."[8]

Fortunately, the Buddhas of the ten directions hear her laments, and a drunken stupor seizes the men who were torturing her and carrying her away; this allows her to flee. To the Homeric patriarchal mentality, Yeshe Tsogyel's determination to follow the path of the Buddha would have appeared suspicious, and the supernatural help she received would have been seen as a form of magic.

After having received instruction from her guru, Yeshe sets out as a beggar for the valley of Nepal, where seven thieves intend to assail her. She sets her gold in front of them as a mandala offering and explains to them that the world is illusion. The thieves are converted and released from the bonds of transmigration.

Another assault, this time from demons, resembles Circe's story more than any other so far. In his *Life of Anthony*, Athanasius, a fourth-century bishop of Alexandria in Egypt, depicts the desert father's temptations in the form of demons who take the shape of enticing women; the story has been famous for fifteen hundred years. The *Life of Yeshe Tsogyel* shows a woman tempted by demons who take the shapes of "charming youths, handsome, with fine complexions, smelling sweetly, glowing with desire, strong and capable, young men at whom a girl need only glance to feel excited." They tell obscene stories and make propositions; they expose their genitals, embrace her, rub her breasts, fondle her vagina, and kiss her, "trying all kinds of seductive foreplay." Yeshe's meditation is, however, powerful enough to transform them, some into nothingness, and some "into black corpses, some into bent and frail geriatrics, some into lepers, some into blind, deformed, dumb or ugly creatures."[9] This story is reminiscent of the episode in which the lewd companions of Odysseus are changed into swine.

But what is wrong with being changed into swine? Zolla shows us that in some places this is considered to be the ultimate experience.[10] Anthropologists classify peoples as "pig lovers" and "pig haters." Judaism and Islam forbid consumption of pork, but Indonesians are great pig lovers. In some parts of the archipelago, infants are given a piglet-twin who shares their childhood. On the Indonesian island of Bali, it is a particularly happy event if during a feast one is possessed by pig-spirits and imitates a pig's voice and mannerisms. Perhaps Circe, a woman belonging to the peaceful civilization of old Europe, was rather trying to do Odysseus's companions a favor. What followed was one of the innumerable genuine anthropological misunderstandings that have occurred—they took her for a sorceress. As far as Circe was concerned, she was certainly right to stay away from these violent, hysterical men whom she correctly assessed for what they were, Indo-European plunderers and rapists.

NEKYIA

In the *Odyssey*, Circe knows the location of Hades; it is across the stream Oceanus, where "into Acheron flows Pyriphlegeton, and Cocytus, a branch of the water of the Styx."[11] She instructs Odysseus to dig a trench there and pour in offerings to the dead of mead, wine, and water in order to attract the ghost of the prophet Tiresias, who can foretell his future. She says that Odysseus must promise Tiresias that once in Ithaca he will sacrifice a spotless black ram to him. Circe advises Odysseus that he should sacrifice a ram and a black ewe at the opening to the underworld, and that their blood will attract the spirits, but that he should keep the spirits away with his sword until the spirit of Tiresias himself appears. Odysseus, now in the mode of a ghost raiser, does all the shaman has told him. This leads to one of the most enigmatic parts of the *Odyssey*, the *Nekyia* (Scene of the dead) in book 11.

As soon as the blood of the slain sheep flows in the trench, spirits begin to swarm. "Brides and youths unwed, and old men of many and evil days, and tender maidens with grief yet fresh at heart; and many there were, wounded with bronze-shod spears, men slain in fight with their bloody mail about them." These are the *bioithanatoi*, people who died a violent death and did not receive proper burial. One of them is Odysseus's former companion Elpenor, who fell off the roof of Circe's cottage when he forgot that he was supposed to use the ladder; he demands to be buried, lest he bring Odysseus bad luck. After the seer Tiresias delivers his message, telling

Odysseus how he will eventually reach his home island,
Odysseus's own mother Anticleia appears. She is extremely
talkative, since she is lonely in Hades. Another flock of women
from the dark mansions of Hades gather around the blood.
Odysseus, both apprentice shaman and host to a parade of
dead celebrities, lets them drink blood one by one, so he can
question each one. After having obtained interviews with
prominent men and women of pre-Homeric Greece, and
having told in turn what gossip he has learned, Odysseus sees
the procession of the dead drawn up by a few of hell's
tormented: Tityus, who mistreated Zeus's mistress Leto, has
his liver eaten by two eagles; Tantalus can neither drink nor
eat, though surrounded by abundance; and Sisyphus continuously rolls a boulder uphill, until it exceeds his power and rolls
back down. After Odysseus and his companions see Heracles,
they sail away hastily.

The Latin poet Virgil, who was also an ideologist of the
grandeur of Rome under the Augustan empire, imitates the
Homeric *Nekyia* scene in the Sixth Book of his epic *Aeneid.* The
epic records the *peregrinatio* of the Trojan hero Aeneas, who
eventually settles in Latium and founds Rome. More enigmatic
than the Homeric *Nekyia,* the Sixth Book of the *Aeneid* reflects
all of the changes undergone by traditional eschatology during
the imperial period.

In his posthumously published *Elysion: On Ancient Greek and
Roman Beliefs Concerning a Life after Death,* W. F. Jackson Knight
shows that ancient Greece had two distinct beliefs about the
spirits of the dead.[12] In general, the Greeks believed that the
dead survived in a shadowy Hades, but that in the case of
special people, the "heroes"—local celebrities, mythological
characters, great warriors, seers, or rulers—their psyche remained on earth and interfered in human affairs. In pre-
Homeric Greece, spirits manifested themselves as *kêres,* "little
flying, insect-like creatures." In Homer, the *kêres* are little

devils; a deadly *kêr* threatens the human beings in the *Iliad.*[13] The Roman generic ghosts were called *manes* (although there were other kinds as well); *manes* were thought to return to earth on such festivals as the Parentalia and the Rosalia.[14]

Greeks offered periodical sacrifices to their dead. Tombs have been found with a pipe opening above so that libations might reach the dead, perhaps through the body soul, which could be strengthened by various kinds of food (we saw blood performing such a function for the vampire souls of the *Odyssey*). The dead had a hearth (*eschara*), where they received uncooked offerings, honey, milk, and cakes. Greek religion took great care to distinguish sacrifices to gods from sacrifices to the dead. Olympian gods had an altar, and unlike the dead they received only burned sacrifices. The name for sacrifice is different in each case.[15]

Heroes were worshipped as dead spirits, not as gods, and had shrines everywhere. Worship was at times meant to propitiate them and was performed often enough to prevent them from doing harm. At other times, worship was used to supplicate them for help. Some of the most typical heroes and heroines were Helen of Troy, Theseus, Amphiaraus, Trophonius, Achilles, Diomedes,[16] Ajax, the Atreids, the Eacides, the successors of Tydaeus and Laërtius,[17] and many others.

The Greeks had oracles at which the dead were conjured by a specialist in order to forecast the future of a client. The procedures and methods were variable. In the sixth book of his *Pharsalia,* Lucan (39–65 C.E.) describes a procedure called *nekyomanteia* (corpse oracle), which consists of the temporary animation of the body of a recently deceased person.[18] Most soothsayers, however, were called *psychomanteis* or *psychopompoi* (soul raisers). As in the *Nekyia* scene of the *Odyssey,* soul raising could be practiced at an entrance to Hades—at Heracleia, at Tainaron, or at Avernus. It could be replaced by incubation in a sanctuary,[19] or in other cases the ghost could indicate to the soul raiser where the traditional black-sheep sacrifice should be performed.[20] In some other cases of popular divination, called *engastrimythos,* ventriloquists probably simulated a dialogue with the dead.[21] Such phenomena should be more accurately studied in comparison with shamanistic performances, where ventriloquism often occurs.

According to Pierre Boyancé, the Pythagoreans enquired about the posthumous fate of their recently dead by using an uncommon method of divination called *alektryomancy.* On a table were traced squares containing the letters of the alphabet, and in each square seeds were placed. After proper incantations, a white rooster was released, and the letters were read in the order in which the rooster pecked the seeds. The interpretation of the oracle is unknown.[22]

The soul raiser par excellence was the god Hermes. He was said to have been born on Cyllene, a mountain in Arcadia. He was associated with stones and rocks, and his symbol was a phallus set on a *herma,* a phallic pillar. Often he was represented with two or three bodies, and sometimes with three heads (tricephalous), by reason of which the allegedly Egyptian Hellenistic god Hermes-Thoth was called *trismegistos* (three times great). One of Hermes' main functions was to act as *psychopompos* (leader of souls) on their way to Hades (see, for example, the *Odyssey* 24:5). But he was equally a soul raiser (*psychagogos*) who could take souls back to this world, for a brief appearance or perhaps even to install them in new bodies. Sometimes, like the Egyptian Thoth[23] or the Iranian Rashnu (see chapter 7, above), Hermes weighed the soul of the dead on a scale (*psychostasy*). He was supposed to take care of the soul during sleep, and he was the leader of the fatuous folk of dreams.[24]

Contact with the ghosts of heroes could also be obtained by incubation, that is, by sleeping in a certain place after ritual preparations. Incubation was practiced at the oracle of Amphiaraus near Thebes (mentioned by Pindar and Herodotus, fifth century B.C.E.), at the oracle of Trophonius at Lebadeia in Boeotia (see below) and at the oracles of Asclepius at Tricca in Thessaly and at Epidaurus (from around 500 B.C.E.).²⁵

Asclepius, the famous *heros iatros* (healing hero) was, according to Pindar, the son of Apollo and the unfaithful mortal Coronis.²⁶ Like Achilles, he was half man and half god; like him, he was mortal. In a moment of anger, Zeus struck him with lightning in punishment for his healing talent: "the dead were continually growing fewer because they were healed by Asclepius."²⁷ Like Heracles, after death he was accepted into the divine pantheon²⁸ and worshiped in temples where he effected cures by sending his patients dreams the meaning of which was sometimes interpreted by a professional physician.²⁹

There are many testimonies and inscriptions praising the healing oracles, especially the one at Epidaurus.³⁰ Asclepius would usually appear in a vision (*opsis*) during dream, promising the patient that he or she would be cured³¹ and giving different prescriptions, some of medicinal drugs and others of actions, such as walking barefoot.³² The inscriptions are usually succinct. "A man with a stone in his *membrum*. He saw a dream. It seemed to him that he was lying with a fair boy and when he had a seminal discharge he ejected the stone and picked it up and walked out holding it in his hands."³³

Some indicate shamanistic dreams of dismemberment and rebirth.

> Aristagora of Troezen. She had a tapeworm in her belly, and she slept in the Temple of Asclepius at Troezen and saw a dream. It seemed to her that the sons of the god, while he was not present but away in Epidaurus, cut off her head, but, being unable to put it back again, they sent a messenger to Asclepius asking him to come. Meanwhile day breaks and the priest clearly sees her head cut off from the body. When night approached, Aristagora saw a vision. It seemed to her

the god had come from Epidaurus and fastened her head onto her neck. Then he cut open her belly, took the tapeworm
out, and stitched her up again. And after that she became
well.[34]

Asclepius's sacred dogs healed wounds by licking, and his
serpent also showed up in dreams, sometimes doing strange
things. "Nicassibula of Messene for offspring slept in the
Temple and saw a dream. It seemed to her that the god
approached her with a snake which was creeping behind him;
and with that snake she had intercourse. Within a year she
had two sons."[35]

The ritual in preparation for incubation in the temples of
Asclepius was simple: the patient had to bathe in cold water
and offer sacrifice.[36] Healing was not the only purpose of
incubation. In the cave of Trophonius at Lebadeia, nine miles
from Chaeronea on the road to Delphi, the hero would send
revelations by means of either a voice or a vision. The
preliminary rites are described at length in Pausanias's *Guide to
Greece* (9.39.4). The postulant must live for a few days in a
building near the sanctuary, taking cold baths in the river
Herkyna and eating the meat of animal sacrifices that are
performed for him so that a professional soothsayer can read
in the entrails whether Trophonius will receive him favorably.
Only the last sacrifice, that of a ram, is decisive. If this omen
is good, the postulant makes further preparations for his
descent (*katabasis*) into the sanctuary, which is symbolically a
descent to Hades. He is bathed at night by two local boys
called Hermai (Hermes was the soul leader) in the cold water
of Herkyna; then he drinks from the water of two springs
called Lethe and Mnemosyne ("forgetfulness" and "memory").
These two springs are also mentioned on ancient gold amulets
for the dead, to which an Orphic origin is often ascribed.[37]

After having worshiped a hidden statue of Trophonius, the
postulant puts on a linen tunic and boots, and climbs down to

the entrance of the cave on a light ladder. There he enters the narrow opening feet first, holding honey cakes—the food of the dead—in his hand. The symbolism of this rite suggests that the performer is given information if and only if he enters the womb of the earth as a dead man. In order to communicate with ghosts, one has to become a ghost.

Lamprias, the brother of the Platonic philosopher Plutarch of Chaeronea (ca. 50–120 C.E.), may have been a priest of Trophonius's sanctuary. If so, he would have had access to the valuable library of wooden tablets on which everyone coming out of the cave was supposed to write down the account of his experience; these records were stored by the priests. If this was the case, then part of Plutarch's story in the tractate *On the Demon of Socrates* may be based on genuine evidence. His hero's name is Timarch of Chaeronea. He goes down into the cave to ask the god about the nature of Socrates' *daimon* and is given a tour of purgatory. We will comment extensively on Timarch's vision presently. Suffice it to say here that, once down in the pitch-dark cave, Timarch receives a violent blow to his head, which loosens his cranial junctures and lets his soul move out freely. The idea that it is through the skull that the soul comes out is surprising; one finds it also in shamanistic and especially in Indo-Tibetan testimonies.[38] Thus freed from the body, Timarch's soul expands happily like a sail in the wind, listening to the music of the spheres and watching the stars like islands floating in the ocean of ether. When the otherworldly journey ceases, the soul is again painfully compressed into the skull.[39]

Apollonius of Tyana, a Hellenistic divine man (*theios aner*) whose exploits were committed to writing by Philostratus before 217 C.E., twice consulted the oracle of Trophonius. Hans Dieter Betz remarks:

> From Philostratus it becomes quite clear that the inquirer does not simply climb down into the crypt but that he

actually descends into the netherworld. As he descends he has
to hold cakes in his hands to appease dangerous underworld
snakes attacking him. The descent is now called *kathodos,* the
traditional name for descending into the netherworld. At his
return, "the earth brings him back to the surface" (Philostratus, *Life of Apollonius,* 8.19). This return may occur in the
vicinity or far away, beyond Locri, beyond Phocis, but we are
told most consultants emerge within the borders of Boeotia.[40]

The second-century satirical writer Lucian wrote a *Nekyo-
mantia* (ghost raising) based on the lost *Nekyia* of Menippus of
Gadara (third century B.C.E.), in which the cave of Trophonius
shows up again. This time, too, it appears to be an entrance to
the netherworld. The Magus Mithrobarzanes shows Menippus
how to return from the netherworld to Greece using Trophonius's cave.[41]

THE GREEK SHAMANS,
OR IATROMANTES

The ancient goddesses of the matrifocal civilization of old
Europe were conquered, but not finished. In western Anatolia
and in ancient Greece, the goddess survived as Kubaba (or
Kybebe, Cybele) as Hekate, and as Artemis. These great
goddesses were connected with the moon, the dead, dogs, and
ecstasy.[42]

Scholars almost unanimously describe Dionysus as a male
heir to the goddesses, lord over a cult of possession whose
main actors were women seized by the madness (*mania*) that
emanates from the god. With "disheveled hair, the head tossed
back, the eyes rolling, the body arched and tense or writh-
ing,"[43] the Maenads wandered around through the Macedonian
mountains (*oreibaseia*), dismembering at times animal victims
(*sparagmos*), and perhaps not loath to feed on members of their
own species, who were treated the same rough way (*homophag-*

eia). In ecstasy (*ekstasis*), a word that in Greek indicated a state of mental illness and dissociation, the Maenads were insensitive to pain and could not be burned by fire.[44]

In the introduction we subjected to criticism some of the usual scholarly distinctions between "possession cult" and "shamanism," noticing that they are often merely external. Among such superficial distinctions, the most important is that between the *collective* character of possession cults and the *individual* character of shamanistic practice. In ancient Greece there were three gods, all of them male, who could possess different categories of people. Dionysus possessed the Maenads, and sometimes also those who resisted him, such as Pentheus in the *Bacchae* of Euripides. Ares, the war god, possessed men in battle. Apollo possessed the Sibyls. Yet, under the name of Apollo of Hyperborea, he also possessed a very special category of seers, the Iatromantes (from the Greek words *iatros* [healer] and *mantis* [prophet]), said to be *phoibolamptoi* or *phoiboleptoi* (possessed by Phoebus-Apollo). These were native Greek shamans, who seldom if ever formed any corporation. (The only exception was probably Bakis; the name refers to an individual seer mentioned by Herodotus, and also to a category of seers.)

Itinerant prophets were known in Greece as well. They were people like Lydas of Arcadia (also known as Aletes the Wanderer), Euvenius of Apollonia, and Lysistratus of Athens.[45] These prophets, however, were not shamans.

The names of a number of Iatromantes were mentioned in a passage of Clement of Alexandria's *Stromata* (1.21; ca. 200 C.E.). They are Pythagoras, Abaris of Hyperborea, Aristeas of Proconnesus, Epimenides of Crete, Zoroaster the Mede, Empedocles of Acragas (Agrigentum, in Sicily), Phormion of Sparta, Polyaratus of Thasos, Empedotimus of Syracuse, and Socrates of Athens. It is interesting that, in Clement's mind, Socrates was a Greek shaman. The list also contains a fictitious

character invented by a disciple of Plato and Aristotle named
Heraclides of Pontus (about whom more, below). To the list
could be added a few other names: Cleonymus of Athens,
Hermotimus of Clazomenae, and Leonymus of Croton.

The most prominent among the Iatromantes have close links
to Apollo of Hyperborea, a northern territory described by a
famous "traveler of the air," Aristeas of Proconnesus. Abaris
comes from the north either *with* an arrow belonging to Apollo
or *on* Apollo's arrow, which is possibly a sunbeam (Apollo is
after all a sun god).[46] Late antique philosophers know him as a
priest of Apollo of Hyperborea. Either at the end of the
seventh or at the end of the sixth century B.C.E., Abaris met
Pythagoras at Olympia. Pythagoras stood in front of the
audience and showed his gold thigh, a symbol that indicated
to Abaris that he was an epiphany of Apollo. (The citizens of
Croton believed Pythagoras to be Apollo of Hyperborea himself.) The symbolic dialogue continued: Abaris gave Pythagoras
his arrow (or Pythagoras took it away from him) in sign of
submission.

Aristeas was the *phoibolamptos* (possessed by Apollo) par
excellence. Due to his close connection with the god, he
traveled as far north as Hyperborea. He wrote a travel description called *Arimaspeia,* which was already in circulation at the
beginning of the sixth century and unfortunately disappeared
before the foundation of the library of Alexandria. Aristeas
died suddenly in a fuller's shop in Proconnesus. The fuller left
to fetch his family, but when they returned Aristeas was not
there any more. Obviously, he had been in a near-death state
but recovered. Then someone saw him on the road to Cyzicus.
Six years later, Aristeas was back in Proconnesus to write his
Arimaspeia, which means that in the meantime he had traveled
as far north as he could. It is no wonder that none of the
dozens and dozens of theories that attempt to reconstruct his
itinerary are satisfactory—his journey was not of this world,

but in another world, the world of shamans, seers, and air travelers.

Two hundred and forty years later, Aristeas appeared again in Metapontum in the guise of a raven, faithful companion of the god Apollo, asking the inhabitants to make a shrine for Apollo and a statue for himself. The Delphic oracle supported his demands, and so the monuments were built; according to Herodotus, they were surrounded by laurels, Apollo's trees. Other testimonies state clearly that Aristeas was an ecstatic whose soul could leave his body, taking the shape of a bird (raven). It was in this guise that he flew over the immense distance between Greece and Hyperborea and back again.[47]

Having established the connection of some of the Iatromantes with Apollo, let us describe a number of other traits they have in common. Only a few fulfill all of the following roles, which added together form the ideal portrait of the Greek shaman: medicine man (*iatros*), seer (*mantis*), purifier (*kathartes*), author of oracles (*chresmologos*), traveler of the air (*aithrobates*), and wonder-worker (*thaumatourgos*).

Stories of sensory deprivation abound in connection with the Iatromantes, unlike other *entheoi* (possessed people) like the Maenads, who clearly used sensory bombardment in their ecstatic methods, such as dance and wine. One master of sensory deprivation was Epimenides of Crete, who as a boy went into the Idaean cave (Zeus's birthplace) and slept for a long time—various authors estimate he slept between forty years (Pausanias 1.14.4) and sixty years (Hesychius). According to Hesychius, Epimenides could dispatch his soul out of his body and call it back again. According to Maximus of Tyre (*Dissertatio* 16), during his long sleep Epimenides was visiting the gods, listening to their conversations, and learning truth and virtue (*aletheia kai dike*).[48]

While in Zeus's Cretan cave, he held hunger in abeyance with the aid of a miraculous plant called *alimos* (hungerbane, which literally means "without hunger"), of which he ate small quantities. We have suggested elsewhere an interesting connection between the word *alimos* and the word *halimos*, which differ only in aspiration. *Halimos* is an adjective from the noun *hals, halos,* meaning "sea." As a noun, *halimos* designates a plant of the *Chenopodiaceae* family (*Atriplex halimus* L.), so called because it grows close to the sea. Antiphanes, a popular author of comedies in the fourth century B.C.E., ascribed to the Pythagoreans the use of *halimos* in their diet.

Alimos has likewise a long story. The fifth-century B.C.E. writer Herodorus of Heraclea, author of a Heracles saga, said that *alimos* was a hungerbane that saved the life of the Greek hero Herakles. In his *Life of Pythagoras,* Porphyry also asserted that the shaman from Samos ate *alimos,* perhaps instead of *halimos.*

Other Iatromantes abstained from food as well: Abaris avoided food, while Pythagoras reputedly died of starvation. Abaris, Aristeas, Bakis, Hermotimus, and Pythagoras were seers, able to forecast the future. Epimenides foretold the Persian War ten years in advance, and was killed by the Spartans because he had prophesied disaster. Abaris forecast an earthquake and a plague. Pythagoras predicted that a white bear would appear in Caulonia, that a ship would have a corpse aboard, and that his Metapontan disciples would be persecuted. Four legends of the fourth century B.C.E. attribute prodigies of the same kind either to Pythagoras or to the prophet Pherecides of Syros. After drinking water from a well, the two were able to foretell an earthquake; they also correctly predicted that a ship would be wrecked on a calm sea and that a certain city would be conquered (Sybaris or Messena). And finally Bakis predicted the invasion of Greece by Xerxes.

Abaris, Bakis, Empedocles, and Epimenides were "purifiers," a business that consisted in driving away *miasma* from a town. *Miasma* could be plague, but it could also be something

entirely spiritual, the result of some moral pollution. Epimenides was the *kathartes* (purifier) par excellence. He drove away
the *miasma* from Athens during Solon's time. Abaris drove away
plague from Sparta and also purified Knossos. Bakis purified
and healed the Spartan women seized by Dionysian furor.

Iatromantes like Pythagoras, Abaris, and Empedocles could
manipulate meteorological phenomena with the aid of charms.
Abaris could sway powerful winds, and Empedocles specialized
in it, for which he gained the title of *alexanemos* (wind repeller).
He actually entrapped winds in leather bags, and he promised
his disciples shamanic power over wind and rain, adding that
they would also be able to recover souls of the dead from
Hades. Pythagoras likewise could stop storms and hail, and
could calm the waves of the sea. This may be why, in
recognition of his power over water, a river greeted him with
a human voice.

Empedocles, Epimenides, and Pythagoras could recall their
previous incarnations. Epimenides believed he had been Aea-
cus, brother of Minos, the king of Crete. Yet the Cretans
worshiped him as a *neos koures,* a local divinity closely connected with Zeus. His long trance in the Idaean cave earned
him the deserved reputation of being an expert in catalepsy
(near-death episodes). When Pythagoras came back from his
voyage to the eastern Magi, he spent three times nine days in
the Idaean cave, with Epimenides as his guide.[49] Iamblichus
rationalized this legend, making Epimenides into Pythagoras's
disciple.

Pythagoras, according to Heraclides of Pontus, was Hermes'
son, and had received from his father the gift of recollection
of his past incarnations. He had been Euphorbus, killed by
Menelaus during the Trojan War, and then Hermotimus of
Clazomenae, the medium who could also remember his former
life. Subsequently he became a fisherman of Delphi, and finally
Pythagoras. An alternative, longer list exists, which adds the

beautiful prostitute Alco to Pythagoras's previous embodiments; the later lists are simplified. Pythagoras could also tell other people and even animals what they had been in their previous lives, and he could talk to the dead. Empedocles possessed the most complete recollection of his past incarnations, extending to plants and animals: he recalled having been a young man, a young woman, a shrub, a bird, and a sea fish.

Catalepsy was a trait characterizing many Iatromantes. We already mentioned the strange traditions concerning Aristeas of Proconnesus, the famous air traveler. Perhaps the greatest expert in catalepsy was Hermotimus of Clazomenae, a seer specializing in out-of-body journeys. Hermotimus would lie naked on his couch, like a professional medium. Leaving the body in a state of near death, his soul would visit various places and then come back. Recovering from his trance, the seer was able to correctly report events he had witnessed while out of the body.

Unfortunately, during one of his trips his wife delivered his lifeless body to his enemies, the Cantharidae, who were probably a Dionysian brotherhood. The Cantharidae burned it, and thus Hermotimus's soul was left without a body. Later the temple of Hermotimus denied access to any woman, by reason of his wife's betrayal.

Several more of our Iatromantes (such as Aristeas, Epimenides, and Hermotimus) mastered near-death states during which they had out-of-body experiences. In general in Greece, catalepsy, called *apnous,* was considered an abnormal phenomenon, and it was sometimes connected with Apollo.

The greatest near-death specialist in ancient Greece was Empedocles of Agrigentum, who was the founder of the first Western school of medicine, the Sicilian school. According to Heraclides of Pontus, cited by the historiographer Diogenes Laërtius, Empedocles wrote a treatise called *On Near Death (Peri ten apnoun),* which he dedicated to his friend Pausanias. After having healed a cataleptic woman, Empedocles organized a banquet. During the night, some guests heard a mysterious voice. The day after, Empedocles disappeared, and Pausanias concluded that he had been called by the gods to heaven. In an alternative legend, of which only the rationalistic interpretation of Hippobotus survives, out of desire to be considered a god—for only gods disappear without trace—Empedocles flung himself into the Etna volcano. The volcano, however, ejected one of his golden sandals, which could be taken to show that Empedocles was not a god, but just a suicide.

Scholars have noticed that the story falls within a Mediterranean pattern of prophecy, according to which it would mean exactly the opposite of what Hippobotus made of it—that the prophet *was* called by the gods, but left an object behind to show that his presence on earth had been real. One such prophet was Elijah (2 Kings 2), who left behind his mantle with his disciple Elisha. The pattern is not only Mediterranean, for we also encounter it in China (see chapter 5, above).

Heraclides himself also specialized in the study of near death and hysteria; according to Pliny, the erudite first-century C.E. Roman, Heraclides wrote the case history of a woman successfully cured after seven days of *apnous,* which he defined as "a disease in which the body is alive, yet breathless and pulseless."

Not only visions and near-death experiences were connected with ancient medicine, as shown above, but also out-of-body experiences or travels in space, such as the legends of Phormion of Croton and Leonymus of Athens. In these stories we find the pre-Homeric character of the *heros iatros* (the healing hero), as well as a homeopathic conception of treatment.

Phormion, a citizen of Croton, took part in the Sagra war against the city of Locri. One of the Dioscuri brethren, who were eminent hero-healers fighting on the side of the Locrians, wounded Phormion in the battle. Phormion consulted an oracle for treatment. It told him to go to Sparta, where the first person to invite him to dinner would also heal his wound. In Sparta, indeed, a young man invited Phormion to dinner and, after having been told the prediction, cured him instantly. Obviously, the young man was the same Dioscurus who had wounded him, and perhaps Phormion never had to go to Sparta, for when he left his host's house he found himself in front of his own house in Croton.

Many garbled pieces of information connect Phormion with the Dioscuri. Thus, while he celebrated the Theoxeniai, a feast in honor of the Dioscuri, two men knocked at his door. Initially he refused to admit them. After they had been seated, the guests stood up and invited Phormion to go to Cyrene, a city in North Africa (present-day Libya), across the Mediterranean Sea from Croton in southern Italy, to meet King Battus. This Battus was known for having instituted rites in honor of the Dioscuri. Obviously, Phormion's guests were the Dioscuri themselves; displeased with his treatment, they wanted to show him a man who had true respect for them. As soon as he stood up, Phormion found himself with a stick of *laser* in his hand. *Laser,* a resin extracted from *silphium* or *laserpitium,* was the principal export product of Cyrene. The meaning of the story is that Phormion had been to Cyrene and back in the blink of an eye, all this through the miraculous powers of the Dioscuri.

As we saw, the Dioscurus who wounded Phormion also healed him. This is a characteristic of the *heros iatros:* he cures the kind of harm he causes. The same ambivalence of the healing hero occurs in the legend of Leonymus of Athens, who took part in the same battle of Sagra and was wounded by Ajax. Like Phormion, he consulted an oracle who set him a difficult task, namely to go to Leuké ("white island"). Obviously Leuké is an otherworldly country where dead heroes live on. Many such places were known in Greece, and their names usually share a reference to brightness, such as Leuké, Lykia (a

Homeric island where the hero Sarpedon was brought after death), and the Leukades rocks, which pegged an entrance to the other world.

Other otherworldly realms existed as well, such as Hyperborea, Aithiopis, and the Isles of the Blessed; all of them were considered to be accessible to the dead, but not to common mortals. If a living person undertook a journey to such a place, it was necessary in some way to go through the initiatory experience of death. After that, like a shaman, the person could visit the other world in search of a ghost, with a goal that was clearly medical. Only here the usual shamanic roles are reversed: instead of taking the otherworldly route in order to find the lost soul of a patient, the shaman goes rather in search of an otherworldly healer who can cure the shaman's own illness. Leonymus found his way to Leuké, where he met Achilles, Ajax, and the beautiful Helen of Troy. When he returned to Athens he was well. Moreover, he took a message from Helen to the poet Stesichorus, who was afflicted with blindness. The explanation for his sickness was that Helen and the Dioscuri brought it about out of anger that he had slandered Helen. It was enough for Stesichorus to write a recantation (*palinode*), and he recovered his sight.

Hyperborea was a northern solar paradise of Apollo. According to Aristeas's *Arimaspeia,* the happy inhabitants of Apollo's realm reach one thousand years of age. A German scholar has connected the name of Apollo with Abalo and with the more prosaic word "apple." Abalo was the "island of apples," the territory of the Hesperides, and the medieval name Avalon is but a variant of both Abalo and Apollo.[50]

So far we have found in Greece beliefs and specialists whose traits are very close to those of shamans and medicine men of other areas of the world. Where did these beliefs come from? This has been the object of a long and inconclusive debate. In the particular case of Hyperborea, Indian influences cannot be ruled out.[51] But in general the problem is far more complicated.

It took scholars some time to recognize the differences between the Iatromantes and the cult of Dionysus. In his epoch-making book *Psyche: Belief in Immortality among the Greeks* (1890–94), Erwin Rohde still could not cope with the idea that the solar genius of the rational Greeks could have such an extensive shadow or *Nachtseite* (nocturnal side); such an idea would have put in jeopardy a century of German classicism that had quietly ignored it. He therefore made of Dionysus a Thracian intruder who brought to Greece a lot of nonsense akin to shamanism and yoga. Seriously indebted to Nietzsche's *Birth of Tragedy,* Rohde preferred to ignore the clear connection between shamanism and Apollo; in his mind, all ecstatic phenomena must have been imported into Greece.

In a 1935 article, the Swiss scholar Karl Meuli revised Rohde's hypothesis in light of the theories of the anthropological Vienna school, led by Father Wilhelm Schmidt. Meuli astutely assessed the similarities among many of the medicine men mentioned in this chapter, and he explained them as a phenomenon of shamanism. This shamanism, he believed, was partly borrowed from the Scythians, with whom the Greeks had been in contact in the seventh century B.C.E., and partly the result of a process of cultural growth that the Greeks, like all other ethnic groups, had to undergo.

We owe to Eric R. Dodds (*The Greeks and the Irrational,* 1951) the word "Iatromantes," and to F. M. Cornford (*Principium Sapientiae,* 1952) the idea that Greek philosophy was an outcome of earlier shamanic speculations on the soul.[52] Dodds was acquainted with Meuli's 1935 article, which he thoroughly critiqued. Incidentally, he did not seem to notice that his own theory was a perfect copy of Meuli's: he explained Greek shamanism partly by Scythian influence and partly as a native development of ancient ideas concerning certain divine men (*theioi andres*).

F. M. Cornford listed other instances of otherworldly journeys among pre-Socratics. Parmenides followed the desires of his own wise heart rather than the desires of the crowd, ascending to heaven in a chariot under the guidance of the daughters of the sun. Beyond the gates of day and night, he met the goddess who promised to instruct him on truth and opinion.

More recently, scholars of Greek religion like Walter Burkert have started treating our Iatromantes as a single category of medicine men.[53] And, the closer we look at the hard core of Platonism, the more we discover how much the Iatromantes influenced Plato's beliefs in afterlife, reincarnation, and otherworldly journeys.

PLATO, THE UNKNOWN

Superficially seen, Plato was a playful dialectician, but deeply understood, he was an extremely religious man. In a certain sense, Platonic philosophy is in its essence a powerful synthesis of Greek shamanistic beliefs that have been systematized and spiritualized.

Platonism is based on a strong anthropological dualism: human beings are composed both of a preexistent, immortal soul and of a perishable body. In the dialogue *Cratylus* (400c), Plato records all sorts of puns on the relationship of soul to body, and he agrees with most of them. Thus the body (*sôma*) is the tomb (*sêma*) of the soul; or, playing on a perfect homonymy, the body (*sôma*) is like the guardian (*sôma*) of the soul's prison.

Embodiment (*somatosis*) of the soul is a painful punishment resulting from a fall. Souls are unhappy in the strong embrace of the body; their purpose is to go back to heaven where they came from and to live forever in enraptured contemplation of the world of ideas, which is absolute truth, goodness, and beauty. Yet it is difficult to reach this state because of the pollution that ensues from prolonged contact between the soul and bodily desires. It depends on this relationship how, when, and where reembodiment (*metensomatosis*) of the soul takes place. Obviously, the lover of truth and wisdom, the philosopher, tries by all means to limit the damage done by the body to the soul. This package of methods by which the soul is kept apart from the body as much as possible Plato calls the "philosophic lifestyle," and it can be defined as a systematic separation of the soul from the pressing needs of the body, the need for food, fighting, and sex. Even when separation is not consciously practiced, people have in themselves innate merits and virtue (their soul being preexistent) that they can increase. The reward in such a case is reincarnation in a superior category of human beings. There are ten such categories, the highest being that of accomplished philosopher, and the lowest that of tyrant. Unfortunately, although in the *Republic* Plato assigns equal social roles to men and women, he thinks women are ontologically inferior. A tyrant can thus fall even lower by becoming a woman, after which the doors of the animal kingdom are open.

Plato shares belief in transmigration with the Greek Iatromantes, and also with many peoples who do not know the use of writing. This allows him to devise a complex system of afterlife retribution based on the quality of one's existence on earth. If one has been sober, frugal, concentrated on the life of one's mind (which is a mirror image of the intelligible world above), one is dispatched to contemplate the Ideas at length, after which a checkup follows in the form of a new incarnation. If the soul leads a strict philosophical life three times in a row, it has a chance to remain in perpetual contemplation.

However, this happens very rarely. Once a downward

movement is started, it becomes increasingly difficult for the soul to resist the urgent pressures of the body. Accordingly, the afterlife is full of movement: souls are continually ascending and descending, spending time in heaven or in the underground Hades described in full detail in the dialogue *Phaedo*. Just as only a few winged souls of philosophers deserve full recompense for their oustanding merits, only a few souls of major profligates deserve eternal punishment in hell. For them there is a special compartment called Tartaros, filled with unspeakable torments from which there is no escape.

Platonic cosmology is further complicated by the fact that the earth is seen as concave, and its bottom—the human world—as having radically different qualities from its surface. This is due to one of the basic tenets of the Platonic system: what is higher is better. Accordingly, the planets, which are made of stellar fire, are much better than the surface of the earth itself, and the world of ideal intelligences is much superior to the planets and stars themselves.

The earth's surface, called "true earth," is beyond our reach, but even if it were not, the experience of getting there would be unbearable, like a fish trying to breathe air. Indeed, ether, the element above the heads of the inhabitants of the true earth, is to air as air is to water. Consequently, people living in this aerial paradise walk on air and breathe ether. Their paradise actually corresponds to Hyperborea or the isles of the blessed, with the difference that it is not on our crumbly earth but above it.

The bottom of the deep clefts in the earth where we live is made of poor-quality materials. Not so the true earth, whose ground is made of precious stones far superior to those known to us, and it is full of gold and silver, and marvelous trees and animals. In the Platonic dialogue *Gorgias* (523a ff.), true earth is called isles of the blessed and is populated by a race that navigates on air, enjoys a mild climate, is not subject to illness or decay, and meets the gods face to face in their temples, for the gods are nothing but shining inhabitants of the upper ether.

Plato was not content only to use ancient shamanistic representations of an earthly paradise, which he moved up to heaven. In the tenth book of the *Republic,* he explains many of the secrets of the universe and of the beyond by having recourse to a near-death scenario that seems to descend directly from the legends of the Iatromantes.[54] Er of Pamphyly in Asia Minor, the son of the mighty Armenius, is wounded in battle with a cranial concussion and appears to be dead for three days. In the meantime, his soul goes to a place in the middle of the universe (probably the true earth's surface), where he sees souls coming down from heaven and up from hell, sees how they draw lots concerning their further destiny, and sees how they are purified by alternate heat and cold and given to drink from the water of Lethe (the river of forgetfulness). There he learns about the law of transmigration and about the eternal sufferings of the murderer Ardiaeus, who is held in the lowest circle of Tartarus in punishment for his unpardonable crimes. Er's body is about to be buried when his soul comes back to animate it, to the astonishment of all those present.

THE SCIENTIFIC REVOLUTION

Plato and his disciples Aristotle and Heraclides of Pontus were heirs to the Greek scientific revolution. Many scholars claim that this change in cosmological beliefs was prepared and perhaps produced by a shamanic sect, the Pythagoreans, whose founder, Pythagoras of Samos, was among the most prestigious Greek Iatromantes before Socrates. We have analyzed the available evidence elsewhere.[55] It appears that one of the most consequential theories in the history of humankind was devised through the genius of a contemporary of Plato, the astronomer Eudoxus of Cnidus.

Eudoxus started from a daring hypothesis, which astonishingly proved to be nearly true. Babylonians and Egyptians had long been practicing astrology and astronomy, but they supposed that heaven was like a concave lid covering the world, on which the planets moved among fixed stars. "Planet" is a Greek word and means "wanderer." In opposition to the stars, the planets were "wandering around" on very complicated paths. In any geocentric system, such as that of Eudoxus, Aristotle, Ptolemy, Thomas Aquinas, or Tycho Brache, "planets" include all visible heavenly lights that move around, such as the moon and the sun.

Here enters in Pythagoreanism, which might have influenced Eudoxus. Pythagoras and his school were interested in numerical proportions, in "golden numbers." Theoretically, this means that they would always try to devise hypotheses showing that natural phenomena and objects that seem chaotic at first sight are actually harmonious and have relatively simple mathematical formulas. Mathematics so far has followed this Pythagorean principle.

Eudoxus was therefore trying to think of a reason that the straight path of a planet could appear so crooked to an observer on earth. In this research he was soon joined by others. Their reasoning followed three steps: the first, which was the most consequential, was to suppose that the planets are not equally distant from the earth. The second, which for some obscure reason of a coincidental nature proved to be nearly correct, was to link the distance of a planet from earth to the length of the revolution of the planet around the earth. This hypothesis did not meet with any obstacle in its application to the moon, nor to the upper planets Mars, Jupiter, and Saturn, whose revolutions respectively take 687 days, twelve years, and almost thirty years to be completed. A problem, however, soon arose: Mercury, Venus, and the sun have different periods of revolution, but they appear to stay close to each other, strangely seeming to move with the same speed and within a certain distance of one another. (We will say more below on the rather complex problem of the planetary orders.) The third hypothesis, meant to show that an apparently random movement can be ascribed to simple and elegant causes, was that either the planets move on a system of concentric, invisible, crystalline spheres, or that they move according to a system of circles.

The problem of the movements of Mercury, Venus, and the sun received different solutions. In the so-called Egyptian order of the planets—which had nothing Egyptian about it at all, having been devised by Eudoxus and adhered to by Plato, Aristotle, and Callippus, a great third-century B.C.E. astronomer—the moon is closest to the earth, followed by the sun. Venus and Mercury are next, in variable order, followed by the superior planets. In the so-called Chaldaean order—which is also purely Greek, and probably as ancient as the Egyptian— the planets are ranged according to the lengths of their revolutions: moon, Mercury, Venus, sun, Mars, Jupiter, and Saturn. This order became current after Ptolemy.

However, as Jacques Flamant has recently noticed,[56] a certain hypothesis often ascribed to Heraclides of Pontus and called "geo-heliocentric" (or "heliosatellitic") has the advantage of conciliating all competing orders of the planets. According to this hypothesis, the planets revolve around the earth, except for Mercury and Venus, which revolve around the sun, being satellites of the sun (*helios*). Flamant shows that, according to whether Mercury and Venus are above or beneath the sun, all variants of both the Egyptian and the Chaldaean order of planets can be reconciled. At least a few philosophers and astronomers must have been aware of this astonishing device that explained away the differences between systems.

The Greek "scientific revolution" achieved a major and lasting change in Western world views. Under the pressure of Eudoxus's hypotheses, heaven suddenly gained a depth in space that had been absent previously. Obviously, Greek speculation on nature was not the first to play with the idea of a multilayered cosmos. The Babylonians conceived of heaven as a multistoried building with a variable number of layers, usually three. Yet for the first time in history, the Greeks elegantly connected the representation of a physically deep heaven with the seven planets, thereby explaining chaotic motion as a result of different simple and harmonic movements. This world view was to dominate for two thousand years.

After Plato

The consequence of a deep heaven was felt after Plato. Despite his innovations, Plato remained committed to a popular, traditional image of the judgment of the dead, which took place partly in an underground Hades and partly in heaven. Some of Plato's successors tried to take advantage of the newly acquired depth of heaven in order to unify chthonic and celestial eschatology and to eliminate the idea of a subterranean hell. This was a slow, gradual process, which achieved a certain uniformity during the first century C.E., a uniformity that was broken especially, if not exclusively, by the Christians.

Plato himself struck the first note of generalization of heavenly eschatology by moving the isles of the blessed from the earth to the celestial zone, called true earth (the earth's true surface). His disciples Xenocrates, Crantor, and especially Heraclides of Pontus continued the process. Among them, the enigmatic Heraclides seems to have been particularly influential.

Born at Heraclea on the Pontus between 388 and 373 B.C.E., Heraclides seems to have tried, without success, to emulate the ancient Iatromantes and to become the head of a mystical school. Apparently his contemporaries, and certainly his successors, ridiculed him. According to the historian Diogenes Laërtius, he frequented Plato's academy (around 364 B.C.E.) and had the ambition of becoming Speusippus's successor (in 338 B.C.E.), but failed. He then returned to Heraclea and supposedly tried to win the admiration of its citizens by attempting to pass for a god, if not in life, at least after death. The publication thirty years ago of Heraclides' extant fragments by the Swiss scholar Fritz Wehrli belatedly exonerated the philosopher from such shameful misinterpretations.[57] It appears that Heraclides was quite an interesting reformer of Greek eschatology, a clever astronomer, and a consequential thinker. He may not have been the only one responsible—as J. D. P. Bolton asserted in a 1963 book—for the vogue enjoyed by heavenly eschatology, but he was certainly instrumental in creating alternative views of the destiny of the dead.[58]

Heraclides was fascinated by the Iatromantes and wanted at least to understand if not to emulate their fabulous exploits such as air travel, otherworldly journeys, and knowledge of previous incarnations. He wrote a dialogue called *Abaris* (the name of the Hyperborean Iatromante who came to Greece riding on Apollo's arrow), a tractate on near-death experiences (*Apnous*), and another one called *On Things in Hell,* all of which have been lost. In one of these works he is said to have told stories of famous Iatromantes such as Abaris, Aristeas, Epimenides, Hermotimus, and Pythagoras. Not content simply to report on past traditions, he also invented an Iatromante of his own, Empedotimus of Syracuse in Sicily, whose mixed name was made up from the names of Empedocles and Hermotimus. This fictitious character intervened in the dialogue and reported his own visions, some of which are preserved in enigmatic fragments scattered among a few late Platonic philosophers and lexicographers.

In Plato's *Republic,* Er contemplates two gates in the region of midearth: the "gate of heaven" by which souls ascend, and the "gate of the earth" by which souls descend. Empedotimus is reported to have seen three gates in one of his otherworldly visions, one located in the zodiacal sign of Scorpio (which was the gate of Hercules, leading to the astral gods), another one located between Leo and Cancer, and a third one located between Aquarius and Pisces. Nothing else is known about this story, except that centuries later the Latin historian Varro wrote a satire whose title, *Triodites tripulios,* contains an allusion to three gates and may therefore ridicule (once again) Heraclides himself.

Empedotimus also called the Milky Way "the way of the souls going through the heavenly Hades,"[59] and he was supposed to believe that the realm of Hades extended from the earth to the sphere of the sun. It is also said that in the middle of a desert he suddenly encountered Pluto and Persephone and then attended the judgment of the dead.

It is very difficult to conclude, from these disconnected fragments, if indeed Heraclides believed that there was no underground Hades at all. It is quite probable that all fragments refer to one and the same vision of Empedotimus obtained during an otherworldly journey. Unfortunately, we miss Heraclides's dialogue, which was probably the most interesting Greek apocalypse to be written after Plato and before Plutarch.

Among Plato's disciples, there seems to have been only one modest report of an otherworldly journey written. It came from Clearchus of Soli, a contemporary of Heraclides. Clearchus told the story of one Cleonymus of Athens, who went through a near-death experience. His· soul flew to astral regions. Looking down on the earth, he saw mysterious rivers that were probably the main rivers inside the chasm of Tartarus. A man from Syracuse, who was experiencing near death at the same time, appeared in the same place, which was very likely the midearth where Er had been too. The two cataleptics witnessed the judgment, punishment, and purification of the souls of the dead under supervision of the Erinyes. Before going back to their countries, and their couches, the two intruders promised each other to try to meet and make further acquaintance.

The Latin writer Cornelius Labeo reported a very similar story, which unfortunately is mistranslated in the latest edition of his *Fragments*.[60] The text simply says that "two persons died the same day and met at a sort of crossroads, after which they were ordered to revert to their bodies; and they decided to become friends until they die."[61] Clearchus must have been the source of Labeo's passage.

NEAR-DEATH AND OUT-OF-BODY EXPERIENCES IN PLUTARCH

Plutarch of Chaeronea in Boeotia (ca. 50–120 C.E.) was a learned Platonic philosopher who was particularly interested in traditional religion—both he and his wife were priests of Greek gods. With immense erudition and literary skill he attempted to update some of the major themes of Platonism, and he chose for this purpose visionary narratives intended to match the myth of Er in Plato's *Republic,* as well as other eschatological passages in Plato. Plutarch often paraphrases Plato, submitting him at the same time to a sophisticated hermeneutics. He makes constant use of ancient popular beliefs, yet gives them entirely new explanations which, according to the criteria of his epoch, were fashionable and even scientific. Plutarch seems also to move the Platonic Hades from the underground space where Plato locates it to a zone beneath and on the moon.

We already saw above that the narrative framework of the myth from the tractate on *The Daemon of Socrates* is connected with the incubations that took place in the cave of Trophonius at Lebadeia. We remember that Timarch's soul was released from the skull and perceived immediately the sights and sounds of heaven, seeing the stars floating as islands in the ocean of ether and listening to the harmony of the spheres. Plutarch is clever enough to describe the vision in vivid and colorful terms; yet behind every element there is some astronomical notion. Thus, the heavenly sphere is represented by a lake in the middle of the islands, the heavenly equator is a rapid stream, and so on. Like the fixed stars, most islands move together with the heavenly sphere, but a few of them, the planets, circulate among the others according to a twisted, unpredictable itinerary. Two streams of fire flow into the lake, and these are the two branches of the Milky Way. (The whole scene is reminiscent of the eschatological landscape in *Phaedo* [111d], with the exception that Plutarch moves the scenery from the Platonic underground to heaven and gives it a clearly astronomical meaning.)

In this vision, Timarch is clearly located somewhere above the earth, and looking down he sees a frightful chasm, which is probably the earth itself. A disembodied voice offers to explain the puzzling things around him, but not those above him, which remain unseen, "for they belong to other gods." Obviously Timarch, like Er, does not have access to the superior, astral gods; the most elevated place about which he can gather information is the moon. Actually, the voice only volunteers information about the zone beneath the moon, and suggests Timarch should ask a question about the river Styx, one of the infernal rivers in Plato's eschatology.

"What is the Styx?" asks Timarch, and the voice answers: "It is the path to Hades. . . . It passes across from you here, cleaving the light with its vertex; it extends upward, as you see, from Hades below, and where in its revolution it also touches the world of light, it bounds the last region of all. . . ."⁶² The moon plays a crucial role in Plutarch's eschatology. "The turning point of birth is at the Moon. For while the rest of the islands belong to gods, the Moon belongs to terrestrial daemons and avoids the Styx by passing slightly above it. . . . As the Styx draws near the souls cry out in terror, for many slip off and are carried away by Hades; others, whose cessation of birth falls out at the proper moment, swim up from below and are rescued by the Moon, the foul and unclean excepted. These the Moon, with lightning and a terrible roar, forbids to another birth, as you see."⁶³

In another dialogue, called *De facie in orbe lunae*, (On the face in the circle of the moon) Plutarch gives a similar description of the moon's function. "For many, even as they are in the act of clinging to the Moon, she thrusts off and sweeps away; and some of those souls too that are on the Moon they see turning upside down as if sinking again into the deep."⁶⁴ The moon is full of hollows and recesses. "The largest of them is called 'Hecate's recess,' where the souls suffer and exact penalties for whatever they have endured or committed after having already become Spirits; and the two long ones are called 'The Gates,' for through them pass the souls now to the side of the Moon that faces heaven and now back to the side that faces earth. The side of the Moon towards heaven is named 'Elysian plain,' the hither side 'House of counterterrestrial Phersephone.' "⁶⁵

With Plutarch, Platonic eschatology is maintained, while all its elements are transferred to heaven. Tartaros seems to be the lower part of the zone between the earth and the moon; Styx is the upper part of this zone, carrying with it the souls that ascend to the moon and the souls that fall back in the cycle of transmigration. The Platonic midearth of the myth of Er is identified by Plutarch as being the moon itself. The moon looks like a perforated coin. One part of it, facing toward the earth, serves as purgatory for the souls in transition to the

Elysian Plain or to upper regions of heaven. The Platonic gates of heaven and earth are nothing but perforations in the moon, one serving the downward movement of souls going back to earth to be reborn, and the other one the upward movement of deserving souls.

Plutarch also authored another apocalypse based on the near-death experience of a certain Aridaeus of Soli, in *De sera numinis vindicta* (On the belated vengeance of the gods; 563b–68f).[66] Unlike Timarch, who volunteered for an otherworldly vision through incubation in the cave of Trophonius, Aridaeus obtained it by accident.

The name Aridaeus is a variant of the name of the greatest criminal in the Platonic inferno, described in the tenth book of the *Republic* (625d, "Ardiaeus"); he was forever detained and tormented in the depth of Tartarus. Like him, Plutarch's character is prodigal and dishonest. The oracle of Amphilochus in Cilicia forecasts that he will be happier after death, which comes true. Yet Aridaeus comes back from among the dead. "He fell from a certain height upon the nape of his neck and died not from a wound, but from the stroke only. The third day he was carried away to be buried when he came back to himself and rapidly recovered, after which he underwent a complete change in his lifestyle. The Cilicians cannot recall anyone more correct in his promises, more pious toward the gods, more terrible for his enemies and more reliable for his friends."[67] The change of habits comes with a change of name, from Aridaeus to Thespesius (meaning "divine, wonderful").

Plutarch's story describes Aridaeus's near-death experience, which is in broad outline similar to that of Timarch, but more vague and also more lengthy. The rational soul of Aridaeus leaves his body (actually, the skull) upon concussion, undergoing a sudden and abrupt transformation (*metabolé*) similar to that which a ship pilot would undergo "falling from his ship in the watery abyss." (Scholars have long noticed Plutarch's

predilection for metaphors connected with the sea and sailing.)
After the initial shock, the soul recovers sight and hearing,
enjoying its freedom and "breathing all over." "Open like a
single eye," it can now "see around in all directions at once."[68]
Carried away by the astral light, which looks like a quiet sea,
Aridaeus's soul (psyche) can "move in all directions easily and
quickly" (563f). This allows it to see the spectacle of the souls
of the dead; like balls of light changing into human shapes,
they move up from the earth, some following a direct path,
but most, frightened, following a disorderly route. At this
point, the soul of a relative who died young comes toward him
and calls him by his new name, Thespesius. Like the voice in
Timarch's myth, this relative has an explanatory function. In
other apocalypses, Jewish, Muslim, and Christian (see chapters
9 and 11, below), this function belongs to an angel or to
someone like Virgil for Dante, that is, to a venerated precursor.

Plutarch's narrative is more complex than the one about
Timarch. It has seven major sequences describing in detail the
punishment of souls and the mechanism of metensomatosis.
The first sequence introduces us to the messengers of justice,
Adrasteia and the three Erinyes, who distribute penances for
different kinds of sins. The second sequence deals with the
"scars" left by sins on the soul (565b), a motif borrowed from
Plato (Gorgias 523d–24e). It is combined here with a more
interesting and original episode, showing that passions not
only produce scars, but leave another kind of mark on the soul
that can only be deleted through thorough purification in the
department of the Erinys named Dike; this mark consists of
color. A soul that has indulged in baseness and greed is dark-
colored; a cruel and harsh soul is red; a soul intemperate in
pleasures becomes green; and a jealous, envious soul is colored
purple. When you see a disembodied soul, the color gives you
a reliable means of rating the soul's "aura." There is no clear
explanation of why these four colors were chosen by Plutarch.

They partly coincide with the colors of the four quarters of Rome, which took part in horse races,[69] and they partly coincide with the colors attributed by Hellenistic astrology to four of the five planets (besides the sun and the moon).[70] If Plutarch had the planets in mind, however, it is impossible to understand why he picked only four and not five or seven colors.

In the third sequence we meet a special category of the dead: those who, during their lifetime, had been initiated into the mysteries of Dionysus (565a–566a). In the afterlife they occupy a "deep chasm," where they spend their time in foolish pursuit of pleasure and entertainment. This occupation causes the rational soul to accumulate moisture and become heavy; it is weighed down by the cycle of rebirth, for birth (*genesis*) is nothing but an inclination toward the earth (*epi gen neusis*). This formidable pun, probably coined by Plutarch and used by him in a famous description of the soul of the initiate,[71] was later used by all major Neoplatonists, from Plotinus to the eleventh-century Michael Psellus. In Greek, it opens associations that are hardly present in English. *Neusis* also means the movement of a rocking cradle; it implies that the baby-soul on high is swinging toward the place of its birth. It also explains why some Platonists would make the Milky Way into a storage place of souls on their way to being reborn: baby-souls probably feed on the same food as physical babies.

Plutarch is especially harsh toward Dionysus's mysteries, for the true initiate, usually initiated in the major mysteries of Eleusis, is never supposed to be reborn again in the world. From a place at the summit, his or her soul contemplates "the mud of the world" below and has absolutely no desire to return there.

A fourth sequence shows that Plutarch was also rough on Orpheus, who visited the beyond in pursuit of his wife Eurydice, but did not remember well what he saw and delivered false information to human beings. A fifth sequence is meant to emphasize that no one has ever visited a region above the moon and lived to tell about it. In particular the region of Apollo, which must be the sun, is far away from the place visited by Thespesius. A sixth sequence gives the description of a number of punishments in the heavenly Hades (probably the lunar zone called "Hecate's recess" in Timarch's myth). Thespesius sees his own father among those who are being dragged away by demons to be tortured. The account, however, is far from the fastidious accounting of crimes and punishments found in other apocalypses (for example in the Middle Persian apocalypse of the Righteous Virâz, covered in chapter 7, above). Plutarch knows only four generic categories of crimes and four types of punishment.

The seventh and last episode takes Thespesius to the place where souls are apportioned the kinds of bodies they deserve in order to go down into the world. The soul of the emperor Nero is initially assigned to animate the body of a poisonous viper, but his sentence is commuted *in extremis* because of one good deed he performed on earth: he restored the Greeks their freedom. For this, he becomes instead an innocuous frog.

Then, as if sucked by a vacuum, the soul of Thespesius himself reverts to his body, preventing the imminent burial from taking place.[72]

PLOTINUS'S MYSTICISM

The greatest philosopher of late antiquity, Plotinus (205–270 C.E.), would certainly share the intensity of mystical concerns with this experiential background of Greek mysticism based on near-death and out-of-body experiences. Plotinus's type of mysticism has, however, been defined as a "subjectification" and "interiorization" of objective otherworldly journeys like those described by Plutarch one and a half centuries earlier.[73]

Plotinus's philosophy is Platonism; yet the solutions now given to many problems left unsolved by Plato are Aristotelian. With the middle Platonists (Philo of Alexandria, Plutarch, Numenius of Apamea, Celsus, and others), Plotinus shares the idea that there are a number of intermediaries between the intelligible and the sensible world. His system has the following hypostases, which emanate downward and are gradual stages, not separate or solid entities:

1. The One (*monos*), the Absolute, the transcendent, which has no perfect equivalent in Plato, but was prefigured by other Platonic philosophers such as Plutarch himself, and derives from the pressure to explain multiplicity from unity

2. The intellect (*nous*), which is the equivalent of the Platonic world of Ideas or intelligible patterns of all things, and is a first step from unity to multiplicity

3. The world soul, which contains *in potentia* the whole universe and represents a further downward movement of unity toward multiplicity

4. Individual souls

Plotinian mysticism is the recovery from the alienation felt by the embodied human being in the world. Nostalgia for unity with the supreme unity, the One, is deeply imprinted in the rational soul, which strives to leave the burden of the physical body and flee toward the One (*phuge monou pros monon*). Ecstasy is the supreme goal of Plotinian mysticism, and it is described in terms that recall the "oceanic feeling" of Hindu mysticism. It is a state of mind in which the knower is identified with the known. All duality being absent, no vision or drama unfolds, unlike most of the apocalypses examined so far. The goal of Platonic mysticism is higher than a visit to the heavenly Hades: it is a visit to the essence of all essences, which is beyond the universe and cannot be described.

9

The Seven Palaces and the Chariot of God

Jewish Mysticism from Merkabah to Kabbalah

The Greek word *apokalypsis* means "uncovering, revelation." It applies to a body of literature belonging to various traditions: Greek, Jewish, Christian, Gnostic, Iranian, and so on.

An American team led by J. J. Collins has tried to establish the morphology of the apocalyptic literary genre. The results were published in 1979 in the journal *Semeia.*[1] J. J. Collins defines apocalypse as a "literary genre." "*Apocalypse* is a genre of revelatory literature with a narrative framework, in which a revelation is mediated by an otherworldly being to a human recipient, disclosing a transcendent reality which is both temporal, insofar as it envisages eschatological salvation, and spatial insofar as it involves another, supernatural world."[2] From this distinction between a "horizontal," historical axis and a "vertical," ontological axis two types of apocalypses follow: apocalypses without an otherworldly journey, and apocalypses with an otherworldly journey.

The team led by J. J. Collins proceeded further to an exhaustive inventory of apocalypses in Judaism, early Christianity, Gnosticism, and even the Greco-Roman and Iranian traditions. Having already examined revelatory journeys in Greece and in Iran, we will focus our attention on the first three religious traditions, which are closely related. Here we will address only apocalypses with otherworldly journeys. They are catalogued in the following way:

In Judaism (covered by J. J. Collins): *The Apocalypse of Abraham, 1 Enoch 1–36 (Book of the Watchers), 1 Enoch 72–82 (Book of the Heavenly Luminaries), 1 Enoch 37–71 (The Similitudes of Enoch), 2 Enoch, The Testament of Levi, 3 Baruch,* and *The Testament of Abraham;* in Rabbinical Judaism and Jewish mysticism (covered by A. J. Saldarini): *Hekhalot Rabbati, Merkaba Rabba, 3 Enoch* or *Sefer Hekhalot, The Apocalypse of Elijah* (Hebrew), *The Chronicles of Jerahmeel, The Revelation of Joshua ben Levi,* and *The Ascension of Moses;* in early Christianity (covered by Adela Yarbro Collins): *The Ascension of Isaiah, The Apocalypse of Paul, The Apocalypse of Esdras, The Apocalypse of the Virgin Mary, The Story of Zosimus, The Apocalypse of the Holy Mother of God, The Apocalypse of James, The Mysteries of St. John the Apostle and Holy Virgin, The Book of Resurrection,* and *The Apocalypse of Sedrach;* and in Gnosticism (covered by F. T. Fallon): *The Paraphrasis of Seem, Zostrianos, The Apocalypse of Paul,* and the *Two Books of Ieu.*

As Collins and other authors frequently note, it is often difficult to ascertain to what extent a Judeo-Christian apocalypse is not just a Judaic apocalypse rewritten to include Christian motifs. This seems especially to be the case with an early Christian apocalypse like *The Ascension of Isaiah.*[3] For this reason, here we will treat at least this particular early Christian apocalypse together with Jewish apocalypses. The decision to examine all other Christian apocalypses as part of a Christian tradition that runs continuously from the end of the first century C.E. to Dante is not an easy one. It is only possible if we interrupt our description to talk about the powerful Muslim tradition of the *mi'râj,* or Muhammad's heavenly journey. On the other hand, since Muhammad's *mi'râj* also depends on Jewish and early Christian apocalyptic literature, the circle is closed, even though the whole is thus divided into chapters 9 and 10.

It is far more difficult to find a place for the examination of Gnostic otherworldly journeys, because they follow two different patterns. The pattern of Zostrianos is close to Judaic and early Christian apocalypses, but has a distinct flavor. The description of heavenly stations in the *Two Books of Ieu* is closer to the Egyptian *Book of the Dead* than to Judaic *merkabah* mysticism, yet within its time period Judaic mysticism is the only frame of reference allowing us to understand the pattern of heavenly ascent in Zostrianos in a broader environment. As the debate about the existence of a "Judaic Gnosticism" and about the relationship between Gnosticism and Judaism is still open, the above-mentioned Gnostic apocalypses are discussed in this chapter, and other aspects of Gnosticism are covered in chapter 10, below, which deals with the powerful Platonic tradition of the "passage of the soul through the planetary spheres."

In 1981, we proposed a parallel classification of apocalypses based on the attitude of the main character going on the otherworldly journey;[4] this classification contains three categories.

1. In "call" or "elective" apocalypses, the hero is elected from above by virtue of special merits he has accumulated in respect to the other world.

2. Some apocalypses take place "by accident," as a result of an accident or a serious illness; in this case, personal merit is unnecessary.

3. In "quest apocalypses," the hero himself or herself strives to obtain the revelation and uses various methods such as incubation, absorption or ingestion of hallucinogens, or bodily and psychological techniques (breath control, fasting, bodily postures, and so on).

This classification allows us to understand some of the major differences between the Judaic (and Christian) tradition of otherworldly journeys, and other traditions, such as the Greek or the Iranian.

JEWISH APOCALYPSES

It is typical for Jewish apocalypses to be call apocalypses.[5] Narratives of quest apocalypses seem to be completely missing in the Jewish tradition, and only one apocalypse, which has no otherworldly journey and, besides, was thoroughly influenced by Greek models, seems to belong to the category of accidental apocalypses.[6]

Studying a number of Jewish apocalypses (*1 Enoch, 2 Enoch, The Testament of Levi, 3 Baruch, The Testament of Abraham, 4 Ezra,* and *The Apocalypse of Abraham*), Mary Dean-Otting, a student of Johann Maier of Cologne, has come to the conclusion that all Jewish apocalypses share a number of traits: they are what we have defined as "call-apocalypses."[7] The ascent takes place in sleep, the ecstatic is the narrator in the first person and is accompanied by an angelic guide, the revelation is obtained in dialogue form, the ecstatic goes through a number of levels of heaven and has a vision of the heavenly Temple, there is a scene of judgment or allusion to judgment, mysteries are revealed, God's glory is described, and the protagonist returns to earth.

The heroes of Jewish apocalypses are biblical characters marked by some special quality that connects them with the heavenly world. Two such characters were taken to heaven by

God: Enoch, who "walked with God" (Gen. 5:24), and Elijah, who ascended to heaven in a chariot of fire (2 Kings 2:1–15). A third one might have been abducted to heaven as well, for "no one knows the place of his burial to this day" (Deut. 34:6); that one is Moses. It should therefore not come as a surprise that most otherworldly journeys in Jewish apocalyptic literature are attributed to two of the three men who went to heaven without dying: Enoch, Elijah, and Moses. Philo of Alexandria (ca. 20 B.C.E.–50 C.E.) interpreted Moses' ascent to Mount Sinai as an ascent to heaven,[8] and Josephus Flavius reports a tradition according to which Moses did not die, but was simply taken to heaven.[9]

The most ancient Jewish apocalypse is *1 Enoch* or *The Ethiopic Book of Enoch,* thus called because its integral version is only preserved in an Ethiopic translation.[10] Based on the Aramaic fragments of *1 Enoch* discovered at Qumran in 1952, J. T. Milik was able to date its most ancient parts to the beginning of the third century B.C.E..[11] *1 Enoch* is a composite work. Two main blocks of text are more ancient than the rest; these are chapters 1–36, called by R. H. Charles "The Book of the Watchers," and chapters 72–82, which he calls "The Book of the Heavenly Luminaries."

In chapter 14, Enoch is visited by a vision in his sleep and taken to heaven by wind and clouds. In heaven he sees a wall of crystal, then a large mansion of crystal, all surrounded by flames of fire; eventually he sees a second mansion made of fire, in which, surrounded by unbearable brightness, is the throne of God. This vision seems to Johan Maier to be "the purest, simplest and earliest ascent description" in *1 Enoch.*[12] The German scholar sees in it the influence of chapter 1 of the vision of the prophet Ezekiel: the chariot (*merkabah*) with God's throne on it. The explanation of the vision, according to Maier, lies in the structure of the Jerusalem temple, which was disposed exactly as in Enoch's description. In other words,

Enoch saw the heavenly temple, which reproduced the archi-tecture of the temple of Jerusalem.[13]

In chapter 17, Enoch is taken on a tour of heaven by angels who can appear as humans when they wish so. Heaven is not multilevel; the tour is strictly horizontal, and it takes him to the extremities of the earth, to witness the punishment of wicked souls after death and even the punishment of angels and stars.

Chapters 72 to 82 contain a similar vision in which the secrets of astronomy are revealed to Enoch. The true calendar thus appears as a powerful, consequential heavenly secret that only Enoch has the privilege to learn and pass on to other human beings.

Enoch is the father of *merkabah* mysticism. It should there-fore not surprise us to see that a whole cycle of otherworldly journeys appears under his name, containing not only 2 *Enoch* (or *The Slavonic Book of Enoch*) and 3 *Enoch* (or *The Hebrew Book of Enoch*), but also traditions that report his name as Metatron ("angel of the throne").[14]

2 *Enoch,* only extant in a late Slavonic version, is a product of the Jewish Diaspora (now with Christian interpolations), redacted during the tormented period between 70 (date of the fall of the Temple of Jerusalem) and 135 C.E. (date of the repression of the revolt of the messiah Bar Kochba by the Roman authorities). Like Plutarch modernizing Plato, the author of 2 *Enoch* had 1 *Enoch* in mind, but changed the horizontal tour of heaven into a vertical journey through seven heavens. This pattern also occurs in the otherworldly journey of Levi (see below).

In 2 *Enoch,* Enoch is asleep on his couch and is in a terrible state of mind when two angels appearing like oversized men come and take him on a heavenly journey. Only two kinds of revelation are imparted to Enoch in each of the seven heavens: cosmological (heavens one, four, and six), and eschatological (heavens two, three, and five).[15] In heaven number one reside the meteorological angels, responsible for weather on earth; in heaven number four are the heavenly luminaries, the sun and the moon, and the divisions of time; in heaven number six are the seven armies of angels who supervise the world's order.

In the second heaven Enoch sees the punishment of the fallen angels; in heaven number three, the paradise of the righteous, where they will dwell in eternity, and the northern hell, where "darkness and gloom" is prepared for practitioners of malevolent arts and for dishonest people; and in heaven number five, the watchers who defected with Satan and await divine penalty.

In the seventh and last heaven, Enoch enters God's court and is adopted as an angel, more precisely as a scribe-angel, to whom the archangel Vrevoel (possibly Uriel) dictates all the secrets of heaven and earth in 360 books. God himself then dictates the secrets of creation, part of which sound like an Eastern European dualistic legend and which must therefore originate from the Slavic context. Enoch is then hurriedly dispatched back to earth with the books, to teach the secrets to his children before the imminent coming of the great flood through which God intends to punish "the idolaters and sodomitic fornicators." After thirty days, the angels take Enoch back to the seventh heaven from the midst of the assembly, concealing themselves and their guest in deep murk and darkness.

The heavenly structure of 2 Enoch also appears in The Testament of Levi, one of the Testaments of the Twelve Patriarchs.[16] The narrative framework of The Testament of Levi is based on Genesis 34: Shechem, son of Hamor, governor of Shechem in Canaan, rapes Jacob's daughter Dinah while traveling with her family through the land. The sons of Jacob accept that Shechem should marry Dinah, on condition that all men in the city be circumcised; while the men are healing, Simeon and Levi attack the city and kill all the males. The same Levi is made by biblical tradition into the ancestor of the priestly tribe of the Levites, although it is questionable whether there is any historical connection between the tribe and Levitic priesthood.[17]

Before the vindication of Dinah, Levi bitterly thinks that all men are wicked and prays for delivery from sin. While sleeping, he is shown three heavens (2:5), which later on (3:4) become seven. The division of heavens is more rational than in *2 Enoch,* for they show increasing holiness according to the Platonic principle that "what is higher is better." In addition to this, cosmological and eschatological elements are all mixed up: in the first heaven the wicked are punished, while in the second are found the meteorological phenomena ready to be unleashed at the final judgment, and in the third "there are the powers of the hosts, those which are ordained for the day of judgment to execute vengeance on the spirits of deceit and Beliar."[18] In the fourth heaven are the thrones and the authorities, in the fifth, the messenger angels, in the sixth, the minstering angels of God, and in the seventh, "the Great Glory in the holy of holies far beyond all holiness" (3:4).

The angel-guide opens to Levi the gates of heaven, and he beholds "the holy temple and the Most High upon a throne of glory" (5:1), after which he receives priestly investiture and the weapons to be used against his sister's rapist. A further episode (8:1–15) contains the heavenly crowning of Levi, which prefigures the eternal installation of the righteous in heaven.

Another otherworldly journey is contained in *3 Baruch,* or *The Greek Apocalypse of Baruch,* possibly mentioned by Origen.[19] The text, of uncertain date, is a product of Hellenized Judaism. During the Babylonian captivity, the prophet Baruch receives his revelation while sitting on a riverbank in front of the gate of a sanctuary. The angel-interpreter Phanuel comes and gives him a tour of heaven, leading him first to the firmament, then to the waters above the firmament, and then to a place of punishment. He crosses into the first heaven through a huge gate and meets there the builders of the Tower of Babel in the monstrous form of hybrid animals. In the second heaven, those who commissioned the tower to be built have feet of stags and the appearance of dogs. In the third there is a serpent (*ophis*) or a dragon (*drakon*), whose belly is Hades and who grinds the bodies of the wicked, and in the fourth heaven the righteous are present in the shape of birds.

Subsequently, Baruch visits the fiery chariot of the sun, led by a crowned man and borne by forty angels. The chariot is preceded by a phoenix with fiery wings called "the guardian of the earth" (6:3). At dusk the chariot of the moon turns up, drawn by bull-shaped angels and containing the moon as a woman surrounded by lamblike angels (9:4). In the fourth heaven, Baruch sees a pool containing heavenly dew and "unearthly birds" beside it (10:2). In the fifth and last heaven, Baruch sees the first of 365 gates and the archangel Michael, supreme commander of the angels, descending with a clash of thunder, a vessel in his hand containing the merits of the righteous to be presented to god. The merits appear in the shape of baskets of flowers carried by angels. In turn, Michael delivers to the angels a quantity of oil allotted by God in proportion to the number of flowers of each righteous one (15:1–4). Michael alone enters the gate that leads to God. When the doors of the inner sanctum close, Baruch's vision comes to an end.[20]

Another otherworldly journey that deserves to be mentioned in this context is taken by Abraham and is the topic of chapters 10 to 14 of *The Testament of Abraham*.[21] Michael gives Abraham a heavenly tour in his chariot. Like Er and Menippus, Abraham looks over the inhabited world below. Then he is led eastward toward the first gate of heaven, where he sees two ways and two corresponding gates, a narrow one leading to paradise and a wide one leading to hell. Abraham follows Michael and two fiery angels through the wide gate. They enter a courtroom where Abel delivers judgment sitting on a crystal throne. The angel Dokiel weighs the souls, and the angel Puriel tests them with fire. Abraham witnesses the judgment of the souls, after which God orders Michael to take him back to earth.

As the beautiful and erudite book by Martha Himmelfarb, *Tours of Hell,* persuasively demonstrates, the matrix of early Christian apocalyptic is undeniably Jewish.[22] Yet, as we have shown in a series of books and articles, Greek influence becomes increasingly important in time, so as to allow one to state that two different apocalyptic traditions developed in Christianity.[23] The case of one early Christian apocalypse, *The Vision of Isaiah,*[24] shows how close the Christians were to Jewish apocalyptic tradition, to the point that it is even possible to postulate the existence of a Jewish apocalypse ascribed to the biblical prophet Isaiah that was subsequently modified in Christian and Gnostic circles.

The *Vision of Isaiah* forms the second part of the apocryphal *Ascension of Isaiah,* consisting of a "Martyrdom of Isaiah" section and of a "Vision" or apocalypse section containing an other-worldly journey. The "Vision" also has two parts: an *anabasis* (ascent) of the prophet (chapters 6–9), which is the only part we will deal with here, and a *descensus* and *ascensus* of the Savior (10:1–11:1 and 11:23). An angel from the seventh heaven comes to take Isaiah on his heavenly voyage. In the firmament, Isaiah meets the angel Sammael (Samael), the chief of Satanic armies that fight against each other; as they fight, the peoples on earth do the same.

To understand this passage, one must know who the angels in the firmament are and who Sammael is. Only Jewish traditions can fully explain. The celestial angels are the angels of the nations, that is, the representatives of all the peoples of the earth (seventy or seventy-two) at God's court. Sammael is simply the national angel of Rome. Yet another tradition, certainly not contradictory, makes of Sammael the angel of death.

This short passage shows us that the "Vision" must have been composed during a period of time when Rome, and therefore its angel, was particularly powerful and thus hateful; such a description certainly coincides with the period traditionally associated with the redaction of the apocryphon, between 70 C.E. (date of the fall of the Second Temple of Jerusalem) and 135 C.E. (date of the definitive defeat of the revolt of the Palestinian messiah Bar Kochba and the death by torture of the chief rabbi of Jerusalem, eighty-five-year-old Akiba ben Joseph).

In the second heaven Isaiah sees an enthroned angel and wants to pay homage to him (probably thinking that he is God). The escort-angel warns him not to worship the enthroned angel. The motif is rabbinical; it receives full treatment below. A similar episode also appears in two other Jewish apocalypses of the same period, 4 Ezra and 2 Baruch, and in a nameless Coptic (Christian) apocalypse.[25]

In the third heaven, Isaiah begins to change into a heavenly being, as Enoch did. In the seventh heaven, an angel who exceeds all others in luminosity shows him a heavenly book in which minute accountability is recorded for every occurrence in the human world. Obviously, this otherworldly journey of Isaiah *is* entirely Jewish and has nothing Christian about it.[26]

EARLY JEWISH MYSTICISM

For a long time, the study of Jewish mysticism was dominated by the imposing figure of a patriarch, Gershom Scholem (1897–1982). As Joseph Dan perceptively noted in his 1987 monograph, Scholem "was first and foremost a historian concerned

with the effect of mysticism on Jewish culture."[27] The conclusion that can be drawn from this remark is that Scholem was
not strictly a scholar of mysticism. He had a unique knowledge
of the bibliography of Jewish mysticism, but he was inclined
to edit out the more technical parts in his descriptions of
mystical doctrines. From the point of view of a scholar of
mysticism, these parts happen to be among the most interesting. We owe to a new generation of scholars the discovery of
the hidden, practical methods of Jewish mysticism that Scholem's generation, being too close to the Enlightenment, was
perhaps ready to dismiss out of a certain embarrassment.
Respectful of the complexity of data and problems, Ithamar
Gruenwald, who never hastens to assert a unilateral position
but always strives toward global understanding, is the safest
guide today to the fascinating world of early Jewish
mysticism.[28]

Early Jewish mysticism is usually identified with two types
of speculation, one more directly "ecstatic" and the other
prevalently "theosophical"; this terminology is used by Moshe
Idel to define the two branches of Kabbalah. The ecstatic
technique is called *ma'aseh merkabah* (work of the chariot). It
derives its biblical legitimacy from the vision of the prophet
Ezekiel (Ezekiel 1), who contemplates the formidable throne
of God transported on a chariot (*merkabah*) carried by various
sorts of angels. The theosophical speculation, which need not
concern us here, is called *ma'aseh bereshit* (work of genesis), and
it consists of a mystical exegesis of the creation of the world.

The first testimonies of *merkabah* mysticism occur as early
as the authorship of *1 Enoch* (14:11–19), in the third century
B.C.E. They are followed in the second century B.C.E. by some
Greek fragments of the Jewish tragedian Ezekiel of Alexandria.
Portions of the *merkabah* tradition are current in Jewish apocalypses such as *2 Enoch* and *The Apocalypse of Abraham*. Later on,
this tradition grows into an impressive body of literature

containing *merkabah* writings, *hekhaloth* writings (from the Hebrew word *hekhal,* meaning "palace"; the mystic is supposed to cross seven palaces before coming to the chariot with God's throne on it), and even works of magic such as the *Sefer ha-razim* (Book of secrets).[29] Among the most important documents pertaining to *merkabah* mysticism are *Hekhaloth rabbati* (The greater palaces) and *3 Enoch,* or *The Hebrew Book of Enoch.*[30] There is no consensus among scholars concerning the dating of these texts. Recent scholarship, however, favors a late date.[31]

Resuming Johann Maier's interpretation of *1 Enoch* as a vision of the heavenly temple, whose structure corresponds with that of the Jerusalem temple, Ira Chernus has recently argued for a close parallel between the preparation of the *merkabah* mystic and the ritual pilgrimage to Jerusalem.[32] Like pilgrims to Jerusalem, who had to purify themselves for seven days, wear white clothes, and bathe before entering the temple, the *merkabah* mystic fasted, bathed, and abstained from sex. Like the pilgrims approaching the temple, who were questioned by the Levites before entering the precinct, the mystics were questioned by heavenly guardians of the various *hekhaloth* (palaces). And, just as certain limits were set on persons approaching the temple in a state of ritual impurity, there were dangerous limits that certain otherworldly pilgrims to the *merkabah* were not supposed to cross.

Merkabah mysticism was esoteric and exclusive. Criteria for would-be practitioners of the "work of the chariot"—generically known as *yorede merkabah* (those who descend to the chariot)—were connected with age, status, moral behavior, adherence to the law, and even certain peculiar bodily signs.[33]

The *yorede merkabah* used a mystical technique whose description was written down only centuries later by the famous Hai Gaon (d. 1038) of the rabbinical Yeshiva (academy) of Pumbeditha in Mesopotamia. The postulant "must sit fasting for a specified number of days, place his head between his knees, and whisper to the earth many prescribed songs and hymns. Thus, he peers into the inner room and chambers as if he were seeing the Seven Palaces (*hekhaloth*) with his own eyes, and he observes as if he were going from Palace to Palace and seeing what is in them."[34]

In the blessed times of the Palestinian Tannaites it was agreeable to God to see the rabbis talking about the mysteries of the chariot and the throne, although this was not without great danger, as fire would descend from heaven during such talks. While the Rabbis Yohannan ben Zakkai and Eleazar ben Araq were sitting under a tree discussing the unspeakable secrets of heaven, a fire came from heaven and angels began dancing before them. Rabbi Yohannan's disciples Eliezer and Yehoshua were surrounded by fire during their study of the work of the chariot.[35] Times changed, however, and the rabbis eventually came to look with suspicion on these esoteric practices and to warn against them.[36]

The tradition of an esoteric teaching transmitted from rabbi to disciple is reflected in the narrative framework of a classic of *hekhaloth* literature, the *Maaseh Merkabah,* a dialogue between master (Rabbi Akiba) and disciple (Rabbi Ishmael).[37] The text emphasizes the astronomical magnitudes of heavenly things and multiplies them beyond necessity. "In the second Palace stand one hundred thousand myriads of Chariots of fire and four thousand myriads of flame are interspersed between them. In the fourth Palace stand a hundred and four thousand myriads of Chariots of fire and four thousand myriads of flame are interspersed between them," and so on. Procedures for ascent are suspiciously simple: by uttering the formula SDYR TYKRY 'M YBY' BYHW SWWSH 'P RWP WYHM and the like, and with no less than forty days of fasting, the Angel of the Countenance descends with his frightening hosts. Prayers should be recited so that the formidable angels do not destroy the mystic, who is then given "permission to catch sight" of the *merkabah*. The description of this experience, ascribed to Rabbi Nehunya ben Hakana, is outstandingly vivid. "When I caught sight of the vision of the Chariot I saw a proud majesty, chambers of chambers, majesties of awe, transparencies of fear, burning and flaming, their fires fire and their shaking shakes."[38] There follows a list of names of the guardian angels of the seven *hekhaloth* and many prayers to be uttered in their presence.

Either in dialogic or, more often, in apocalyptic form, *hekhaloth* literature describes the details of the otherworldly journey, designated as a "descent to the *merkabah*" despite the indisputable fact that it is a heavenly ascent. Once in possession of the secret technique, the mystic can come and go as he likes. "What is it like [to know the secret of the *merkabah*]? It is like having a ladder in one's house (and being able to go up and down at will)."[39] Again, "Rabbi Ishmael said: All the *haverim* [companions, that is, initiated disciples] liken this to a man who has a ladder in the middle of his house, who ascends and descends on it and there is no creature to stop him."[40]

The operation, as we have already seen, was probably performed by conjuring up an important angel, the Angel of the Countenance (or of the Presence) of God. "When anyone would want to descend to the Chariot, he would call upon Surya, the Angel of the Presence, and make him swear [to protect him] one hundred and twelve times in the name of Tutruseah-YHVH who is called Tutruseah Tsortak Totarkhiel Tofgar Ashruleah Zevudiel and Zeharariel Tandiel Shokel Huzeah Dahivurin and Adiroron YHVH, Lord of Israel."[41]

The mystic then crosses a total of eight *hekhaloth,* each provided with a gate. Each gate has two guardians, one on the right and one on the left side, and each palace has a total of eight guards. God's name has to be pronounced in front of each guardian of each of the seven palaces, once for the descent and once for the ascent, which, based on the preceding paragraph, gives us the figure of 112, or eight times seven times two. The guardians themselves have their own hidden names, which are the subject of a tedious description.[42]

The mystic crosses the first *hekhal* armed with the seals of Surya and Tutruseah-YHVH, which he shows to the guardians on the right and the left of the gate. The entrance to each new palace presupposes the knowledge of a new set of names.

The function of the guards of the sixth palace is to kill those who are "unworthy of the task."[43] If Dumiel, the chief guard of the sixth *hekhal*, decides that the mystic has enough knowledge of the Jewish tradition, he leads him before the throne of glory.

The formidable names of the guardians of the seventh *hekhal* derive directly from the unutterable name of God. The attendant prince is Anaphiel, who "is like the Creator of the World."[44] He opens the gates of the seventh palace, opposite to which are 256 *hayyot* (living creatures, a rank of *merkabah* angels) who lift the mystic. "Five hundred and twelve eyes, and each and every eye of the eyes of the Holy *hayyot* is hollow like the holes in a sieve woven of branches." The eyes of the Cherubim and Ophanim (the angelic wheels of the chariot) "are similar to torches of light and the flames of burning coals."[45]

The twenty-sixth chapter of *Hekhaloth rabbati* deals with those who are not worthy to enter the *merkabah*. Whereas one who is worthy politely declines to enter at the first invitation and only accepts at the second invitation, one who is not worthy enters immediately. The guards of the sixth *hekhal* produce before the unworthy one the mirage of "a million waves of water," and if he asks any questions about the water "they throw a million bars of iron on him."

This crushing "danger of water" that succeeds the "danger of fire" is connected in a strange yet very precise way with the

cycle of Enoch's otherworldly journeys, and with some enigmatic episodes concerning the fate of four Tannaitic rabbis.

"Four were those who entered Paradise: Ben Azzay and Ben
Zoma, Aher and Rabbi Akiba."[46] Only "Rabbi Akiba ascended
and descended in peace,"[47] while the other three met with an
ill fate because of the "danger of water," which the *Greater
Hekhaloth* places in the sixth palace. They mistook for water
"the pure marble stones" of paradise, which look like waves,
and thereby incurred the wrath of God, who does not tolerate
lies before Himself (*Babli hagigah* 14b). Johann Maier deciphers
from this riddle of paradise a clear allusion to the temple of
Jerusalem, whose walls were built in marble of different colors
that "looked like sea waves."[48] The sixth heavenly *hekhal* is
nothing but an image of the Jerusalem *hekhal,* which, in its
turn, is only a reproduction of the celestial model. According
to the *Greater Hekhaloth,* Ben Azzay paid for his mistake by
death, and Ben Zoma by madness. "Only Akiba ascended and
descended in peace."

What happened to Aher (the other, that is, the apostate),
whose real name was Elisha ben Abuyah, and who, after his
otherworldly experience, became a heretic and the paradigm
of the atheist in rabbinic Judaism? His fate is closely related to
the fate of Enoch.

According to the early tradition transmitted by *1 Enoch,*
Enoch was a Jewish culture hero; he had been to heaven,
learned the secrets of astronomy, watched God's court, and
obtained information on the coming of the Messiah. He had
received instruction in all the secret doctrines concerning past
and future, things on earth and in heaven. He had taught
human beings the alphabet and science. According to the *Book
of Jubilees* (4:23), God gave him an extremely important job,
which he performed sitting in the Garden of Eden: he was
God's scribe and archivist. In *2 Enoch,* this story is reported in
full detail: Vrevoel, the angel-minister of God, gives Enoch the

pleasant news of his assumption and promotion, and another angel and then God himself teach him the secrets of creation and the secrets of heaven. This section is actually the equivalent of the "work of Genesis" and of the "work of the chariot." *The Testament of Abraham* (10:8–11:3) makes Enoch into an angel; the Cherubim carry his books and registers. Successive *merkabah* writings give Enoch the angelic name of Metatron. *3 Enoch* (15) vividly describes the metamorphosis of the human being Enoch into an angel made of celestial fire; his flesh and hair changes into flames, his muscles into fire, his bones into burning charcoals, his eye pupils into embers, and his limbs into fiery wings. The same happens to Moses in a Hebrew medieval apocalypse known as *The Revelation of Moses* (*Gedulat Mosheh*).

Yet Metatron retains one characteristic of Enoch the human being: he can sit. This is important to know, for angels cannot sit because they have no joints. When Elisha ben Abuyah goes to heaven, he—like Isaiah and others mentioned above—sees a being sitting on a glorious throne and mistakes him for God himself, knowing that only God can sit and the angels cannot. In reality, he has been misled by Enoch-Metatron, and he becomes a ditheist, thinking: "Perhaps—God forfend!—there are two Powers [in heaven]."[49]

The *Sefer ha-razim* (Book of secrets), reconstructed in 1966 by Mordecai Margalioth, is a composite text dated variously between the fourth and the seventh century C.E. It contains magical recipes within a *merkabah* framework. The fictive disclosure of heavenly secrets is not presented here as the otherworldly journey of a deserving biblical character, but as a heavenly book transmitted to Noah by the angel Raziel and inscribed by the patriarch on a sapphire stone. The major difference between the *Sefer ha-razim* and *hekhaloth* literature is that, whereas the latter makes the otherworldly journey into a goal in itself, the former uses knowledge about heavenly beings for a magical purpose, that is, in order to ask of angels "success in each thing."[50]

"Noah learned from it rituals that cause death and rituals that preserve life, . . . to interpret dreams and visions, to arouse combat, and to quiet wars, and to rule over spirits and demons, to dispatch them around as if they were your slaves, to watch the four winds of the earth, to be learned in the speech of thunderclaps, to tell the significance of lightning flashes, to foretell what will happen in each and every month, . . . and to comprehend the songs of heaven,"[51] which are the songs of the holy creatures (*hayyoth hakodesh*), the animal-shaped angels of the chariot.[52] This is none other than the famous book of magic of King Solomon, who used it to rule over the spirits. The main body of the text is a fastidious description of the many names and capabilities of the angelic hosts in each of the seven firmaments, together with the preparations, ceremonies, and formulas that propitiate the angels. The tractate does not have a theoretical astrological framework.[53]

Noticing analogies between Gnosticism and early Jewish mysticism, Gershom Scholem holds that the latter is derived from the former; he therefore calls *merkabah* mysticism "Jewish Gnosticism."[54] This contention is quite debatable, for a series of reasons that will be analyzed below. It has been challenged by Ithamar Gruenwald from a perspective different from ours. His previous book, *Apocalyptic and Merkavah Mysticism* (1980), already commends him as Scholem's main successor in the study of Merkabah mysticism. In that book Gruenwald made important discoveries that present *merkabah* mysticism and *hekhaloth* literature in a new light. Yet, with particular discretion, Gruenwald never polemicizes against his predecessors or boasts about his discoveries.

As we know, Scholem's main thesis is that *merkabah* mysticism is a form of Jewish Gnosticism, and he bases this assumption on the occurrence in both of them of techniques of permutation of the letters of the alphabet, arithmological speculations, and the importance of divine names, passwords, and badges for opening the gates to the many abodes of heaven. Obviously, Scholem is wrong on one point only: far from being Gnostic in themselves, all of the above-mentioned motifs are already present in Hellenistic magic, from which, it is legitimate to assume, both Jewish mystics and Gnostics borrowed. Therefore, no claim of precedence can be made, either by Gnosticism over *merkabah* mysticism or vice versa.

Yet in several of the essays contained in his latest book, Gruenwald, working with the often subtle boundary between apocalypse, *merkabah* mysticism, and gnosis, thoroughly argues that a theory of Judaic origin would explain many Gnostic motifs. Unlike many of his colleagues, however, Gruenwald does not reverse the traditional explanation, which derives Gnosticism from early Jewish mysticism. His arguments are sound and convincing; they seem to enforce the view that the problem of the historical origins of Gnosticism is actually based on a theoretical fallacy. While this is true, it does not take away the probability that a whole series of mythical motifs were borrowed by the Gnostics from Judaism, if only because the anti-Judaic attitude of some of them presupposes an active confrontation with Judaism (this is Birger Pearson's thesis). Therefore, I think that Gruenwald's position in the debate is the most balanced. "In fact," he argues, "even in the case of the Gnostic use of the Jewish material, one has to be on guard not to confuse an actual borrowing from Jewish sources with a mere echo, or indirect reflection, of Jewish ideas and biblical interpretations. In addition, Judaism should not be viewed as the only source for Gnosticism. There are other factors besides Judaism that contributed to the formation of Gnosticism. . . ."[55] This position is stated in such essays as "Jewish Merkavah Mysticism and Gnosticism," "Jewish Sources for the

Gnostic Texts from Nag Hammadi?," "Aspects of the Jewish-Gnostic Controversy," "The Problem of the Anti-Gnostic Polemic in Rabbinic Literature," and "Halakhic Material in Codex Gnosticus V,4 (2 ApJ)?"

Only a survey of Gnostic otherworldly journeys can show to what extent the main pattern of ascent is similar in both of these religious trends in late antiquity.

GNOSTIC OTHERWORLDLY JOURNEYS

Today there are two inventories of Gnostic apocalypses,[56] as well as two surveys of Gnostic otherworldly journeys, the latest one, by Giovanni Casadio, being also the most complete.[57] Any further research should take into account Casadio's thorough analysis.[58]

Thanks to such recent research, we are today in a better position than a few years ago to understand the preliminary practices used by Gnostics in order to obtain acquaintance with the heavenly realm. One of these practices was visualization. We cannot understand this practice outside the framework of Gnostic doctrine, in particular the doctrine of a group of Gnostics that the early third-century heresiologist Hippolytus of Rome called Sethians.[59] Two Nag Hammadi Gnostic tractates—*Zostrianos* and *Paraphrasis of Seem*—show important connections with this type of Gnosis.[60]

The Sethians of Hippolytus, whose doctrine must have had a fundamental impact on Manichaeism, postulate the existence of three principles: light, darkness, and pneuma (or spirit), which mediates between the first two. The three probably derive from Aristotelian psychology, where pneuma is the intermediary between soul and body.[61] Like the Platonic archetype of space (*chôra*), these principles are intelligible but not perceptible, and they can only be understood through meditative practice. Pneuma is diffuse, like a fragrance.

Darkness is made of irrational yet self-reflective water, which anxiously desires to come in contact with pneuma and light, in order not to remain "lonely, invisible, deprived of light, impotent, inert and weak."[62] This is why darkness does anything in her power to retain in herself the splendor of light and the fragrance of pneuma.

The three principles contain in themselves innumerable atomic forces in perpetual collision among themselves. From their impact, molds and patterns come into being, which like Aristotelian forms act on matter as "seals" or imprints. One of these imprints is the form of the universe, which looks like a huge female womb or matrix "with an *omphalos* in the middle." As Casadio shows, the Greek word *omphalos,* commonly meaning "navel," is here a euphemism for *phallos* (phallus).[63] It is possible to visualize the world's matrix by meditating on the shape of the matrix of a pregnant animal. Everything that is has a matrix of this sort, say the Sethians, thereby giving an illustration *sui generis* to the Aristotelian theory of forms.

Here enters the fecundating principle, the *membrum virile* that caused the world to be produced in the matrix, that is, the Demiurge of the World. He is a terrible serpentlike wind, who raises a huge wave in the female waters below. We understand that this wave is the female womb, and the serpent is the male organ that penetrates it. From this primordial intercourse a son is born, Nous or Intellect, who is superior to his parents for being made of light and pneuma. He is tragically caught in this world, from which he wants to be freed; he is "Light in Darkness, who strives to be liberated (*lythênai*) from the bodies and cannot find liberation (*lysis*) or escape (*diexo-dos*)."[64] In order to save Nous subsumed in the middle of darkness, light dispatches Logos-Christ to save him by "entering the repugnant mysteries of the maternal matrix."[65]

This cosmogonic process can be understood by the adepts

of the Sethian Gnosis by means of analogy and meditation. The objects of this mystic activity are the pupil of the eye and the matrix of a pregnant animal. The pupil reveals a substratum of darkness polished by the presence of the bright spirit. The matrix reveals the cosmogonical process, and intensifies the horror that sexuality inspired in these ascetic Gnostics.[66]

According to the same Hippolytus, another group of Gnostics, the Peratae, practiced visualization of the primordial serpent in a portion of the sky.[67] The late fourth-century heresiologist Epiphanius, bishop of Salamis (Cyprus), gives us further details about Gnostic practices involving a serpent, with particular reference to the sect called Ophites, from the Greek word *ophis* (serpent).[68] According to him, these Ophites worshiped the serpent as a god, for he revealed knowledge to human beings. Epiphanius reports only one out of what must have been a long series of analogies between the serpent and natural shapes. "Are not our entrails also, said the Ophites, by which we live and are nourished, shaped like a serpent?"[69] Yet worship goes much further than that. "They have an actual snake, and keep it in a sort of basket. When it is time for their mysteries they bring it out of the den, spread loaves around on a table, and call the snake to come; and when the den is opened it comes out. And then the snake . . . crawls onto the table and coils up on the loaves. And this is what they call a perfect sacrifice. And . . . they each kiss the snake besides."[70]

Many Gnostics obtained otherworldly journeys through ritual activities. Marcus the Gnostic and the (probably fictitious) group to which the late tractate *Pistis Sophia* refers performed many kinds of baptismal rites. Others resorted to strenuous sexual practices;[71] these were disavowed by the majority of the Gnostics, who were generally on the contrary exceedingly ascetic. (Nonetheless, the difficult character of the sexual exercises reported by Epiphanius rather indicates that the Gnostics conceived them as another form of asceticism, and not as "libertinism," as Hans Jonas asserts in his famous book, *The Gnostic Religion;* one single report alludes to a libertine and communal Gnostic sect, but the extent to which this sect was "Gnostic" is debatable.) We will not describe such rituals here.[72] Basilides and Marcus the Gnostic also resorted to artifices of grammar and numerology very akin to the methods used later in the Jewish Kabbalah under the names of *gemmatria, temurah,* and *notarikon.* Such methods were not typically Gnostic. They belonged to Hellenistic magic in general and were practiced from immemorial times, for the Assyriologist Alasdair Livingstone could trace them back as early as a number of Assyro-Babylonian tablets already employing numerology and permutational philology.[73]

Baptism rituals return in a spiritualized, heavenly form in one of the most interesting Gnostic reports of otherworldly journeys, contained in the narrative framework of the Nag Hammadi tractate *Zostrianos* (Codex 8:1), written in the first person. Goethe would have liked it, for Zostrianos, like his Faust, was on the brink of nervous exhaustion and suicide when he received the ultimate revelation.

Zostrianos is a typical intellectual, who, while scrupulously practicing the rigorous ascetic exercises he preaches to his community (Zostrianos is a prominent character in his group), secretly longs for an experiential illumination he never attains. To his dismay, many of his comrades resort to sexual rituals, which help to further alienate Zostrianos from the surrounding world. In his meditations, Zostrianos often senses otherworldly presences visiting him, but even these meditations are exceedingly abstract. They concern some of the deepest questions that human beings have ever been able to formulate: Why do existing things exist? Why is there multiplicity?

Unable to answer these questions, distressed and desperate from his lack of actual knowledge of a superior reality, Zostrianos takes to the road of the desert in order to let himself die of starvation or be food for the lions. This final resolution produces the expected result: a messenger is dispatched by the world of light, who scolds him for his suicide attempt and enjoins him to return to his community and preach, but not as before. The messenger offers him an otherworldly tour on a bright cloud of gnosis that moves fast in space. Baptized, that is, adopted, in all successive aeons, Zostrianos reaches the summit of the otherworld and receives final revelation from the great Authrounios and from a being of light called Ephesech.

The Sethian system is more colorfully presented in another Gnostic apocalypse with an otherworldly journey, *The Paraphrasis of Seem* (Codex 7:1), where we meet innumerable female matrices endowed with eyes, along with wind-matrices and colored clouds of gnosis representing the heavenly aeons.[74]

It is easy to tell from these reports that so far Gnostic otherworldly journeys seem to have scarcely anything in common either with Jewish apocalypses or with *merkabah* mysticism. However, two late third-century Coptic writings known as the *First and Second Books of Ieu*[75] certainly resemble *merkabah* mysticism in so far as they contain a long and fastidious description of celestial stations through which the soul of the Gnostic is supposed to find its way after death.

The Gnostics using these books were supposed to learn by heart the names, maps, and diagrams of sixty such heavenly stations, called "treasures," in which at least sixty Ieus resided, all derived from a primordial Ieu (that is, YHVH). It was not enough to learn by heart the topography of each treasure and the name of each Ieu. Each treasure had a name, three guardians, several occupants, and several gates, and each gate had its own keepers. A seal and a magical number (*psephos*) were required at each station. The exercise of learning all these formulas by heart must have exceeded the powers of most Gnostics, for at the end of the book the Savior is said to have taken pity on them and therefore reveals a master set of powerful names, numbers, and seals that can by-pass all other heavenly customs. The book thereby ends by canceling its own usefulness.

The *Books of Ieu* are probably translated from Greek (given the number of Greek words they contain, unusual even among other Gnostic writings in Coptic translation), but their origin must be Egyptian. If we look around, no religion had such an extended inventory of otherworldly descriptions as the Egyptian, not to mention that—with the exception of the fact that the Egyptian journey of the dead was horizontal and the Gnostic was vertical—the system of fastidious enumeration of stations is the same in both cases, and is much like *merkabah* mysticism as well.

If *merkabah* mysticism and certain Gnostic documents have anything in common, it is the method of listing names and magical formulas to be used in the other world. We can ascertain beyond any doubt that such a method was first used in Egyptian mortuary practices, and it is quite likely that it was borrowed from there by Egyptian Gnosticism. The following sample from the Theban *Book of the Dead,* spell 150, is one of the least elaborate; others involve many more elements, including colors and formulas.

> The Field of Rushes. The god who is in it is Re-Horakhty. The Horns of Fire. The god who is in it is Lifter of Braziers. The Very High Mountain. The Mound of Spirits. The Cavern. The god who is in it is Feller of Fish. Iseset. Hasret. The god who is in it is He who is on high. The Horns of Qahu. Idu. The god who is in it is Sothis. The Mound of Wenet. The god who is in it is Greatest of the Mighty Ones. The Mound of Kheraha. The god who is in it is the Nile. The River of Flaming fire. Ikesy. The god who is in it is He who sees and takes. The Beautiful West of the gods who live in it on shens-cakes and beer.[76]

Compare this with the following passage from the *First Book of Ieu:*

> Again we came to the sixtieth Treasure: Oaxaex come out, it's me and my Taxis [order] that surrounds me. I told my disciples: "Behold the structure of this Treasure: There are six Topoi [places] around it, and in their middle is Oaxaexo. These two lines above his Topoi are the roots of the Topoi in which he dwells. The two other lines, in which there are all these Alphas, are of the same kind; there are two of them above and two of them below, they are the routes which you must follow when you wish to reach the Father in his Topos and within it. These Alphas are the curtains pulled in front of him."[77]

EARLY CHRISTIAN MYSTICISM

As far as otherworldly journeys are concerned, the mysticism of the fathers of the Egyptian desert is a Christian transformation of Jewish mysticism. We find in it many themes common to Jewish apocalyptic literature: sleep, the arrival of a messenger, the vision of the predestined place in heaven, and so on.[78] These themes are reinterpreted in a context that, however strong in faith, was certainly poor intellectually. One innovation is that a saint can experience an otherworldly journey during martyrdom. Saint Eusebius, while tortured "until his flesh and his blood fell scattered upon the ground," took a heavenly journey in the company of the angel Suriel, who showed him his throne, crown, and glory; this story conforms to the simplest pattern of expectations of a Jewish righteous one.[79] The same occurred to Apa Lacaronis,[80] among others. Sometimes visions occurred during mass.

Apa Macarius taught a sort of primitive *Book of the Dead* that he had learned when abducted to heaven by two angels.[81] Angels detach the soul of a dead Christian from the body and leave it in the air for three days "to go everywhere it wishes.

If it has a desire for its body, it goes for a time by the body in the tomb, for a time by familiar associations as it was accustomed. And thus these three days pass while it flies and circles and seeks those who love it as a bird seeks its nest. In this way also a virtuous soul goes to those places where it had the custom to practise righteousness." On the third day the soul rises to heaven, worships God, and has a view of paradise for the next six days. After that, it is shown *sheol* (hell) for thirty days. On the fortieth day, the soul comes before the judgment of God and is allotted the posthumous destiny it deserves. If the soul does not belong to a baptized Christian, then its lot obviously will be "fire and eternal darkness." This representation of the afterlife is certainly primitive to the extent that it allows *any* Christian, no matter how sinful, a glimpse of heaven before judgment. This other-world view is infinitely more democratic than the view prevalent in Jewish mysticism or in Gnosticism.

KABBALAH

Kabbalah is a form of Jewish mysticism rooted on the one hand in the grammatologic and numerologic speculations that led to the *Sefer yetsirah* (Book of creation; perhaps fourth century C.E.) and on the other, in *hekhaloth* literature. The study of Kabbalah has greatly profited from the recent works of Moshe Idel, who distinguishes two Kabbalistic trends throughout history: a "theosophic-theurgic" and an "ecstatic" Kabbalah.[82]

The *Sefer yetsirah* already features a cosmological system that becomes classic in Kabbalah; the ten *sephirot* (heavenly spheres) probably correspond to the ten commandments, and the twenty-two paths that connect them correspond to the twenty-two letters of the Hebrew alphabet. Creation takes place through these thirty-two primordial elements. The *Sefer yetsirah* and *hekhaloth* literature are the intellectual focus of the German Pietist Jews (Hasidei Ashkenaz), among whom the Kalonymus family is especially famous; this family included Samuel ben Kalonymus of Speyer (twelfth century), his son Judah ben Samuel (ca. 1150–1217), and the son's disciple, the famous Eleazar of Worms (ca. 1165–1230). Classical Kabbalah appears, however, in Provençal Sefardi circles among the authors of the *Sefer ha-bahir* (Book of splendor); in this book, the *sephirot* are for the first time designated as attributes of God. Isaac the Blind (ca. 1160–1235), son of Rabbi Abraham ben David of Posquières (ca. 1120–98), was the first Provençal mystic to study the *Bahir*. In Catalunya, Kabbalah flourished in the Gerona circle of the rabbis Ezra ben Solomon, Azriel, and the famous Moses ben Nahman or Nahmanides (ca. 1195–1270). In Christian Castilla, the immediate precursors of the author of the *Zohar* were the brothers Jacob and Isaac Cohen. The Kabbalists of this period used *temurah, gematria,* and *notarikon,* ancient techniques of permutation and combination of the letters of the alphabet and numerology whose proto-types seem to be Hellenistic, although they were already in use in Babylonia.

The major representative of ecstatic Kabbalah was the great thirteenth-century Sefardi mystic Abraham Abulafia, whose goal was *devekut* or *unio mystica* with God. Idel contends that Abulafian Kabbalah is a theoretical synthesis of Maimonidean Aristotelianism and Sufi mysticism, and is based in practice on a series of methods called *hitbodedut* (concentration), consisting of grammatology and the pronouncing of divine names. As in Sufism, for Abulafia *unio mystica* (*devekut*) is the experience of transformation of the human being into God.[83]

Abulafia's generation produced two of the fathers of classical Kabbalah: Joseph ben Abraham Gikatilla (1248–1305) and Moses of Leon (ca. 1250–1305), author of the pseudepigraphic

Sefer ha-zohar (Book of splendor), which he attributed to the second-century *tanna* (master) Simeon bar Yohay.

Classical Kabbalah integrates the cosmology of the *merkabah* literature into one of the four spiritual universes that follow each other from above, that is, *atsilut, beriyah, yetzirah,* and *asiyah.* The universe *atsilut* (emanation) contains the ten *sephirot* (Keter, Hokhmah, Binah, Gedullah or Hesed, Geburah or Din, Tiferet or Rahamim, Netsah, Hod, Yesod or Tsaddik, and Malkhut or Shekinah), which altogether form the heavenly body of Adam Kadmon, the primordial man. The universe *beriyah* (creation) contains the seven *hekhaloth* and the *merkabah.* The universe *yetsirah* (formation) contains the angelic hosts. The universe *asiyah* (making) is the prototype of the visible world. In *asiyah,* the ten *sephirot* are present in the shape of the rainbow, the sea waves, the dawn, grasses, and trees.

Kabbalah has developed many mystical techniques, such as visualization of colors and the like, in order to facilitate access to the universe *atsilut.* This operation is difficult because of the presence of "the other side" (*sitra ahra*), that is, of evil, in *asiyah.* Kabbalah does not share the Platonic dualism of soul and body or Platonic contempt for this world, at least not systematically. Sexuality is considered to be good, since it produces the merger of entities that were separated at the descent of the souls into their bodies.[84] The actions of the Kabbalist have three goals: *tikkun,* or the restoration of a primeval unity and harmony (both within the individual and in the universe), *kavvanah,* or contemplative meditation, and *devekut,* or ecstatic union with God.

Isaac Luria, *Ari ha-kadosh* (The Holy Lion of Safed; *Ari,* "lion," is the acronym of "Ashkenazi Rabbi Ishaq") and his disciples, the most important of whom was Hayyim Vital, 1543–1620, were the authors of a synthesis, revolutionary in so far as it conceives of creation as a process of contraction (*tsimtsum*) of God into Himself, while evil is the active presence of spiritual refuse (shells, or *qelippot*), fallen due to the breaking of the vessels (*shevirat ha-kelim*) that were expected to contain the Sephirot. Luria valued positively the reincarnation of the soul, or metensomatosis, which allows the sage to gain an additional number of souls or "sparks of soul" belonging to illustrious masters.

In his latest book, *Kabbalah: New Perspectives,* Moshe Idel has provided breathtaking new descriptions of actual mystical techniques used by the Kabbalists, some of which Gershom Scholem had only mentioned *en passant,* if at all, in his work, *The Major Trends of Jewish Mysticism.* These include weeping and visiting a grave,[85] ascent to heaven,[86] combining the letters of the divine name,[87] and *kavvanah* (prayer) accompanied by internalization of the ten *sephirot* visualized as colors.[88]

Ascent of the soul was practiced in Kabbalah as part of an ancient mystical inheritance, that of the *merkabah* literature preserved by the Hasidei Ashkenaz of the twelfth and thirteenth centuries. Like the Tannaim of old, Rabbi Michael the Angel (mid-thirteenth-century France) "asked questions, and his soul ascended to heaven in order to seek answers." His body remained motionless like a stone for three days.[89] Rabbi Ezra of Moncontour went to heaven and heard the songs of the *hayyoth.* At nighttime the soul of Isaac Luria visited the *yeshivot* of famous Tannaitic rabbis in heaven. Luria's disciple Hayyim Vital also ascended to the seat of glory in a swoon.[90]

LATE JEWISH MYSTICISM

Later Jewish mysticism is connected with Shabbetai Tsevi (1626–76), a seventeenth-century mystic but not a Kabbalist. The identification of Shabbetai Tsevi as the expected messiah was the work of the Lurian Kabbalist Abraham Nathan ben Elisha Hayyim Ashkenazi (1643 or 1644 to 1680), known as Nathan of Gaza, who discovered in this mystic of Smyrna the signs of divine election, among which were predictable weaknesses of character and temptations stemming from the *qelippot*. In his monumental work *Sabbatai Sevi: The Mystical Messiah* (1973), Gershom Scholem reconstructed the history of Shabbatianism.

When the messiah was thus revealed in 1665, Nathan of Gaza replaced mourning ceremonies with joyful feasts in honor of Shabbetai, to the dismay of the orthodox Jewish community. Nathan predicted that the messiah would take the crown of the Turkish sultan and become world emperor. When Shabbetai set foot in Istanbul in February 1666, the sultan had him arrested. In September he gave him the choice between the gallows and conversion to Islam. Shabbetai chose the latter, but Nathan and many Shabbatianists of the Ottoman empire accepted his choice without losing their faith, and decided to follow him in a *pro forma* conversion to Islam, while continuing their antinomian practices. Later, the radical Shabbatianist Jacob Frank (1726–91), who believed himself to be the reincarnation of Shabbetai, preached messianic rejection of the Torah in Poland.

Polish Hasidism is one of the most recent and richest Jewish religious syntheses, containing elements from all trends of Jewish mysticism. The founder of Hasidism was Israel ben Eliezer, called the Baal Shem Tov (acronym Besht; d. 1760), a man who performed miracles. The Besht was followed by the *maggid* of Meseritch, itinerant preacher Dov Baer (1710–72); during his time the movement won many adepts, to the exasperation of the Jewish authorities (*kehillah*), who favored the ideology of the Enlightenment (represented by the Jewish *mitnagdim,* the Enlightenment's representatives). After one hundred years of conflict, the differences between the two factions were smoothed out; while the Hasidim lost much of their revolutionary impetus, the *mitnagdim* learned a lesson in ethics.

Contrary to traditional Ashkenazi pietism, which consisted

of a relentless and strict asceticism, the Hasidim would rather emphasize the joy of the omnipresence of God. They experience *devekut* as *aliyat ha-neshamah* (ascent of the soul in the divine light). They identify the presence of God in the humblest activities of their bodies and practice physical worship (*avodah ba-gashmiyut*), praising God not only in prayer or during sacred ceremonies, but also in the middle of profane activities such as sexual intercourse, eating, and sleeping. Any action fulfilled with *devekut* in mind can lead to ecstasy. Thus, ecstatic dances, songs, and even rotatory movements like those of the whirling dervishes have *devekut* in view. The accomplished Hasid descends from contemplative heights to rescue his community, thus practicing *yeridah le-tsorekh aliyah* (descent in view of the ascent).

The practice of heavenly ascent was frequent with the founder of Hasidism, Rabbi Israel Baal Shem Tov. In a letter to his brother in law, he wrote:

> On *Rosh ha-Shanah* of the year 4407 (1746), I performed an incantation for the ascent of the soul. . . . And in that vision I saw wondrous things. . . . But when I returned to the lower Paradise, I saw the souls of living and of dead persons, both of those with whom I was acquainted and of those with whom I was not, . . . numberless, in a to-and-fro movement, ascending from one world to the other. . . . And I asked my teacher and master that he come with me, and it is a great danger to go and ascend to the supernal worlds, whence I had never ascended since I acquired awareness, and these were mighty ascents. So I ascended degree after degree, until I entered the place of the Messiah.[91]

Although ascent of the soul was less fashionable under the *maggid* and his followers, a theory of ecstasy was expounded in a tractate ('*Qunteros ha-hithpa'aluth*') by Dov Baer of Lubavitch (1773–1827), the leader of the Hasidic sect of Habad, founded by his father Schneor Zalman of Liady (1747–1813).[92] Like other Hasidim, those of the Habad sect did not object to ecstasy induced artificially, for example through song, dance, and consumption of alcohol. Dov Baer's successor and son-in-law Menahem Mendel "would drink large quantities of alcohol when his followers were gathered round his table and he would then expound the most profound Habad themes."[93] Dov Baer did not, however, discuss such means of achieving ecstasy in his tract, with the exception of music and song. He writes that it is important to distinguish true ecstasy, which is ecstasy of the soul, from false ecstasy, which is "external ecstasy," ecstasy of the flesh and "self-worship."[94] "External ecstasy" comes "with an inflammatory enthusiasm of strange fire which stems only from the inflammation of the blood and possesses nothing whatever of the fire of the Lord."[95] There are five types of true ecstasy, or "ecstasy of the soul," just as there are five types of soul and five psychological types of human being. Deep authentic ecstasy is completely unconscious. Familiar themes from Kabbalah and even from Renaissance Platonism are present in Dov Baer's excellent treatise. He praises melancholy and contrition, and believes that the true mystic who has experienced the superior form of ecstasy seeks annihilation of the self and becomes immune to mundane values such as "fame, clothes, good food and other coarse lusts."[96]

10

Interplanetary Tours

The Platonic Space Shuttle, from Plotinus to Marsilio Ficino

THE SOUL AS SPACE SHUTTLE

The soul, having started on its downward movement from the intersection of the zodiac and the Milky Way to the successive spheres lying beneath, as it passes through these spheres, not only takes on the . . . wrapping in each sphere by approaching a luminous body, but also acquires each of the attributes which it will exercise later, as follows: in the sphere of Saturn it obtains reason and understanding, called *logistikon* and *theoretikon;* in Jupiter's sphere, the power to act, called *praktikon;* in Mars' sphere, a bold spirit or *thymikon;* in the Sun's sphere, sense-perception and imagination, *aisthetikon* and *phantastikon;* in Venus' sphere, the impulse of passion, *epithymetikon;* in Mercury's sphere, the ability to speak and interpret, *hermeneutikon;* and in the sphere of the Moon, the power of sowing and growing bodies, *phytikon.*[1]

Thus wrote the late fourth-century Latin Platonist Aurelius Theodosius Macrobius in his *Commentary* on Cicero's *Dream of Scipio.* A nostalgic Roman aristocrat, he was close to Symmachus and those who desperately tried to revive pagan religion in a Roman Empire that was rapidly moving toward religious totalitarianism; in fact, all pagan cults, public and private, were forbidden between 381 and 392. Macrobius was, however, certainly not the inventor of what we are calling here the "Platonic space shuttle."[2]

The history of this consequential doctrine is the subject of this chapter. In essence, the doctrine states that in its descent into the body the soul is wrapped in planetary influences that constitute a "vehicle" to carry it down and permit it to become embodied. Conversely, after death the "vehicle" takes off with the soul in it and is gradually discarded during a passage through the planets, which now pick up again what they previously contributed to form the wrapping. Freed from its "vehicle," the soul goes to the place of its origin, awaiting rebirth or perhaps a better fate.

In order to understand the background of this bizarre and important doctrine, which shaped ideas about the interplanetary journeys of the soul down to the seventeenth century, we need to move back in time a few centuries, to a period ranging from the first decades of the second century to the late fourth century. The most outstanding philosophers of the second century—Basilides the Christian Gnostic, Numenius, Celsus, and the two Julians (Julian the Chaldaean and his son, Julian the Theurgist, authors of the *Chaldaean Oracles*)—were obsessed by a question that has now lost much of its appeal: How does the soul descend from its heavenly realm to be incarnated in the body, and by what means does it return to its origin?

THE GNOSTIC "COUNTERFEIT SPIRIT"

The first to answer this question coherently were the Gnostics, groups of radical, generally Christian Platonists who were rebellious toward the conventional world order of Platonism and Judaism. They asserted that this world and its creator are, if not evil, at least inferior, and that human beings are superior to the world and its creator. The Gnostics, who were not constituted in large organizations but formed small independent groups, left numerous tractates, some of which survived in Coptic translations later found by scholars in the nineteenth and twentieth centuries.[3] One of these tractates, extant in four Coptic versions, is the *Apocryphon of John; apocryphon* means "secret book," and John is John the Apostle.[4]

In the *Apocryphon of John,* anthropogony ("birth of man") is preceded by a long prologue set in heaven. Suffice it to say here that the laments of Sophia, who is a lonely female entity at the edge of the *pleroma* (wholeness) of divine emanations, are heard by the wholeness (*pleroma*) on high. Two major aeons are dispatched to come to the rescue of the world created by Ialdabaoth-Authades, the Arrogant Creator, who is Sophia's miscarried son. These aeons are called Primordial Man and Son of Man, and the latter is prefigured by an image reflected by the waters.

The rulers (*archons*) see this image and tell each other, "Let us make man in the image of God and in His [or our] resemblance."[5] They then fabricate a creature (*plasma*) in imitation (*mimesis*) of the image reflected in water, which is nothing but an imperfect simulacrum of the perfect (*teleios*) man.[6] This creature's name is Adam, and each one of the seven powers (*exousiai*) fabricates for him a soul (*psyche*), so that the angels can subsequently build his heavenly body based on this structure. Divinity creates the osseous soul, Lordship creates the fibrous or nervous soul, Jealousy (or Fire) creates the flesh (*sarx*) soul, Providence (Pronoia) the marrow soul and the body shape, Kingship the blood soul, Intelligence (Synesis) the skin soul, and Wisdom (Sophia) the hair soul.[7] Starting from this psychic basis laid by the seven *exousiai,* the 360 angels make the limbs (*melos, harmos*) of the heavenly Adam, from the top of the skull to the nails on his toes.[8] Technically, this is a long episode of anatomical "melothesia," reminiscent of the attribution of parts of the body to the seven planets and the twelve signs of the zodiac in Hellenistic astrology. Obviously the presupposition of the group of texts to which the *Apocryphon of John* belongs (which I would be quite opposed to calling "Sethian") is that the seven cosmic rulers are the planets; this needs no demonstration here.[9] When we read that thirty demons are ascribed to the different parts of the body, it becomes even clearer that we are dealing with the basic Gnostic antiastrological polemic.[10] Thirty is the number of degrees of an astrological sign. Other didactic notions are combined in this episode; Michel Tardieu sees them as being derived from Stoicism.[11]

The next sequence of the narrative has often been related to the rabbinical tradition of the amorphous and imperfect primordial man. One would, however, hesitate to make any pronouncement as to the Jewish origin of this story. The myth is so widespread and is found in so many contexts that it is far from compelling to seek its derivation in a specific tradition. Briefly, the scenario is that this heavenly Adam does not have enough power to walk, which shows how restricted are the creative capacities of the seven Rulers, the 360 angels, and the thirty demons of the zodiac. Only after Sophia's intervention does the supreme Father communicate to Ialdabaoth the secret of animating this Golem, which is to blow in his face some of the spirit (*pneuma*) inherited from Sophia. Only at this point does Adam stand up.[12] Thanks to this pneuma that originates in wholeness, Adam becomes superior to the seven powers who created him and even to Ialdabaoth himself. But the archons, sensing this, want to get rid of him and throw him down into the region (*meros*) of matter (*hule*), which is diametrically opposed to the wholeness.

At this point the ungenerated Father shows compassion for the exiled Adam; He sends to him as an aid (*boethos*) His own breath, the intelligence (*epinoia*) or light, who is Zoe or Life.[13]

Catching sight of the spiritual spark that shines in Adam, the archons devise a further means of keeping him prisoner of matter—they create a physical body for him.

Adam's physical body is composed of the four material elements (earth, water, fire, and wind), to which are added darkness and concupiscence (*epithumia*). "This is the tomb of the modeled body! This is the vesture in which those evildoers have clothed Adam, the object [engendering] forgetfulness! And thus he became a mortal man. This is the primordial fall and the primordial failure!."[14] At this point a crucial element is added to this miserable creation of the archons, an element of paramount importance not only among the Gnostics, but also among Manichaeans and late Neoplatonists: the *antikeimenon pneuma* (evil spirit) or, more frequently, the *antimimon pneuma* (the counterfeit spirit; BG, 2).

This fundamental Gnostic notion, the counterfeit spirit, is defined as the quintessence of the evil astral powers and the epitome of fate (*heimarmene*). The demiurge Ialdabaoth "has a meeting with his Powers. They generate Fate and chain down heavenly gods, angels, demons and men to measures, moments and times, so that all of them should be tied with bonds by [Fate] who rules all things; what a pernicious and deadly plan!"[15] Again, "Indeed from this Fate all iniquities, abominations and blasphemies have come, all the bonds of hatred and ignorance, and likewise the tyrannical commandments and the oppressive sins and the great fears. And thus all creation was blinded in order that she could not recognize the God who is above all."[16]

In another place the counterfeit spirit is explained more precisely: it is astrally originated genetic information that accompanies every soul coming into the world. The relation of a person to his or her *antimimon pneuma* determines the result of the judgment undergone by the soul after physical death.[17]

Possibly more optimistic than other Gnostic tractates, the

Apocryphon of John rejects the theory of metensomatosis: *all* souls, including those that have been led astray by their counterfeit spirit, partake of salvation, although those who have strayed are saved only after having been instructed by other souls who possess the living spirit.[18] Only sacrilegious blasphemy against the spirit entails eternal punishment.

The counterfeit spirit is further presented as the "tree of iniquity," the quintessence of the bonds of astral fatality, and as the most influential factor in determining personal destiny. In this sense, it is one with the "appendages" (*prosartêmata*) described by the Christian Gnostic Basilides, according to Clement of Alexandria (*Stromata* 2:112). These appendages are planetary accretions that lure and push the soul toward evil. Clement also quotes the title of a lost work by Isidorus, son or perhaps major disciple of Basilides (2:113. 3–114.1), called *Peri prosphuoùs psuchês* (On the appended soul); in this text, Isidorus opposes the perfectly Gnostic idea that astral fatality can hinder the free will of human reason. Note that this discussion of free will must have taken place before 150 C.E. Isidorus, whom we have every reason to think was a Christian Gnostic, also engages in polemics against other Gnostics, perhaps of the kind illustrated by the *Apocryphon of John,* who made the counterfeit spirit into a serious obstacle to free will. Isidorus already takes the stance later taken by Pelagius or Julian of Eclanum, who were the opponents of Augustine's predestinationism at the beginning of the fifth century; the *Apocryphon of John* is closer to what would later be the position of the Manichaeans and of Augustine.

I have analyzed the diffusion of the Neoplatonic doctrine of the astral vehicle (*óchêma*) of the soul in two books and a series of articles.[19] Basilides is placed at the inception of this doctrine. In the late 1970s and early 1980s, however, this theory was the subject of an amicable polemic between Jacques Flamant, the learned author of the book *Macrobe et le Néo-platonisme latin,* and me. The several phases of this polemic are summarized in the articles both of us contributed to the volume on concepts of salvation in mystery religions of late antiquity, edited by Ugo Bianchi and Maarten J. Vermaseren. The disagreement was over whether the Middle Platonist Numenius of Apamea was the father of the influential doctrine of the passage of the human soul through the planetary spheres; during this passage the soul acquires certain qualities, or, in a negative version, certain vices from the planets. All testimonies have in the meantime been gathered and discussed in my book *Expériences de l'extase*. The negative version of the doctrine is especially present in the Hermetic treatise *Poimandres* (chapter 25) and in a few enigmatic passages of the grammarian Servius (*Commentary to the Aeneis*), a younger contemporary of Macrobius. In a late phase of the debate, Flamant and I agreed that, although Numenius was not the father of the doctrine, which was already known to Basilides of Alexandria, there is no serious reason to doubt that he shared its positive variant.

This conclusion leaves us with the Gnostics as authors of the doctrine of the passage of the soul through the spheres; however, this explanation seems improbable, because the Gnostics commonly reacted by semantically inverting a Platonic theory originally presented in a positive key. In other words, such a doctrine could have been first produced in Middle Platonic circles steeped in Hermetic astrology out of the desire to understand how the planets communicate their qualities to human souls, and then reinterpreted by the Gnostics in a negative key, and this hypothesis would be easier to understand than the reverse. We are certain that the Gnostics dealt with the passage of the soul through the spheres before Numenius, which means that an early second-century or even a late first-century origin of the theory is more probable.

No matter who produced it first, the Gnostic version reflects a constant antiastrological polemic that is at the core of the Gnostic and Manichaean message. The most elaborate result of such a polemic is the late treatise *Pistis sophia,* whose relation to Manichaeism awaits further study. In *Pistis sophia,* the theory of the counterfeit spirit is clearly the main link between cosmology, anthropology, and soteriology.

The *antimimon pneuma* shows up first in chapters 111 to 115 of the second book of *Pistis sophia.* It derives from the vices of the cosmic archons, and it pushes the soul toward the fulfillment of the same vicious impulses, which are for it like food (*trophai*). "The *antimimon pneuma* seeks all the evils (*kakia*), the concupiscences (*epithumiai*) and the sins,"[20] thus compelling the soul to commit errors. After physical death, the soul whose counterfeit spirit is strong is dispatched again in the cycle of metensomatosis, thus propagating sin; the soul is not able to move out of recurrent incarnations (*metabolai*) before passing through the last cycle (*kuklos*) that befalls her.[21] On the contrary, when the counterfeit spirit is weak, the soul can shed it after earthly embodiment on its ascent through the spheres of the rulers of astral fatality. Thus liberated, the soul is entrusted to the good Sabaoth and eventually reaches the treasure of light. In order to free the soul from the bonds of the counterfeit spirit, *Pistis sophia* proposes two methods: baptism, which, like a purifying fire, loosens the seals of the sins with which the soul is burdened and separates the soul from her *antimimon pneuma;*[22] and the prayer of intercession for the dead.[23]

The myth of the fabrication of the soul together with the counterfeit spirit is reported in detail in chapters 131 and following,[24] which are an impressive parody of Plato's *Timaeus* (41dff.). The five archons of astral fatality (*heimarmene*) send preexistent souls into the world or create new souls. In the first case they give the soul that goes down into the world a drink from the seed (*sperma*) of evil (*kakia*) and from the covetousness (*epithumiai*) contained in the cup of forgetfulness. From other sources (discussed elsewhere) it appears that in some cases the cup of forgetfulness could simply be identified with the constellation of the Krater or Chalice. This deadly beverage becomes a sort of body (*soma*) in which the soul (*psyche*) is wrapped and which is akin to the soul; this is why it is called counterfeit spirit (*antimimon pneuma*), and is like a vesture[25] for the soul.

In the second case, that is, when the archons make new souls, the five rulers of heimarmene or astral fatality, that is, the planets Saturn, Mars, Mercury, Venus, and Jupiter,[26] create a new soul from the sweat, tears, and breath (presumably bad) of all their heavenly colleagues. This new soul matter, which also contains parts derived from each planet in addition to many of the other celestial demons impersonating the concepts of astrology, is further combined, squeezed, and rolled like dough; it is cut like bread into little pieces, which become the individual souls not yet wrapped in their personal *antimimon pneuma*.

Like Adam in the anthropogonic myth of the *Apocryphon of John,* the new souls do not have enough strength to stand up, which means that they cannot animate a body. The five planetary rulers, together with their colleagues, the sun and the moon, therefore blow their breath over the souls, and with their breath a spark of spirit penetrates the souls, thus enabling them to go in search of the eternal light.[27]

The *antimimon pneuma* is attached to the soul with the seals (*sphragides*) of the rulers. It compels (*anankazein*) the soul to immerse itself in all the passions (*pathe*) and iniquities (*anomiai*), and holds her under its power during all her transmigrations (*metabolai*) in new bodies. When the souls have been thus prepared, they are transmitted further by the rulers to the 365 ministers (*leitourgoi*) of their aeons. Based on the structure of the soul (*tupos*), the ministers build a bodily mold (*antitupos*), a recipient capable of receiving every single "package."

A package, as we will see shortly, consists of several things. It is first dispatched by the ministers to the archons of the Middle, who put its destiny (*moira*) into it. Destiny is, more properly, the blind predestination of actions on earth, including the hour of death. Every package is composed of *moira*, *migma* (mixture), spirit, soul, and counterfeit spirit. Every package is cut in two, and the two halves are placed in a man and a woman. "They give one part to the man and another part to the woman, hiding it in food (*trophe*), in the breeze, in water or in something to drink."[28] Even if they are far away from each other, the man and the woman are supposed to look for each other in the world (*kosmos*) until they find each other and thus they realize their basic accord (*symphonia*); but, obviously, this wandering in search of one's spouse is secretly predestined by the heavenly ministers. The counterfeit spirit then flows into the male's sperm and from there into the woman's womb (*metra*).

At this point the 365 ministers penetrate into the matrix, reunite the two halves, feed them on the mother's blood for forty days, and during the following thirty days form the limbs (*mele*) of the infant to be. Then they distribute the counterfeit spirit, the soul, the *migma*, and the *moira*; finally, they close them all in a new body marked with their seals. They mark the conception day on the left palm of the hand; the day of the completion of the limbs on the right palm; and other memorable dates on the tip of the skull, on the two temples, on the nape of the neck, on the brain, and on the heart. The number of years the soul will be embodied is finally stamped on the forehead. Having thus exhausted their bureaucratic activity, the ministers entrust their seals to the avenging archons (*erunaioi*), who distribute punishments (*kolaseis*) and trials (*kriseis*). In their turn the avengers pass them on to the *paralemptai* (collectors), whose role is to separate the soul from the body when the person meets his or her preestablished death according to her or his *moira*.[29]

The doctrine of the counterfeit spirit is further extremely influential in Manichaeism, a radical Gnostic religion founded by the Persian Mani (216–76). Manichaean astrology is a complex topic that has been only marginally treated so far. Astrology itself is a sector that requires specialization.[30] Scholars acquainted with Hellenistic astrology have so far failed to understand the profound connection between antiastrological polemic in Gnosticism and the foundation of the Manichaean system of classifications.

Two more or less recent books have shed new light on this system: Michel Tardieu's *Le Manichéisme* (1981), and Peter Bryder's *The Chinese Transformation of Manichaeism* (1985). Tardieu's book recognizes a pentad-based classification system as being one of the formal keys to understanding the Manichaean system. The fact that Mani worked from a basic scheme of five elements can help us understand how all further classifications were built. Peter Bryder's excellent book further details the Manichaean pentads in the four main traditions of Manichaean texts: the Western, the Near Eastern, the Middle Eastern, and the Far Eastern, found respectively in Rome and North Africa, Medinet Madi, Turfân, and Tun-huang.

Here I will proceed in three steps. First I will refer to a number of researches I carried out on Gnostic texts, which show that one of the most basic doctrines of Gnosticism, that of the *antimimon pneuma* or counterfeit spirit, was derived from astrology. Second, I will refer to the major Manichaean texts that try to establish a Manichaean astrology, which though twisted is not beyond recognition. Third, I will show that Manichaean classification by pentads, or series of five, which is essential to the Manichaean system as a whole, is but a version of the Gnostic doctrine of the *antimimon pneuma* and a variant of the Gnostic antiastrological polemic.

Thus, I will attempt to show here that the formal system of Manichaean classification is ultimately and polemically derived from astrology and is based on the doctrine of the counterfeit spirit, which is the most ancient version of what I have called the "Platonic space shuttle" or vehicle of the soul.

As I have collected evidence on otherworldly journeys in Hellenism, late antiquity, and the Middle Ages, I have found that there is not much in the theories of the once powerful German school of religion (*religionsgeschichtliche Schule*) that conforms to the standards of modern research. I have attempted to show this in a number of books and articles dating back to 1978.[31] I will summarize here the results of my research in one area only: the theory of the embodiment and disembodiment of the preexistent soul envisioned as a passage through the seven planetary spheres. As already stated above, chronologically the first to make use of this theory was the Christian Gnostic Basilides of Alexandria, followed by his son (or major disciple) Isidorus. Later on the theory may have been used by the Middle Platonist Numenius of Apamea; it is certainly present in those parts of the *Apocryphon of John* that precede Ireneus's *Against Heresies* and in other Gnostic doctrines summarized by Ireneus around 180 C.E. It becomes a common motif in Neoplatonism starting with Iamblichus of Coelé-Syria; it is present in the Greek Neoplatonists Proclus, Hierocles, Damascius, Simplicius and Priscianus of Athens, and Hermeias and Olympiodorus of Alexandria. It is also very important in the Latin Neoplatonist Macrobius and in his younger contemporary Servius. The theory is of paramount importance in Hermeticism, occurs in a modified version in Manichaeism, and informs one of the most luxuriant Gnostic myths in the late tractate *Pistis sophia*. Finally, it reappears in a sporadic episode of Bogomil mythology.

I will try to point out briefly all the variants of this theory.

1. Possibly in Middle Platonism, and certainly in later Neoplatonism, this doctrine simply means that at birth the soul descends from the Milky Way through the spheres of the seven planets and from each of them assumes certain qualities necessary for the new being to exist on earth. These planetary qualities are those commonly ascribed to the seven planets by Hellenistic astrology.

2. In Gnosticism, starting with Basilides (who does not use the expression *antimimon pneuma* but its equivalent *prosartemata,* "appendages"), the doctrine is negative: from the seven planetary rulers (archons) the soul at her embodiment assumes seven vices that form its *antimimon pneuma* (counterfeit spirit). Hermeticism in this respect can be treated as a simple variant of Gnosticism.

3. In Neoplatonism we find a positive version of the counterfeit spirit in the doctrine of the *óchêma* (vehicle) of the soul, which is vaguely present in Plotinus himself and consists of a blending of Platonic Aristotelian, and astrological elements.

The source of this doctrine is the pseudo-Hermetic treatise *Panaretos,* which belonged to the Hermetic astrological vulgate and probably dated to the second century B.C.E. It is no longer extant, but is summarized in the *Eisagogika* of Paul of Alexandria (after 378 C.E.) and is further expounded on in the commentary on Paul of Alexandria written by Heliodorus, an Athenian disciple of Proclus, between 475 and 509. These two works were published by Boer and Neugebauer in 1958 and 1962 respectively.[32] Very briefly, the *Panaretos* is concerned with the theory of the *kleroi* (lots) of the different planets, that is, certain qualities that the planets confer on a human being. These lots can be inferred from the reading of the horoscope after performing a few mathematical operations that are not exceedingly complicated. The lot of the sun is said to be one's *agathos daimon* (good angel) and the lot of the moon good fortune. The lot of Jupiter determines one's rank and social position, the lot of Mercury one's "natural necessities," the lot of Venus one's erotic life, the lot of Mars one's courage and spirit of adventure, and the lot of Saturn one's inescapable fate (*nemesis*).

Let us now come to Manichaean testimonies. I will briefly summarize a few of them, concentrating on those that make sense in this context.[33] Coptic Kephalaion 57, *On the Question of Adam,* expands on the five kinds of leaders of the sphere of the zodiac. These are the *kronocratores* (rulers of time) in a large sense (and not in the technical sense this word acquires in astrology in the second century B.C.E.); they are related to the measuring of time, which is a part of astrology.

Kephalaion 47, *On the Four Great Things,* speaks of a class of archons tied to the zodiac. Kephalaion 69, *On the Twelve Signs of the Zodiac and the Five Stars,* puts the twelve zodiacal signs and the five leaders of the archons tied to the zodiac, which are none other than the five planets (we will see below why there are five, not seven), under supervision of an *apaitetes* (supervisor). *Apaitetes* is synonymous with *paralemptes,* which is used in the Gnostic tractate *Pistis sophia;* this tractate shows heavy influence from Manichaeism.

The five archons are the dark rulers of the five elements: Jupiter rules over smoke, Venus over fire (this is ironical, since in traditional astrology Venus is rather watery), Mars over wind, Mercury over water, and Saturn over darkness. Two additions are made to the list, corresponding with the constellations Caput and Cauda Draconis, generically called here *katabibazontes.*

The five archons are the rulers of the twelve signs of the zodiac according to an order of distribution that is again quite specific to Mani himself. Smoke rules over Gemini and Sagittarius; fire over Aries and Leo; wind over Taurus, Aquarius, and Libra; water over Cancer, Virgo, and Pisces; and darkness over Caper and Scorpio. The sun and moon, as already said, are entirely beneficent.

Now that we know who the five and the twelve are, we can proceed to the analysis of the Manichaean genesis. A very common Manichaean myth, in the versions reported by Augustine and by his disciple Evodius, says that the twelve virtues appeared in the middle of heaven in order to instill desire in the archons. This purpose is achieved, and the male archons run amok: they scream and become agitated, and their sweat pours abundantly over the earth. (This last is the explanation for rain and storm.) Evodius goes further in specifying that this state of sexual arousal ends up in ejaculation *per genitalia*. This sperm (or soul) of the archons contains light, which is picked up by the *tertius legatus* ("third messenger"), the envoy of the Supreme Father, who separates light from darkness and drops the residual substance over the earth. There the substance is further divided up into a part that falls on dry land and gives birth to the five trees, which become the ancestors of the plants, and a part that falls in water and gives birth to a monster, the earthly embodiment of the king of darkness.

What we have here is the transformation of a Gnostic doctrine. The five trees are simply the *antimimon pneuma* (defined in Gnostic texts as the tree of iniquity), that is, the negative influences of the five evil planets, of the twelve evil signs of the zodiac, and of all troops of heavenly archons. Being a quintessence of the worst of vegetal and animal life, human beings are also a quintessence of the *counterfeit spirit*.

In conclusion, as we well know, the number five serves as a constant basis for classification in Manichaeism: we have five

trees, five archons, five elements, five planets, and so on. This
is the systematic expression of what the Gnostics called
antimimon pneuma, that is, the negative aspects derived from the
planets. Thus the five planets became central and primary in
the Manichaean system and forced their number on other
realms of reality that were not commonly classified according
to a pentad-based scheme, such as the four elements (which
obviously in Manichaeism became five).

Thus the number five was first the number of darkness, of
the evil planetary rulers. It was further extended to the world
of light, which is seen as a *typos* to which darkness is the
antitypos or mold.

If in the Manichaean system light and darkness were both
eternal, we can state with certainty that in Mani's mind
darkness came first.

There is a late sequel to the Manichaean myth. It is even
more repellent than the original.[34]

Around 1050, the monk Eutymius of Our Lady the Venerable (Theotokou tes Peribleptou) in Constantinople reported
the following myth of the Byzantine Bogomils. The ruler of
this world fabricated Adam's physical body and wanted to
implant the soul in it, but as soon as the soul entered through
the mouth it would come out through the opposite orifice,
and when introduced through the rectum it would come out
the mouth. For three hundred years Adam's body stayed
soulless, until the ruler had the brilliant idea of eating unclean
animals such as serpent, scorpion, dog, cat, frog, and so on,
and spitting this awful mixture over the soul. Then, plugging
up Adam's anus, the ruler blew the soul into his mouth. Due
to its disgusting wrapping, the soul hung on to the body.

One is rather puzzled by this crude myth, until one
recognizes in it a garbled version of the ancient Gnostic-
Manichaean doctrine of the *antimimon pneuma.* What we have
here is a popular and negative version of the clean, intellectual

Neoplatonic *óchêma* or vehicle of the soul, and ultimately of the Aristotelian *proton organon,* the astral body that wraps the soul before it can be introduced into the body.

THE VEHICLE OF THE SOUL

In late antiquity it was widely believed that the soul ascends to heaven, whether after death or as the result of some initiation, particular favor, or accident. This belief was possibly as wide-spread—although not based on the same kind of empirical evidence—as our conviction that we can go to the airport whenever we want and fly wherever we wish.

The two preceding chapters of this book, dealing respectively with Greco-Roman and Jewish otherworldly journeys, were sufficient to give us a general idea of the whole. A few other testimonies should be added here; these I have analyzed at greater length elsewhere.[35]

First of all, all mysteries of late antiquity without exception promised their initiates a sort of heavenly immortality after death, a doctrine which historically may appear strange when one thinks that some of the divinities of these mysteries, such as Cybele and Persephone, were traditionally goddesses of the underworld. Now they were relocated somewhere in heaven, fulfilling the function of heavenly host.

During late antiquity mystery cults proliferated, allegedly coming from the Near East, but actually representing a Roman blending of love of exoticism and esotericism, Platonism and astrology. A mystery cult, such as the ancient mysteries of Eleusis practiced by the Athenians, is an institution that imparts secret initiations. Indiscretions were always partial, and therefore we lack reliable information as to the ultimate goal of the mysteries. Nevertheless, a number of allusions to an otherworldly journey of the candidate or the initiate appear.

One such case is the mystery cult of the Egyptian goddess

Isis. In his novel *Metamorphoses,* or *The Golden Ass,* the African Apuleius of Madaura, who wrote in Latin, described in enigmatic yet vivid terms the initiation of Lucius into the cult of Isis. "I crossed the border of death and, moving beyond the threshold of Proserpina, I came back, carried through the elements; I saw, in the middle of the night, the bright sun full of light; I came before the inferior and the superior gods and worshiped them from close-by."[36] So far, scholars have not been able to resolve the difficulties already pinpointed in a 1900 dissertation (in Latin) by the Dutch scholar K. H. E. De Jong, according to whom it is impossible to decide of the meaning of this passage. Briefly, there are three hypotheses: that the initiate was indeed shown some supernatural scenery, with the aid of expensive machineries, as is known from other mystery cults; that the initiate was through suggestion made invulnerable by exposure to the elements (less plausible); or that the meaning of all this is that the initiate was offered an otherworldly trip as a visionary experience, and the passage through the elements simply meant that he was crossing the sublunar zone before coming to the lunar Persephone. Some scholars have even sought an Egyptian model for this otherworldly journey, but their attempts have not been convincing thus far.

Even more enigmatic is a passage from the *True Discourse* of the pagan Platonist Celsus (second half of the second century C.E.), preserved by the Christian Platonist Origen of Alexandria. This passage concerns the mysteries of Mithra, a Roman god with nothing Iranian about him but his name.

> Plato taught that, in order to descend from heaven to earth and to ascend from earth to heaven, the souls pass across the planets. The Persians represented the same idea in their mysteries of Mithra. They have a symbol that represents the two movements taking place in heaven, that is, the movement of the fixed stars and that of the planets, and another one to

figure the journey of the soul across the heavenly bodies. This latter symbol is a tall ladder with seven gates (*heptapylos*) and an eighth gate above the others. The first gate is made of lead, the second of tin, the third of copper, the fourth of iron, the fifth of an alloy, the sixth of silver, and the seventh of gold. They ascribe the first to Saturn, and lead refers to the slowness of this planet; the second to Venus, of whom the softness of stain reminds; the third, which, made of copper, cannot but be firm and hard, to Jupiter; the fourth to Mercury, who among humans passes as a hard and resourceful worker, like iron; the fifth, which, being composed of different metals is unpredictable and varied, to Mars; the sixth to the moon, white like silver; and the seventh to the sun, whose beams recall the color of gold. This disposition of the planets is not haphazard, but follows certain musical relations.[37]

For the many difficulties of this passage I must again refer to my previous commentaries.[38] Only one point ought to be emphasized here: the fact that the planetary "gates" are listed in the opposite order from that of the weekdays; the planetary week had appeared in the first century B.C.E. and had become common by Celsus's time. This reversed order does not correspond to any known order of the planets in the universe. This does explain, however, Celsus's allusion to "musical relations," for the order of the planets thought to dominate the seven days of the week can be obtained from the order of the planets in the universe through two operations, one of which had to do with Pythagorean heavenly music. Consequently, either Celsus's assumption that the Mithraic ladder referred to the ascent of the soul through the planetary spheres is wrong, or his description of the subject is mistaken. The misattribution and misinterpretation of the ladder seems, however, more likely. Scholars have recently attempted to explain the ladder in reference to an unknown Iranian doctrine, but these theories have not met with general consensus.

What is more, the planetary order of the ladder also does

not match another Mithraic doctrine, the attribution of planetary dominations (*tutelae*) to the seven grades of initiation.[39] The series of correspondences runs as follows:

1. Mercury: Korax
2. Venus: Nymphus
3. Mars: Miles
4. Jupiter: Leo
5. moon: Perses
6. sun: Heliodromus
7. Saturn: Pater

Although Saturn, the most distant planet from the earth, rules here over the highest initiation and is therefore endowed with unmatched dignity, the other planets are not disposed in any known order, and Jacques Flamant's ingenious observation that we are dealing with an Egyptian series split in two and aligned in erratic order does not quite solve our problem.[40]

To conclude this part of our story, it is by no means certain that the initiates in Mithraic mysteries truly simulated an interplanetary journey of some sort, although this is by no means implausible.

Among the magical papyri there is a document, erroneously called "the Mithra liturgy" (which has nothing to do with the mysteries of Mithra, however), describing the otherworldly journey of the initiate after death beyond the celestial pole, and even beyond the sphere of the fixed stars, as far as the throne of the Supreme God who sets in motion the stars of the Big Dipper.[41]

Even more interesting are the testimonies relating to the second-century *Chaldaean Oracles* of Julian the Chaldaean and Julian the Theurgist. Two of the fragments advise the soul not to look down into a precipice (presumably the earth?), which would attract it "far away from the threshold (*bathmidos*) with seven roads (*heptaporos*)."⁴² The eleventh-century Byzantine Platonist Michael Psellus thus explains this enigmatic passage: "The threshold with seven roads represents the planetary spheres. Thus, when the soul swings down from above (*neusasa goun anothen*) toward the earth, it is carried onto the earth across these seven spheres."⁴³ Hans Lewy doubts the authenticity of Psellus's interpretation, for elsewhere in the *Chaldaean Oracles* the descent of the soul does not take place across the planetary spheres, but across four zones: the ether, the sun, the moon, and the air. The ascent occurs in reverse order, and is a ritual process performed during the life of the initiate, not after death. Knowledge of watchwords to tell the heavenly guardians is as important as the help of the sun, whose beams allow the initiate to climb to heaven.⁴⁴

After a brief examination of all these testimonies, it does not come as a surprise to find out that Neoplatonism, grounded in Plotinus (205–70), tried to perfect the doctrine of the descent and ascent of the soul and make it as "scientific" as possible. This result was achieved by adopting a theory that was already present in medical circles at the beginning of the third century C.E.

Aristotle, possibly starting from a suggestion made by Plato (*Laws,* 898c), invented a wrapping for the soul, made of astral fire, that would allow the soul to enter the body (*On the Generation of Animals,* 736b). The major medical authority at the beginning of the third century, Galen, recognized the existence of this "light-like and ether-like spirit," and even the term Vehicle (*ochema*) referring to this external wrap of the soul was invented as soon as the second century C.E.⁴⁵ Plotinus knows the doctrine of this subtle body (*leptoteron soma*), but does not yet adopt the word "vehicle" to describe it, nor does his disciple Porphyry. It is designated as such only after Iamblichus, by late Neoplatonists like the Athenians Proclus, Damascius, Simplicius, and Priscianus and the Alexandrians Hermeias and Olympiodorus. Proclus (end of the fifth century C.E.) gave the doctrine as a whole synthetic expression in his *Elements of Theology*.

> The vehicle of every particular soul descends by the addition of vestures (*chitones*) increasingly material; and ascends in company with the soul through divestment of all that is material and recovery of its proper form, after the analogy of the soul which makes use of it: for the soul descends by the acquisition of irrational principles of life; and ascends by putting off all those faculties tending to temporal process with which it was invested in its descent, and becoming clean and bare of all such faculties as serve the uses of the process.[46]

Thus the Platonic space shuttle, meant to carry the soul to the earth from its heavenly dwelling and from the earth back to its origin, was continually perfected. It started in Hellenistic astrology, was adopted by the rebellious Gnostics, and attained its climax in late Neoplatonism. Thanks to Macrobius, who wrote in Latin, it was never completely forgotten in the early Christian Middle Ages. And it became once more extremely influential in the Italian Renaissance.

THE WORLD VIEW OF
EARLY MODERN EUROPE

Aristotle's "first instrument" (*proton organon*) is made of spirit (*pneuma*) or stellar fire, and the soul uses it in its communication with the sensory world. In this function, it is located in the heart and is called "common sense" or "internal sense." It has the role of collecting all messages stemming from the peripheral sense organs. There in the heart these messages are translated into a language accessible to the intellect present in the soul, that is, into images (*phantasmata*). For the soul "cannot understand without the help of images" (*aneu phantasmatos*);

this doctrine remained compelling until the seventeenth century. Aquinas summarized it in his *Summa Theologica,* "It is beyond the capabilities of the soul to understand without conversion [of sensory messages] into images (*phantasmata*)."[47]

This "synthesizer" of perceptions, now located in the heart and now in the brain, was a central concept in Stoicism and in all schools of ancient medicine. Physicians did not believe in the existence of an immaterial soul. Aristotelian philosophers did, and it appealed to them to make the synthesizer into a double organ that changed external perceptions into images and also performed a similar function with respect to the extrasensory world, which thereby became knowable. The idea that the vehicle of the soul is the organ that acts as a medium is as old as the Neoplatonist Iamblichus. It was perfected by the Platonist Synesius of Cyrene (end of the fourth century) in his tractate *On Dreams,* where the "internal sense" is thus praised. "I do not know if this sense is not more saintly than others, for it is because of it that we can communicate with the gods, either through sight, through conversation, or by other means. One should not be surprised if, for many people, dreams are their most precious treasure. If, for example, one sleeps quietly and, during sleep, speaks to the Muses and listens to what they have to say, one can, upon awakening, become unexpectedly a good poet."[48]

Marsilio Ficino (1433–99), the most influential philosopher of the Renaissance, whose doctrines were put into verse by the French poets of the Pléïade and by the English Elizabethan poets, based his own theories of magic on Synesius's views. Ficino firmly believed in the "Platonic space shuttle," and he described the process of embodiment and disembodiment of the soul in the following terms.

> Souls descend into bodies from the Milky Way through the
> constellation of Cancer, wrapping themselves in a celestial and

luminous veil which they put on to enter terrestrial bodies. For nature demands that the very pure soul be united with the very impure body only through the intermediary of a pure vehicle, which, being less pure than the soul and purer than the body, is considered by the Platonists to be a very convenient means of uniting the soul with the terrestrial body. It is due to that descent that the souls and bodies of the Planets confirm and reinforce, in our souls and our bodies respectively, the seven original gifts bestowed upon us by God. The same function is performed by the seven categories of demons, intermediaries between the heavenly gods and humans. The gift of contemplation is strengthened by Saturn by means of the Saturnian demons. The power of government and empire is strengthened by Jupiter through the ministry of the Jovian demons; similarly, Mars through the Martians fosters the soul's courage. The Sun, with the help of the Solar demons, fosters the clarity of the senses and opinions that makes divination possible; Venus, through the Venereans, incites Love. Mercury, through the Mercurials, awakens the capacity for interpretation and expression. Finally, the Moon, through the Lunar demons, increases procreation.[49]

This passage derives from Macrobius, as the reader can easily ascertain, although Ficino makes some changes (for example, he introduces the "planetary demons" from popular magic).

Although this doctrine was suspicious in the eyes of the Catholic Church (in effect, Ficino elsewhere exposed it as a "Platonic fable"), or perhaps for that very reason, it became extremely influential in the Florentine Platonic academy, and by the end of the sixteenth century it was known all over Europe. In the aftermath of the Reformation, however, Europe was unwilling to accept it as a scientific doctrine. It lingered for quite a while in literary and esoteric circles, and could still be found in nineteenth-century occultism and theosophy, having survived for two thousand years in the history of Western culture.

ᕫ11

The Apogee of Otherworldly Journeys

From Muhammad to Dante

Paul was one of the most famous ecstatics of the Christian Middle Ages. His apocalypse, originally composed in Greek in the third century C.E., was translated into many vernacular languages: French, Provençal, English, Welsh, German, Danish, Bulgarian, Serbian, and Romanian. In the process of translation, the apocalypse was often amplified as well. At least two early Latin translations survive through copies and variants.[1]

The narrative framework presents the account of Paul's vision as having been written down by himself, hidden in a box together with his apostolic shoes, and buried under the foundation of his house at Tarsus. An angel reveals the presence of the relic to an "honorable man" who lives in the house. The pattern of discovery of Christian apocrypha seems in certain cases to be very close to the much later tradition of discovery of the Tibetan *gter-mas* (hidden-treasure) texts.

In the apocalypse, God chooses Paul as his spokesman in order to remind human beings that they are living in sin. Everything—the sun, the moon, the sea—complains about human iniquity. An angel takes Paul and shows him a terrifying vision of bottomless hell. He then leads him to the first heaven, where evil and hideous angels are located; they are responsible for the evil that befalls humankind and for the tortures in Hell. "There was Forgetfulness, which deceives and draws human hearts to itself, and the spirit of Slander, and the spirit of Fornication, and the spirit of Wrath, and the spirit of Insolence; and there were the princes of Wickedness." These heavenly beings are nightmarish, with "teeth stuck forward in their mouths, and . . . eyes like the morning star of the east," charged with electricity that sends forth sparks from their hair and out of their mouths.[2]

Like many other apocalypses, *The Apocalypse of Paul* is a rather unsophisticated Christian *Book of the Dead*. Its purpose is not to disclose the illusory character of the "intermediary state," but on the contrary, to create the illusion of posthumous retribution of deeds accomplished during one's lifetime. When the soul of the departed goes through the lower region of Heaven, the evil angels check to see if there is in it any trace of the vice that each of them carries with him and represents. If this is not the case, the soul passes through and is received by the good angels and then led by its guardian angel to the presence of the Lord. On the contrary, when a vicious soul is intercepted by an evil angel, the guardian angel can do nothing for it. An angel-judge dispatches it to the Prince of Darkness for eternal punishment. This would not have occurred had that soul repented at least one year before death.

The angelic guide leads Paul further to the third heaven, to the Mansions of the Just, where he meets Enoch and Elijah. Then he is led to the New Jerusalem, where he watches King David playing harp and singing hallelujah. Then follows a detailed visit to the great western Hell beyond the great ocean surrounding the world. Eventually, Paul is shown Paradise, where he is greeted by the Virgin Mary.

The number of episodes and the order in which they occur are slightly different in the most common Latin version of the *Apocalypse*. Widely known, the *Apocalypse of Paul* was the object of numerous imitations. One of the most interesting comes from a woman mystic, the Béguine Mechthild of Magdeburg (ca. 1207–82), who took trips to heaven on various occasions. According to her writings, in the earthly Paradise she met Enoch and Elijah, in the first heaven she found another Paradise, in the second heaven she discovered the multistoried building where the angels abide, and in the third heaven she found God's own palace and throne, together with Christ's bridal chamber, where he receives the souls of virgins in intimate union. Mechthild herself was received and was met with a tender kiss that elevated her above the ten ranks of the angels. Another time she entered "the bed of love" and was stripped by Christ of all "garments of fear and shame and all outward virtue."[3]

Together with the *Ascension of Isaiah* (see chapter 9, above), the *Apocalypse of Paul* is the most important among early Christian heavenly revelations containing an otherworldly journey. It is, however, only one of the nearly twenty Jewish and Christian "tours of Hell" analyzed in a beautiful book by Martha Himmelfarb,[4] many of which—like the *Apocalypse of Peter*—are not based on an otherworldly journey. In the early centuries, the Christian notion of heaven oscillated between two distinct conceptions. One of them, represented by the late second-century author Irenaeus, bishop of Lyons in Gaul, envisages heaven as a kind of "glorified material world"; this view seems very close to the Marxist idea of a technological paradise, except that it includes extreme longevity and fertility for human beings. The other one, which prevailed with

Augustine of Hippo (354–430), depicts Heaven as a Platonic spiritualized realm, "devoid of human interaction and family concern." Later this was modified into a "semispiritual heaven" in which saints have social exchanges and there is even room for lustless admiration for the beauty of women's bodies.[5]

THE EARLY MIDDLE AGES

In 594, Pope Gregory I, known as Gregory the Great (590–604), wrote a text of unsurpassed interest for the study of the early Middle Ages called *Dialogi de vita et miraculis patrum Italicorum* (Dialogues about the lives and miracles of the Italian fathers).[6] Among the many curiosities he reports are three cases of near-death experience, which he uses to show that not all people who are shown the beyond in a vision take the threat of hell seriously or repent and thus improve their posthumous fate. Two near-death experiences are interwoven: an unnamed soldier at the point of death is said to have witnessed in a vision the sad fate of a certain Stephen, who had had his own glimpse of Hell three years previously, but had not repented. The soldier reported that in Hell he saw a bridge over "a smokey river . . . that had a filthy and intolerable smell." The bridge led to "pleasant green meadows full of sweet flowers" that emitted "such a delicate odor that the fragrant smell gave wonderful pleasure to all who dwelled and walked in that place." As in the later Iranian *Book of Ardâ Virâz* (see chapter 7, above), the main opposition between good and evil, Paradise and Hell, is strongly olfactory, being expressed in the sensory opposition between fragrant and foul. The bridge is interesting, for, like the one in the Middle Persian vision of Virâz, it widens to let the righteous pass and narrows to fling the wicked down into the infernal river."If anyone wicked attempted to cross, down he or she fell into the dark and stinking river. Those who were just and not hindered by sin, however, safely and easily crossed over to those pleasant and delicate places."[7] The visionary soldier sees the soul of Stephen venturing onto the bridge. "He was about to go over when his foot slipped and his body hung in half over either side of the bridge. Terrible creatures rose out of the river and drew him down by the legs," but good angels were also fighting for the wretched soul.[8] The earliest date we encounter the motif of the "narrow bridge" in early medieval literature is before 577. It occurs in the tour of Hell of the abbot Sunniulfus of Randan (Puy-de-Dôme, France), as described by the historian Gregory of Tours in his *History of the Franks*.[9]

If the above-reported visions show that a relationship exists between Jewish-Christian and Iranian eschatology, it is difficult if not impossible to ascertain which comes first, since it all depends on the dating of a particular motif in the *Book of Ardâ Virâz*, that is, the motif of the "narrow bridge."[10] Another early medieval vision shows that during these times of relative isolation the memory of Platonic eschatology still persisted. Indeed, the vision of Furseus the Irishman, reported by the ecclesiastical historian Bede the Venerable (672–735) and placed in 633 B.C.E., is based not only on the widely known *Apocalypse of Paul,* but also on the inaccessible (to Bede) story of Timarch of Chaeronea in Plutarch's dialogue *On the Demon of Socrates.* Furseus had two out-of-body experiences. During the second, the angels who took him up showed him the world below, which "seemed to be a dark and obscure valley. . . . He also saw four fires in the air, not far from each other. Then asking the angels what those fires were, he was told they were the fires that would kindle and consume the world. . . . These fires, increasing by degrees, extended to meet one another, and being joined, became an immense flame." The angel explains that it is the fire of the celestial purgatory, which "tries everyone according to the merits of his or her works."[11] The episode occurring here is too characteristic to be ex-

plained by a fortuitous coincidence. Somehow Plutarch's apocalypse must have survived in seventh-century England.

A few details are supposed to authenticate Furseus's story.
A demon throws at him the flaming body of a damned soul
(under the pretext that Furseus has not rejected a gift from
him), and Furseus is badly burned. After he comes back to
life, he cannot bear to wear any thick garment and sweats even
in the middle of a hard winter.

Another vision reported by Bede also contains an episode
that occurs in Timarch's apocalypse as part of the near-death
experience of a certain Drythelm of Cunningham in North-
umberland, which allegedly took place in 696.[12] Like another
character of Plutarch's, Thespesius of Soloi, Drythelm began
leading a saintly life as result of a vision that he had while his
family thought him dead. Coming back to life, he gave his wife
and children an endowment, distributed a third of his wealth
to the poor, and became a monk in the monastery of Melrose
on the river Tweed, where he lived in perpetual silence.
According to the usual pattern, Drythelm was taken to heaven
by an angelic guide, the *angelus interpres,* who first showed him
a limbo in which souls not so wicked as to be sent to hell
were purified by an alternation of heat and cold, and then
took him to a pitch-dark place.

> As we went on through the shades of night, all of a sudden
> there appeared before us frequent globes of black flames,
> rising out of a great pit and falling back again into it. When I
> had been conducted there, my guide suddenly vanished and
> left me alone in the middle of darkness and this horrid vision,
> while those same globes of fire alternately flew up and fell
> back into the bottom of the abyss without intermission. As
> they ascended, I observed that all the flames were full of
> human souls, which were sometimes thrown up high like
> sparks flying up with smoke and again, when the vapor of the
> fire ceased, dropped down to the depth below.[13]

When the souls dropped, they fell into the stinking abyss. Similarly, Plutarch's Timarch saw the souls in the heavenly river of fire ascending and descending as glowing globes, some lucky enough to climb to the surface of the moon, others falling back into the cycles of rebirth.[14] Drythelm was further shown the Elysian Fields and, preceded by an intense fragrance, the mansions of the blessed, where a place was prepared for him after death. Such was the beauty of this place that Drythelm did not want to go back to his life on earth, but he had to. To hasten his return to heaven, he performed penances worthy of a Houdini: he said his prayers in the ice-cold water of a river, and "when he came ashore, he never took off his cold and frozen garments until they grew warm and dry on his body."[15]

The tour of Hell of the monk Wetti of the monastery of Reichenau, which took place on 3 November 824, and was written down by Heito, shows special concerns for sins of a sexual nature. It does not contain a heavenly journey.[16] The *Voyage of Saint Brendan,* like the *Odyssey,* can be read as an otherworldly journey and is probably based on a Celtic narrative pattern of travel by sea (*imrama*), although in the tenth century, when the legend seems to have originated, other models of *navigatio* were also available.[17]

THE MUSLIM LEGENDS OF THE *MI'RÂJ*

The tradition that the founder of Islam went on an otherworldly journey crystallized around an early nucleus. The *Laylat al-isrâ' wa-l-mi'râj* (Night of the journey and the vision) of the Prophet Muhammad is supposed to have taken place on the twenty-seventh of Rajab. In the Quran, *sûra* 17, called *Sûrat al-isrâ',* seems to allude to the "nightly journey."

In the ninth century, there were already two traditions of the *isrâ'* (journey) and three different traditions of the *mi'râj* (vision).[18] The scenarios of the *isrâ'* were simple. In one of them, Muhammad, like the characters of Jewish apocalypses, is asleep when a man takes him by the hand to a mountain, which they climb together. At the top, he is shown the tortures of hell and the joys of paradise. Raising his eyes to heaven, he sees Abraham, Moses, and Jesus. According to the other scenario, Muhammad is taken by two men or angels to Jerusalem, and on his way he meets people who are tortured for the sins committed during their lifetimes. He also sees Abraham under a huge tree in the garden of paradise, as well as then the mansion of the believers and the mansion of the martyrs. At this point, Muhammad's two guides identify themselves as Gabriel and Michael. Raising his eyes, the Prophet contemplates the heavenly palace that will be his after death.

The three variants of the *mi'râj* are more complex, and involve ascent to heaven. Abû Ja'far Muhammad al-Tabarî (839–923 C.E.) collected twenty-six traditions of the nocturnal trip of the Prophet in his *Tafsîr al-Qur'ân*. One of them relies on the early authority of Abû Huraya and belongs to the first type of *mi'râj* scenario; it is similar to the version given by the traditionalists Bukhârî and Muslim (ninth century). The Archangels Jibrîl and Mîkâil pay Muhammad a visit. Mîkâil brings water from the sacred source, Zamzam of Mecca. Jibrîl opens Muhammad's abdomen and breast, takes out his heart, washes it three times in water, fills it with goodness, wisdom, faith, certainty, and *islâm* (submission to God), and marks him between his shoulders with the seal of prophecy (*khâtîm al-nubuwa*). After this episode, which has authentic shamanistic flavor, the Prophet mounts his famous winged, human-faced, female ass Burâq and follows Jibrîl to various places, where people are either rewarded for their religious zeal or punished for their indolence. In Jerusalem, Muhammad converses with the souls of some of the most famous representatives of the

Jewish tradition, such as Abraham, Moses, David, Solomon, and Jesus himself, of whom it is said that he could create a bird of clay and bring it to life with his own breath. Then Jibrîl takes the Prophet on a tour of the heavens: in the first he meets Adam, in the second Jesus and John the Evangelist, in the third Joseph, in the fourth Idrîs-Enoch, in the fifth Aaron, in the sixth Moses, and in the seventh Abraham. They subsequently come to the lotus of the border line (*sidrat al-muntahâ*), where Muhammad contemplates God's glory and talks to Him, receiving from Him his mission of *rasûl* (messenger of the revelation), together with the eight parts of the true religion: *islâm, hajj* (pilgrimage to Mecca), the *jihâd* (sacred war), almsgiving, ritual prayer, Ramadan fasting, and the commandments to perform good and to avoid evil deeds. Initially God commands Muhammad to have the community recite fifty prayers daily, but on the advice of Moses, who knows how weak human beings are, this number is drastically cut to five.[19]

Burâq is variously described in different traditions of the *mi'râj*. Thus, in a Persian version compiled in 510 H./1116 C.E.) by Abû'l Futîh al-Râzî, Burâq is now male and is "a horse bigger than a donkey yet smaller than a camel. He has a camel tail, the body of a horse, the face of a human being, the limbs of a camel, the hooves of a cow, the breast red like ruby, the back white like pearl. . . . He has two wings like those of a peacock and is lightning-swift."[20]

The second scenario of the *mi'râj* is similar to the one reported above, with the insertion of a long episode in which Muhammad is shown the first of seven stories of hell by a huge, fiery angel who is the supervisor of hell. The third scenario, which probably owes its origins to Persian imagination, is also the longest. The structure of the heavens is different, as are the seven stations that follow after Muhammad reaches the eighth and last heaven, the residence of God.

This Muslim legend penetrated into Christian Spain from the ninth century on. The first Latin summary of two versions of the *mi'râj* is borrowed from Bukhârî and Muslim, and enlivens the fifth chapter of the *History of the Arabs* by the archbishop of Toledo, Rodrigo Ximenez de Rada (1170–1247). A long version of the *mi'râj* was translated in 1264 from Arabic into Castilian by a certain Abraham Alfaquim, a converted Jew, at the order of Alphonse X, the Wise. The notary Bonaventura of Siena translated the Castilian version into Latin. A French translation from Latin followed.[21] At the end of the fifteenth century, the converted theologian Juan Andrés de Jativa acquainted the Christian West with a third, different version of the *mi'râj*. It is not our intention to report here the many variations of these legends. Their popularity was certainly comparable to that of the many Jewish and Christian apocalypses. Early in the history of Islam, they became one of the favorite subjects of allegorical interpretation among the Sufi mystics.

Among the Sufis, the most famous for his own *mi'râj* was certainly the Persian Abû Yazîd al-Bîstâmî (d. ca. 874 to 877 B.C.E.), the founder of ecstatic or "drunken" Sufism. Al-Bîstâmî, who had the reputation of flying in the air and walking on water, wrote a description of his journey to heaven that survives in two variants, one by the Persian poet Farîd al-Dîn 'Attâr (d. ca. 1220 to 1230 C.E.),[22] and another one by al-Sahlajî.[23]

Many other mystics interpreted the *mi'râj* of Muhammad according to a Sufi key, changing the objective levels that Muhammad had visited in his ascent into internal levels of mystical achievement. One of the greatest among them was 'Abd al-Karîm ibn Ibrâhîm al-Jîlî (ca. 1365 or 1366 to 1406 or 1417), who combined the *mi'râj* and the *Divina commedia* and interpreted the heavens visited by Muhammad as the astronomical spheres of the planets.[24] Sufi masters (*shaikh*) often combined a personal ascent like Abû Yazîd's with an allegorical interpretation of Muhammad's *mi'râj*. One such example comes from the *shaikh* Imâm Muhammad Nur-Bakhsh, founder of the order of the Nur-Bakhshian in Kashmir, as interpreted by Mohsin Fani, who was a contemporary of the seventeenth-century Sufi prince Dara Shikoh of the Mughal imperial family.[25]

A few words are necessary in order to conclude this brief presentation of the *mi'râj* tradition. Initially it was based on Jewish and Christian apocalypses, but it did not lack its own originality. In none of the many variants analyzed elsewhere[26] are the eight to ten heavens crossed by Muhammad identified with the planets.

The large number of allegorical interpretations of the *mi'râj* legends shows that in Islam they enjoyed a higher status than the various apocalypses did in Christianity. Using mystical hermeneutics, the Sufis were distancing themselves from the popular, exoteric traditions of Islam and were propounding their own version of the stages by which union with God is reached.

THE TWELFTH-CENTURY RENAISSANCE

As a consequence of the weakening of Muslim power during the period of the "party kings" (*reyes de taifas*), who were petty rulers of city-states in permanent conflict with each other, the city of Toledo was conquered in 1085 by the Christian armies of northern Spain. Toledo, the former capital of the Visigothic kingdom of Spain, was a symbol of domination on the Iberian peninsula. This event marked the beginning of the end of Muslim power in Spain; despite two long occupations by Berber dynasties, by 1250 all of Spain had been conquered by the Christians, with the exception of a strip running from Granada to Gibraltar and crossing over to Ceuta. As a result,

Muslim culture deeply penetrated Christian Europe. Although some translations of works from Arabic or Greek were done sporadically in Syria, Constantinople, and Sicily, at the end of the eleventh century Toledo became the major center of diffusion of Greco-Roman culture by means of Arabic translations and commentaries that now found their way into Latin Europe.

Shortly thereafter, the conquest of Toledo was followed by the even more consequential conquest of Jerusalem (1099), which became a kingdom of the crusaders a few years later. Half a century earlier, monasticism had been subjected to a major reform. By the time Bernard of Clairvaux (1090–1153) was born, the main intellectual transformations of Europe that came to be referred to as the Renaissance of the twelfth century had already begun.

This epoch, which bore fruit in the thirteenth century, saw the rise of the cult of the Virgin, the building of the Gothic cathedrals, the emergence of universities from cathedral schools, the triumph of Aristotelian philosophy, the foundation of new religious orders (some of them military), the beginnings of the heresy of the poor and Catharism, the appearance of the phenomenon of courtly love and the Arthurian romance, the "birth of purgatory" (as Jacques Le Goff called it in an influential book), the definition of sacraments (including marriage), and so on. These extraordinary changes went together with a renewed interest in otherworldly revelations and journeys that culminated in Dante's masterpiece, *Divina commedia*.

It is difficult to assess to what extent otherworldly journeys in the twelfth century were influenced by the Muslim legends of the *mi'râj*. Very influential seems to be a Latin reworking of the *Apocalypse of Paul*, known under the name of the *Vision of Paul*.[27] Before the twelfth century, other apocalypses were reworkings of a no-longer-extant Greek translation of the Hebrew or Aramaic apocryphon known as 4 Ezra.[28] The hypothesis that the Arabic legends were borrowed from seems therefore superfluous, although in some cases it could have been possible.

One of these cases is the *Vision of Alberic of Monte Cassino,* based on a near-death experience of a ten-year-old boy that took place in or after 1111. Born in the castle of Settefrati, diocese of Sora, province of Caserta, Alberic became a Benedictine monk immediately after his recovery. Girardo (1111–23) was then abbot of Montecassino, and he asked a certain brother Guido to write down the boy's story. By 1127 there were already two redactions thereof that Alberic himself thought unreliable. Together with his young friend Peter the Deacon (1107–60), Alberic proceeded to revise the report of his otherworldly journey. It appears that Guido had inserted many spurious episodes borrowed from such apocrypha as the *Life of Adam and Eve* and the *Voyage of Brendan.*[29] Yet, even when expurgated, Alberic's *Vision* seems to be—with the exception of one episode that has authentic shamanistic flavor—only another compendium of apocalyptic commonplaces. Obviously, intertextuality played an important role in the reelaboration of a childhood experience that must have been largely forgotten after Alberic grew up in the monastery.[30]

Before we proceed further, we should note that, in this case at least, an Islamic influence could be plausibly argued. The greatest translator of medical works from Arabic into Latin, Constantine the African (1020–87), spent the last seventeen years of his life in the monastery of Monte Cassino.[31] Alberic's friend, Peter the Deacon, who helped with the 1127 version of the vision, is known in the history of medicine for his tabulation of the works of Constantine. It is certainly possible that an oral tradition going back to Constantine himself could have existed in Monte Cassino. Steeped in Muslim culture, Constantine must have known about the *mi'râj,* and he could have talked about it.

However, Alberic's vision does not bear the clear imprint of the Islamic legends. The boy saw a dovelike bird insert its beak in his mouth and pull out something (the soul?) from his insides. Then the bird seized his hair in its beak and raised him above the earth, showing him the torments of hell and the joys of paradise. In hell, he saw the "narrowing bridge," which by then had become a standard feature of all Christian apocalypses, starting with the tenth-century Latin *Vision of Esdra*.[32]

More influential than Alberic's vision were two other twelfth-century apocalypses, the *Vision of Tundal* and the *Purgatory of Saint Patrick*. Tundal's vision was written in 1149 by the Irish monk Marc of Munster for the abbess of the Saint Paul monastery in Regensburg. Its hero is the Irish nobleman Tundal (or Tnugdal) from the southern city of Cashel, who goes through a three-day near-death experience, and after recovery distributes his wealth to the poor and joins a monastic order.[33] According to this story, after a period of confusion in the middle of a hideous crowd, an angel like a bright star takes Tundal's soul on a tour of hell and heaven. Tundal expiates some of his worldly transgressions by leading a wild cow over a two-mile-long bridge. This bridge is as narrow as the palm of the hand and is covered with sharp nails that lacerate his feet (they are chopped into pieces and then put back together again). He further expiates his transgressions by being devoured by beasts with "burning iron heads and the sharpest beaks"; by being roasted in a forge; and by being abandoned in a deep, dark, stinking pit, where the Prince of Shadows, Lucifer himself, dwells. Here Tundal's soul is pardoned and taken first to the purgatorial fields and the fountain of life, and afterwards to the heavenly abodes of saints and virtuous people. A similar pattern is followed by the narrative of another near-death experience that is said to have befallen a monk of the Evesham monastery in England in 1196.[34]

The *Purgatory of Saint Patrick,* written by the monk H. of
Saltrey around 1189, is based on the existence of a famous cave
at Lough Derg in Ireland, similar to Trophonius's cave at
Lebadeia (see chapter 8, above).[35] Reports about the strange
properties of that vision-producing cave range over a period of
one thousand years, ending in 1497, when it was temporarily
closed by Pope Alexander VI; after that reports resume and
continue until the eighteenth century. Permission to visit the
cave was difficult to obtain. Its reputation was based on the
legend of an apparition of Christ to Saint Patrick. In the
Purgatory of Saint Patrick, during the reign of King Stephen, the
Irish knight Owein is given license by the bishop to visit
purgatory, and spends fifteen days in the church in prayer.
After celebrating mass and administering the eucharist to him,
the prior leads him to the entrance of the cave and dispatches
him on his adventure. Uttering the name of Jesus Christ,
Owein resists a multitude of demons who drag him to a plain
of torments, then into a fiery stinking pit, and finally to a long,
narrow, high, slippery bridge running across "a broad and
stinking river, covered with flame and fire of brimstone and
full of demons."[36] After that he reaches the earthly paradise
and is shown the gate of the heavenly paradise. Back at the
church, Owein remains fifteen days in prayer, after which he
goes on a pilgrimage to Jerusalem. Upon his return, he is sent
to Ireland by King Stephen and serves as an interpreter for an
abbey of settlers from England.

In the *Vision of Thurkill* (1206), a curious parallelism is
established between the structure of heaven and a cathedral.[37]
Led by Saint Julian to the place where the souls of the dead
are collected, Thurkill, a poor laborer of Tunsted, Essex,
ascertains that the beyond looks like "a church of wonderful
structure," dedicated to the Virgin, and in which the archangel
Michael and the apostles Peter and Paul judge the deceased
and weigh their souls on a scale. The stinking pit of hell is

beyond the northern wall, the fire of purgatory is "on the eastern side of this church between two walls," and the mount of joy is across a glacial lake and can only be reached over a bridge "planted all over with thorns and stakes" that hurt the feet.

In other cases, heaven looks like a city. Urbanization was another trait of the twelfth-century Renaissance. According to Colleen McDannell and Bernhard Lang, the growth of European urban centers between 1150 and 1250 is paralleled by the promotion of a highly urban concept of heaven. The large Gothic cathedrals built during this period were the embodiment of the ideal of an urban heaven.[38] As an example of this trend, the authors cite the vision of the Camaldolese tertiary Gherardesca da Pisa (1210–69), who saw the heavenly city of Jerusalem, with streets made "of the purest gold and the most precious stones" and flanked by golden trees, surrounded by seven rich castles of the Virgin Mary in which chairs were prepared for all the inhabitants of heaven. Gherardesca's new Jerusalem, conclude the authors, looks like a *contado* (region) in upper Italy, or a city surrounded by castles.[39] This conclusion, however, cannot be generalized for all the apocalyptic texts of this extraordinary period. On the contrary, some of the most important do not have an urban setting. We already examined the *Purgatory of Saint Patrick,* which is based on an ancient pattern of cave incubation. Another example is the vision of Gottschalk.

Gottschalk was a poor and sickly but free German peasant who lived in Holstein (located between Kiel and Hamburg) in the second half of the thirteenth century. On 12 December 1189, a Tuesday, he was drafted by his lord, Heinrich Duke of Saxony and Bavaria, to help surround the soldiers of his enemy Adolf of Dassel who were holding the fortress of Segerberg, but Gottschalk got seriously ill in his tent. Between 17 and 20 December he entered a comatose state, and on 20 December his soul left his body altogether. The draftees moved away on 24 December (Christmas vigil), taking their nearly lifeless colleague with them. It took him five weeks to recover, but thenceforth he had frequent hallucinations and headaches, and also suffered very severely from the wounds he had incurred during his otherworldly journey. He was not quite human any more: once his leg got caught in the chimney, but fire did not harm him. Two religious men took interest in his visions and wrote two reports, one shorter than the other, but showing no notable discrepancies between them.[40]

Separated from the body, Gottschalk's soul was intercepted by two angels dressed in snow-white robes, who took him southward to a great meeting of souls that looked like human beings. From the canopy of a lime tree, one of the angels got fourteen pairs of shoes and handed them to fourteen people in the assembly. All the others, including Gottschalk, had to cross barefoot, in agony, over a two-mile-long field full of sharp thorns. After a while, Gottschalk fell to the ground and could walk no more. The angel showed mercy on him and brought him a pair of shoes. On the other side of the field, the wounds of twenty-five of the sinners were miraculously healed, as a sign that they had repented on their way.

They then came to a wide river, and there was no other way to cross it than by walking on the tips of terrible swords and spears. For the fourteen righteous and the twenty-five repentants, however, there were rafts floating on the river, so that they could remain unharmed. The others were incredibly mutilated; all but six were restored to the community of the righteous because of their sincere repentance. The people then came to a crossroad; there, five of those who had received shoes went directly to heaven and were transfigured into glorious beings. Most of the others took the "midway" leading to purgatory. Only Gottschalk and the six sinners were led by the angels to contemplate the formidable tortures in the fire of hell. Gottschalk recognized in there several people from his province, mainly notorious criminals. But punishment appeared not always to be eternal. After being roasted and cooled again many times in a row, some of the sinners were released. The angels, Gottschalk, and two of the six people who had come all the way down proceeded to the green midway, which slowly began widening. They walked past three mansions, each more beautiful than the one before, with dignified people inside who sang hymns of glory and praise. Then they came to the promised land, the wonderful sight of which was heralded by a fragrant breeze. Contemplating the intensely green valley and the light that now surrounded his companions, Gottschalk was afflicted by the thought that he would have to leave this place and revert to his ailing body. But before leaving, he had time to see a great shining cloister where the righteous, under the supervision of Saint John the Evangelist, spent all their time in happy prayer. The apostles paid them regular visits, and it was now the turn of Saint Andrew, whom Gottschalk watched as he was directing the chorus of the blessed. All of them looked young and peaceful. They were awaiting the day of resurrection, when all of them would go to heaven in order to enjoy a form of existence nine times more glorious than in purgatory. Before he came back to where his body was being watched by his companions, Gottschalk had time to see a wonderful city of praising righteous ones. Their houses actually had no walls, and everything was open to anyone in an openhearted, unearthly communality.

THE DIVINE COMEDY

No one has done more for the popularity of otherworldly journeys than the Florentine poet Dante Alighieri (1265–1321). His masterpiece, *Divina commedia,* is a classic of descent to hell and ascent to heaven. Heaven is divided into seven stories corresponding to the seven planets. Guided first by the ghost of the Latin poet Virgil and then by Beatrice, a mysterious celestial being whose counterpart on earth was a woman who died young and to whom Dante vowed mystical love and devotion, the poet crosses all the levels of hell and reaches the dark pit of Lucifer himself; he reemerges on the mountain of purgatory and then visits the spheres of paradise one by one. A product of unparalleled poetical ingenuity as well as great theological sophistication, the *Divine Comedy* has been the object of innumerable interpretations.

I do not intend to take a position in the debate concerning the "origins" of the *Divine Comedy*. All the apocalypses listed above are, in a certain sense, its "sources." The case for the dependence of the *Divine Comedy* on the *mi'râj* is, of course, extremely meager. The closest earlier parallels of Dante's scenario are probably the *Vision of Paul* and the many other tours of hell available at the time. The idea of making the planetary spheres into abodes of the saints was ancient and prestigious. Dante's contemporaries had revived the Aristotelian-Ptolemaic universe, which was masterfully described in the *Summa* of Thomas of Aquinas (1225–74). Besides, it was an error of modern scholarship to believe that Dante could have borrowed the journey through the "astronomical heavens" from the *mi'râj* legends, for the simple reason that the heavens in these legends are never associated with the planets.

With Dante our survey of otherworldly journeys comes to a conclusion. Surprisingly enough, it is an entirely circular conclusion, and the end of this book leads us again to its beginning. Stripped of its cultural complexity, Dante's story seems to fall within a pattern we looked at before we started our historical overview. It is the story of a man visited by the spirits of a poet long dead and of a young woman endowed with supernatural powers. The two show him around the world of ghosts, where Dante meets many people from his own town who are being tortured for their sins and witnesses the glorious fate of meritorious ones who have made it to heaven.

Reduced to its nucleus, Dante's story is a shamanistic story that could have taken place in any space or time setting among those we have surveyed above. This is probably why it continues to captivate our attention, in an epoch in which there is no less interest in near-death and out-of-body experiences than there was in the thirteenth century. Although we have our own popular literature on near-death and out-of-body experiences, Dante's poem continues to move us.

Conclusion

This book is meant to be a survey of otherworldly journeys according to place and time, and it therefore arrives at no particular conclusions. Nonetheless, despite their variety, most if not all of the traditions studied here share a number of basic traits. First, there is the belief in a "free soul" that survives after death as a ghost. This soul can, under certain conditions, separate itself from the body and visit the ghost world. Swooning, dreaming, experiencing near death, being in states of consciousness altered by means of hallucinogens, and undergoing sensory deprivation or its opposite, sensory bombardment, are some of the situations in which separation can occur.

The shaman is a specialist in separation, and can, therefore, function as a soul raiser. Soul raising is one of the activities we have come across almost constantly, in all the ancient traditions of humankind. Due to repeated visits to the abodes of the ghosts, the shaman knows exactly the geography of dead land; he or she can describe it and often dramatizes encounters with the dead. Between the medium's description of the inferno in the soul raising of Singapore and in Dante's *Divine Comedy* there is only a difference of discourse and theology; both of them share the idea of infernal punishment and the narrative device of conversation with familiar ghosts.

Does this mean that the origin of otherworldly journeys has to be sought in shamanism? It is more reasonable to believe that it precedes the crystallization of the shamanistic complex as such. In fact, it may have Palaeolithic roots.

How can we explain its continuity from that remote time period to ours? It is useless, in this case, to look for a general pattern of historical diffusion. All traditions of humankind developed parallelly from analogous premises, although beliefs inevitably interacted and coalesced. The result is a surprising unity in the variety.

The variety consists of the great number and types of ghost lands, and of the often puzzling kinds of ethical transgressions that are punished or of achievements that are rewarded in the worlds of the dead. Yet the idea of the existence of such lands and of reward and punishment is very widespread.

The more complex a religion, the more complex dead land becomes. In some cases, the notion of the beyond is submitted to extremely sophisticated interpretations. In Tibetan Buddhism, for example, the afterlife, despite its concrete appearance, is just another creation of the mind. Learning this may enable one to avert the pitfalls of the afterlife and leave the world. In a certain sense, what we have here is the widespread notion of "second death," which in Buddhism is an important goal to strive for, whereas in other religions it is a horrible fate encountered by certain unfortunates among the dead.

Studying complex series of otherworldly journeys belonging to the same tradition, it is possible to reach some typological conclusions. Thus, for example, it appears that the Jewish tradition has a number of constant traits, one of the most important of which is that the character who is shown other worlds does not take drugs and does not postulate a vision in any way. He simply lies on a couch asleep, usually in a state of depression. On the other hand, in the Greek tradition visits to other worlds often occur in a near-death state, or as a result of incubation, and in the Iranian tradition consumption of hallucinogens is part of the scenario. Early Christian apocalypses are but a continuation of the Jewish pattern, whereas late medieval otherworldly visions are far more often obtained through near-death experience, which becomes a quasi-standard feature of twelfth- and thirteenth-century apocalypses.

Most of the reports of otherworldly journeys that have been examined above can still satisfy our aesthetic sensibility, but they bring a smile to our lips if we consider their veracity and their timeliness. None can satisfy our expectations of the afterlife, neither the Platonic isles of the blessed nor Dante's astronomical paradise. Examining the accounts of near-death and out-of-body experiences that have been produced during the past thirty years, we ascertain that one of the basic features of most of the ancient apocalypses is often lacking: there is neither punishment nor reward after death. On the other hand, science itself has opened amazing perspectives in the exploration of other worlds, and sometimes in other dimensions of space. Accordingly, our otherworldly journeys may lead to parallel universes or to all sorts of possible or even impossible worlds.

Is this a sign that belief in a ghost land has ceased? That soul raising is an affair of the past? Not necessarily. The only conclusion we can draw from the multiplicity of current representations of other worlds is that we live in a state of advanced other-world pluralism. Through science fiction, representations of other worlds have reached an unprecedented expansion, not coordinated by any basic world view. Indeed, even Isaac Asimov's universe, which is among the most "classical" and coherent, is sometimes unpredictable and can reserve encounters with invisible dimensions. Whatever our convictions about the universe may be, one thing seems to be certain: only a few of us still share the coarse hypothesis of a "separable soul." Other models of mind, more sophisticated and inspired by cybernetics and artificial intelligence, are replacing the old ones. Although in many cases we still mistake the space of our mind for the space outside of us, we are increasingly inclined to understand that the former is no less interesting than the latter, and that in it all sorts of mysterious encounters may take place. Yet, the exploration of our mind space is only at the beginning.

In the meantime, no ancient otherworldly beliefs have been completely abandoned; at least a few people still seem to share them. Psychotherapy recommends the exploration of imaginary universes for multiple purposes and in multiple ways, from the flight dreams of Robert Desoille to Senoi dream interpretation (one of the therapeutic hoaxes of the century). One of the most popular New Age therapeutic techniques is "past-lives regression" based on mind travel which is supposed to be time travel. Similar otherworldly journeys abound in New Age literature.

It is unlikely that we will ever return to the certainties of the past, which might have been reassuring but were usually cheap as well. Other worlds without limit will continue to be multiplied by our minds, which in so doing will be exploring their own limitless possibilities.

Notes

Introduction

1. The results of these polls are summarized in George Gallup, Jr., with William Proctor, *Adventures in Immortality,* (New York: McGraw Hill, 1982), pp. 31ff. and 183ff.
2. See my *Eros and Magic in the Renaissance,* trans. into English by Margaret Cook, (Chicago and London: University of Chicago Press, 1987), pp. 244–45, n. 21.
3. Gallup and Proctor, *Adventures,* pp. 6–15 (passage quoted is on p. 15).
4. J. G. Frazer, *The Belief in Immortality and the Worship of the Dead,* vol. 2: *The Belief among the Polynesians* (London: Macmillan, 1922), pp. 148ff.
5. See my *Psychanodia I: A Survey of the Evidence Concerning the Ascension of the Soul and Its Relevance* (Leiden: Brill, 1983); and my *Expériences de l'extase: Extase, ascension et récit visionnarie de l'Hellénisme au Moyen Age* (Paris: Payot, 1984).

Chapter 1. A Historian's Kit for the Fourth Dimension

1. Albert Einstein, *Relativity: The Special and General Theory,* trans. R. W. Lawson (New York: Peter Smith, 1920), 3:30, from Milton K. Munitz, *Theories of the Universe: From Babylonian Myth to Modern Science* (New York: Macmillan, 1965), p. 276.
2. On Einstein's life and activity, see the excellent work of

Abraham Pais, *'Subtle is the Lord . . .': The Science and the Life of Albert Einstein* (Oxford: Oxford University Press, 1982).

3. For the "guided tour of the higher universes" they provided I am much indebted to Rudy Rucker's books *Geometry, Relativity and the Fourth Dimension* (New York: Dover, 1977), and *The Fourth Dimension: A Guided Tour of the Higher Universes* (Boston: Houghton Mifflin, 1984). For stimulating discussion I am particularly grateful to H.S., and to the students who attended my "Fourth Dimension" seminar at the University of Chicago: Michael Allocca, Margaret Arndt-Caddigan, Beatrice Briggs, Nathaniel Deutsch, Julia Dulocq, Jennifer Jesse, Shannon Robinson, Stephanie Stamm, Leslie Steinfeld, and Greg Spinner.

4. In *A Reader: A Selection from the Writings of Jorge Luis Borges,* ed. Emir Rodriguez Monegal and Alastair Reid (New York: Dutton, 1981), pp. 111ff.

5. For related literature, see my *Eros and Magic.*

6. These biographical details are drawn from Rudy Rucker's introduction to *Speculations on the Fourth Dimension: Selected Writings of Ch. H. Hinton,* ed. R. Rucker (New York: Dover, 1980), and on Rucker's *The Fourth Dimension,* pp. 64–68.

7. Fragments from Hinton's writings were published by Rudy Rucker (see note 3 above). Strangely enough, although Hinton was not an outspoken occultist and, apart from the extraordinary difficulty of his challenging operations with cubes, his main fault being rather that he was one hundred years ahead of his time, his *Scientific Romances* and his *The Fourth Dimension* (Allen & Unwin's 1912 edition) were reprinted in the collection "The Occult" of Arno Press (New York).

8. See Pais, *Science and Life of Einstein,* p. 520.

9. Ibid., p. 13.

10. See Edwin Abbott, *Flatland,* with a preface by Isaac Asimov (New York: Harper & Row, 1983).

11. Astrians can actually move in only one direction, by analogy with human beings who can scarcely move in more than two directions.

12. On time as perception of the third dimension in flat beings, see especially Hinton, *The Fourth Dimension,* pp. 23ff.

13. The consequence of Einstein's world view is that space-time can

be envisioned as a solid four-dimensional continuum, temporarily being a pure illusion. It is not at all clear why time flows only one way. And there is no absolute reason why one should not be able to move back and forth on the continuum to any point in space-time one would like. In other words, it appears impossible to explain many of our limitations rather than some of our freedoms.

14. See Rucker, *Geometry*.

15. See a good survey of these problems in Paul Davies, *Superforce: The Search for a Grand Unified Theory of Nature* (New York: Simon & Schuster, 1984).

16. See *Lewis Carroll: The Complete Works,* intro. by Alexander Woolcott (Modern Library Giants, n.d.); for chronologies, see Sidney Herbert Williams, *A Handbook of the Literature of the Rev. C. L. Dodgson (Lewis Carroll)* (London: Oxford University Press, 1931). Dodgson's diaries are exhaustively used and commented upon by Anne Clark, *Lewis Carroll: A Biography* (New York: Schocken Books, 1979).

17. Ruth Brandon, *The Spiritualists: The Passion for the Occult in the Nineteenth and Twentieth Centuries* (New York: Alfred A. Knopf, 1983).

18. See in this respect the rather debatable book by Stephen E. Braude, *The Limits of Influence: Psychokinesis and the Philosophy of Science* (New York and London: Routledge & Kegan Paul, 1986). Braude sees in the Franciscan saint Giuseppe Desa da Copertino (1603–63), who often levitated and occasionally took others with him on his trips, the champion of paranormal phenomena.

19. See the perceptive book by Janet Oppenheim, *The Other World: Spiritualism and Psychical Research in England, 1850–1914* (Cambridge: Cambridge University Press, 1985), p. 23.

20. Oppenheim, *The Other World*, pp. 23–24.

21. Braude, *The Limits of Influence*, p. 160.

22. Braude, *The Limits of Influence*, p. 160.

23. See especially P. D. Ouspensky's *Tertium Organum: The Third Canon of Thought; A Key to the Enigmas of the World.* Trans. N. Bessaraboff and C. Bragdon (New York: Vintage Books, 1970).

24. For an account of Ouspensky's discipleship under Gurdjieff, see

Ouspensky, *In Search of the Miraculous: Fragments of an Unknown Teaching* (New York: Harcourt & Brace, 1949).

25. P. D. Ouspensky, *A New Model of the Universe: Principles of the Psychological Method in Its Applications to Problems of Science, Religion, and Art* (1931; reprint New York: Vintage Books, 1971).

26. Bombay: Jaico Publishing House, 1975. This book was first published in 1946 and was revised in 1951.

27. Yogananda, *Autobiography,* p. 79.

28. Ibid., pp. 141–42.

29. "The Aleph," in Borges, *A Reader,* p. 161, trans. N. T. di Giovanni.

30. See Robert A. Monroe, *Journeys Out of the Body,* preface by Charles Tart (Garden City, N.Y.: Doubleday, 1971).

31. Flora Courtois, *An Experience of Enlightenment* (Madras and London: Theosophical Publishing House, 1986), p. 11.

32. Ibid., pp. 34–35.

33. See Charles T. Tart, ed., *Altered States of Consciousness: A Book of Readings* (New York: John Wiley & Sons, 1969).

34. See *Readings from Scientific American,* ed. Timothy J. Tyler "Altered States of Awareness" (San Francisco: W. H. Freeman, n.d., but after 1972).

35. See A. Brierre de Boismont, *Hallucinations: The Rational History of Apparitions, Visions, Dreams, Ecstasy, Magnetism, and Somnambulism* (Philadelphia: Lindsay & Blakiston, 1853), ch. 19. Modern research still retains the concept of "hallucination": see Ronald K. Siegel, "Hallucinations," in *Readings from Scientific American: The Mind's Eye,* intro. by Jeremy M. Wolfe (New York: W. H. Freeman, 1986), pp. 108ff.

36. See Traugott Konstantin Oesterreich, *Possession: Demoniacal and Other* (Secaucus, N.J.: Citadel Press, 1974).

37. Raymond Moody, *Life after Life* (Atlanta: Bantam, 1975).

38. Kenneth Ring, *Life at Death: A Scientific Investigation of the Near-Death Experience* (New York: Coward, McCann, and Geoghehan, 1980) seems to be the best-known among them; see also a more recent and excellent survey by Carol Zaleski, *Otherworld Journeys: Accounts of Near-Death Experience in Medieval and Modern Times* (New York and Oxford: Oxford University Press, 1987).

39. Moody, *Life after Life,* pp. 21–22; Zaleski, *Otherworld Journeys,* pp. 102–3.
40. Zaleski, *Otherworld Journeys,* pp. 107–8.
41. Ibid., p. 189.
42. See Weston La Barre, *The Peyote Cult* (Hamden: Shoe String Press, 1964), p. 232.

Chapter 2. Free Spirit Seeks Free Spirit

1. See the studies by H. G. Kippenberg quoted in my "Mircea Eliade at the Crossroads of Anthropology," in *Neue Zeitschrift für Systematische Theologie,* 1985.
2. J. G. Frazer, *The Belief in Immortality and the Worship of the Dead,* vol. 1: *The Belief among the Aborigines of Australia, the Torres Straits Islanders, New Guinea, and Melanesia;* vol. 2: *The Belief among the Polynesians;* vol. 3: *The Belief among the Micronesians* (London: Macmillan, 1913, 1922, 1924).
3. Hans Fischer, *Studien über Seelenvorstellungen in Ozeanien* (Munich: Klaus Renner, 1965).
4. These two kinds of soul are often mixed up, and the "body souls" may perform otherworldly journeys as well, but the distinction holds in general.
5. Frazer, *Belief in Immortality,* vol. 2, p. 85.
6. Ibid., vol. 1, p. 466.
7. Ibid., vol. 1 pp. 464–465.
8. Ibid., vol. 3, p. 49.
9. Ibid., vol. 1, pp. 464–465.
8. Ibid., vol. 3, p. 49.
9. Ibid., vol. 3, p. 355.
10. Ibid., vol. 3, p. 167.
11. Ibid., vol. 3, p. 118.
12. Fischer, *Studien.*
13. L. Leertouwer, *Het beeld van de ziel bij drie sumatraanse volken* (Groningen: Drukkerijen bv, 1977).
14. Ibid., p. 222.
15. Ivar Paulson, *Die primitiven Seelenvorstellungen der nordeurasischen Völker: Eine religionsethnographische und religionsphänomenologische Untersuchung* (Stockholm: Ethnographical Museum of Sweden, 1958).

16. Åke Hultkrantz, *Conceptions of the Soul among North American Indians: A Study in Religious Ethnology* (Stockholm: Ethnographical Museum of Sweden, 1953).

17. Lawrence E. Sullivan, *Icanchu's Drum: An Orientation to Meaning in South American Religions* (New York: Macmillan, 1988).

18. Vilmos Dioszegi, *Tracing Shamans in Siberia: The Story of an Ethnographical Research Expedition* (Oosterhout: Anthropological Publications, 1968).

19. V. Basilov, "Shamanism in Central Asia," in Agehananda Bharati, ed., *The Realm of the Extra-Human: Agents and Audiences* (The Hague and Paris: Mouton, 1976), pp. 150–53.

20. Paulson, *Die primitiven*, pp. 331ff.

21. Hultkrantz, *Conceptions of the Soul*, pp. 259ff.

22. Ibid., p. 280.

23. Sullivan, *Icanchu's Drum*, p. 425.

24. Ibid., p. 451.

25. Ibid.

26. A. P. Elkin, *Aboriginal Men of High-Degree* (New York: St. Martin's Press, 1978), p. 47.

27. Ibid., p. 53.

28. Ibid., pp. 53–57.

29. In my *Iter in silvis*, vol. 1 (Messina: EDAS, 1981), pp. 97–108.

30. Ibid., p. 107.

31. Ioan M. Lewis, *Ecstatic Religion: An Anthropological Study of Spirit Possession and Shamanism* (Harmondsworth: Penguin Books, 1971).

32. See Felicitas D. Goodman, *Speaking in Tongues: A Cross-cultural Study of Glossolalia* (Chicago: Chicago University Press, 1972), p. 60; Barbara W. Lex, "Altered States of Consciousness in Northern Iroquoian Ritual," in Bharati, *Realm of the Extra-Human*, pp. 277–300; and Vincent Crapanzano and Vivian Garrison, eds., *Case Studies in Spirit Possession* (New York: John Wiley & Sons, 1977).

33. Carlo Ginzburg, *I benandanti* (Torino: Einaudi, 1966).

34. Carlo Ginzburg, *Storia notturna: Una decifrazione del Sabba* (Torino: Einaudi, 1989); see my review in *Times Literary Supplement*, December 15–21, 1989, "Liber" Section, p. 14.

35. As an example of the views of other historians, see the recent

book by Robert I. Moore, *The Formation of a Persecuting Society* (Oxford: Blackwell, 1987).

36. See my *Eros and Magic*, p. 245.

Chapter 3. Dark Treasures

1. A. Leo Oppenheim, *Ancient Mesopotamia: Portrait of a Dead Civilization* (Chicago and London: The University of Chicago Press, 1964).

2. Thorkild Jacobsen, *The Treasures of Darkness: A History of Mesopotamian Religion* (New Haven and London: Yale University Press, 1976).

3. Sumerian and Akkadian texts are from James B. Pritchard, ed., *Ancient Near Eastern Texts Relating to the Old Testament* (Princeton: Princeton University Press, 1955), vol. 1; Sumerian translations by S. N. Kramer and Akkadian translations by E. A. Speiser (hereafter ANET). Some of the materials contained in this invaluable collection are included in the more accessible *The Ancient Near East*, vol. 1: *An Anthology of Texts and Pictures*, ed. J. B. Pritchard (Princeton: Princeton University Press, 1958), and in other anthologies such as Walter Beyerlin, ed., *Near Eastern Religious Texts Relating to the Old Testament* (London: SCM Press, 1978). Convenient summaries are contained in S. H. Hooke, *Middle Eastern Mythology* (Harmondsworth: Penguin Books, 1963). The Gilgamesh epic is widely accessible in the translation by N. K. Sandars, *The Epic of Gilgamesh* (Harmondsworth: Penguin Books, 1972). Jacobsen's *Treasures* contains enlightening comments on all these texts.

4. See Jacobsen, *Treasures*, p. 195.

5. Translated by Speiser, in Pritchard, ANET, p. 75.

6. Ibid., tablet 9:1, p. 88.

7. Ibid., tablet 9:2, verses 4–5, p. 88.

8. Ibid., tablet 10:3, p. 90.

9. Jacobsen, *Treasures*, p. 57.

10. Ibid., p. 60.

11. J.-M. Aynard, "Le jugement des morts chez les Assyro-Babyloniens," in *Sources orientales: le jugement des morts* (Paris: Seuil, 1961), pp. 90–91.

12. E. A. Speiser, in Pritchard, ANET, p. 97.
13. Ibid., tablet 12:84–85, p. 98.
14. Ibid., p. 118.

Chapter 4. Puppets, Playhouses, and Gods

1. Marie Weynants-Ronday, *Les Statues Vivantes* (Brussels: Fondation Egyptologique, 1926).
2. A. Rosalie David, *The Ancient Egyptians: Religious Beliefs and Practices* (London and New York: Routledge & Kegan Paul, 1982), p. 59.
3. Raymond O. Faulkner, trans., *The Ancient Egyptian Pyramid Texts* (Oxford: Clarendon Press, 1969).
4. Raymond O. Faulkner, trans., *The Ancient Egyptian Coffin Texts,* 3 vols. (Warminster: Aris & Philips, 1973–78); Paul Barguet, *Les textes des sarcophages égyptiens du Moyen Empire* (Paris: Éditions du Cerf, 1986).
5. Raymond O. Faulkner, trans., *The Ancient Egyptian Book of the Dead,* ed. Carol Andrews (New York: Macmillan, 1985).
6. Faulkner, *Pyramid Texts,* utterance 302.
7. Ibid., utterance 467.
8. Ibid., utterance 509.
9. Ibid., utterance 539.
10. Ibid., utterance 317.
11. Ibid., utterances 273–274.
12. Ibid., utterances 515–522.
13. Ibid., utterance 467.
14. Barguet, *Textes des sarcophages,* p. 13.
15. Faulkner, *Coffin Texts,* spell 473, part of a fishnet series that extends from spell 473 to 481.
16. Ibid., spell 479.
17. Barguet, *Textes des sarcophages,* p. 28.
18. Faulkner, *Coffin Texts,* spell 441.
19. Ibid., spell 443.
20. Barguet, *Textes des sarcophages,* p. 27.
21. Faulkner, *Coffin Texts,* spells 1029ff.
22. Ibid., spell 1131.
23. Ibid., spell 1156.
24. This was shown already by Raymond Weill, *Le Champ des Roseaux*

et le Champ des Offrandes dans la religion funéraire et la religion
générale (Paris: Paul Geuthner, 1936).
25. Ibid., p. 19.

Chapter 5. Crane Riding, Soul Raising, and Ghost Brides

1. Isabelle Robinet, *Méditation taoïste* (Paris: Dervy Livres, 1979), p. 68.
2. Ibid., p. 69.
3. Ibid., pp. 249–50.
4. After Berthold Laufer, *The Prehistory of Aviation*, Anthropological Series 18:1, Publication 253 (Chicago: Field Museum of Natural History, 1928), p. 29.
5. Ibid., p. 26.
6. Ibid.
7. Reported by J. J. M. de Groot in *The Religious System of China: Its Ancient Forms, Evolution, History and Present Aspect; Manners, Customs and Social Institutions Connected Therewith*, vols. 4–6 (Leiden: E. J. Brill, 1901–10), pp. 320–23.
8. Laufer, *Prehistory*, p. 28.
9. Ibid., p. 18.
10. Ibid., p. 15.
11. Ibid., pp. 14–17.
12. Ibid., p. 19.
13. Ibid., p. 23.
14. See note 7.
15. De Groot, *Religious System*, pp. 51–53.
16. Ibid., pp. 126–27.
17. Ibid., pp. 100–2.
18. Ibid., p. 103.
19. Ibid., pp. 103–4.
20. Ibid., pp. 105–6.
21. Ibid., pp. 134ff.
22. Ibid., pp. 190–91.
23. Alan J. A. Elliott, *Chinese Spirit-Medium Cults in Singapore* (London: School of Economics, 1955).

24. Ibid., p. 139.
25. David K. Jordan, *Gods, Ghosts and Ancestors: The Folk Religion of a Taiwanese Village* (Berkeley and Los Angeles: University of California Press, 1972), p. 141.
26. John Blofeld, who claims to have spent seventeen years in China prior to World War II, visited Taoist hermitages in which the most serious among the adepts were working toward the transmogrification of their flesh "into a shining adamantine substance, weightless yet hard as jade," although most Taoists commonly "fashion spirit-bodies that will be perfected before they die" (John Blofeld, *Taoist Mysteries and Magic,* Boulder: Shambhala Publications, 1982, pp. 47–48).
27. Michael Saso, *The Teachings of Taoist Master Chuang* (New Haven and London: Yale University Press, 1978).
28. Robinet, *Méditation,* p. 308.
29. John Lagerwey, *Taoist Ritual in Chinese Society and History* (New York and London: Macmillan-Collier, 1987).
30. Ibid., p. 53.
31. Ibid., pp. 53–55.
32. Ibid., p. 66.
33. Ibid., p. 69.
34. Ibid., p. 78.
35. Ibid., p. 80.
36. Ibid., p. 81.
37. Ibid., p. 83.
38. Ibid., p. 88.
39. *Tao tsang* 1221 (*Shang-ch'ing ling-pao ta-fa*), translated in Lagerwey, p. 156.
40. Lagerwey, *Taoist Ritual,* pp. 191–92.
41. Ibid., p. 197.
42. Ibid., pp. 216–28.

Chapter 6. Journeys through the Mind

1. R. Gordon Wasson and Wendy Doniger O'Flaherty, *Soma: Divine Mushroom of Immortality* (New York: Harcourt, Brace, Jovanovitch, n.d.); part 2, "The Post-Vedic History of the Soma," pp. 95–151, is by O'Flaherty.

2. See S. G. F. Brandon, *The Judgment of the Dead: The Idea of Life after Death in the Major Religions* (New York: Scribner's Sons, 1969), pp. 166–67.
3. See Geoffrey Parrinder, *The Indestructible Soul: The Nature of Man and Life after Death in Indian Thought* (London: Allen & Unwin, 1973), p. 88.
4. Herbert Günther [Guenther], *Das Seelenproblem in alteren Buddhismus* (Konstanz: K. Weller, 1949).
5. See Gherardo Gnoli, "Ashavan: Contributo allo studio del libro di Ardâ Wirâz," in *Iranica*, pp. 427–28.
6. Hemacandra, *Trisastisalakapurusacarita* 1, vols. 852–62, cited by William Norman Brown, *The Indian and Christian Miracles of Walking on the Water* (Chicago and London: Open Court, 1928), p. 16.
7. Patanjali, *Yogasutra* 3:42; see Brown, *Miracles*, p. 16.
8. See Mircea Eliade, *Yoga: Immortality and Freedom* (New York: Sheed & Ward, 1964), ch. 8.
9. J. Moussaieff Masson, *The Oceanic Feeling: The Origins of Religious Sentiment in Ancient India* (Doordrecht: Reidel, 1980), p. 33.
10. June McDaniel, *The Madness of the Saints: Ecstatic Religion in Bengal* (Chicago: The University of Chicago Press, 1989), p. 93.
11. Ibid., pp. 94–95.
12. Ibid., p. 101.
13. *Digha nikaga* 2; cited in Günther, *Seelenproblem*, and in Brown, *Miracles*, p. 15 (translation mine).
14. *Digha nikaya*, "Mahaparinibbana," sutta 16, cited by Brown, *Miracles*, p. 18.
15. *Lalita vistara*, cited by Brown, *Miracles*, p. 18. For other references, see above.
16. John S. Strong, "Wenn der magische Flucht misslingt," in H. P. Duerr ed., *Sehnsucht nach dem Ursprung* (Frankfurt: Syndicat 1983), pp. 503–18; see my *Expériences de l'extase* (Paris: Payot, 1984), pp. 99–101.
17. J. R. Haldar, *Early Buddhist Mythology* (London: Luzac & Co., 1977); Bimala Charan Law, *The Buddhist Conception of Spirits* (Calcutta: Thacker, Spink & Co., 1923).
18. See *The Tibetan Book of the Great Liberation or The Method of Realizing Nirvana through Knowing the Mind*, ed. and intro. by

W. Y. Evans-Wentz (London, Oxford, and New York: Oxford University Press, 1968).

19. Two translations of the *Bardo thödöl* are now available: the traditional one, *The Tibetan Book of the Dead, or The After-Death Experiences on the Bardo Plane,* trans. Lama Kazi Dawa Samdup, ed. W. Y. Evans-Wentz (London, Oxford, and New York: Oxford University Press, 1957); and a more recent and more accurate one, *The Tibetan Book of the Dead: The Great Liberation through Hearing in the Bardo,* by Guru Rinpoche according to Karma Lingpa, trans. Francesa Fremantle and Chögyam Trungpa (Berkeley and London: Shambhala Publications, 1975).

20. Fremantle and Trungpa, *Tibetan Book of the Dead,* p. 40.

21. Ibid., pp. 39–40.

22. See Law, *Buddhist Conception,* pp. 2ff.

23. Fremantle and Trungpa, *Tibetan Book of the Dead,* p. 60.

24. Ibid., p. 69.

25. Ibid.

26. Ibid., pp. 216–22.

27. Lama Kazi Dawa Samdup, trans., *Tibetan Yoga and Secret Doctrines, or Seven Books of Wisdom of the Great Path,* ed. and intro. by W. Y. Evans-Wentz (London, Oxford, and New York: Oxford University Press, 1958).

28. Ibid., pp. 216–22.

29. See J. J. L. Duyvendak, *A Chinese "Divina Commedia"* (Leiden: Brill, 1952), p. 8.

30. Ibid., pp. 18–20.

31. Ibid., pp. 25–27.

32. Ibid., p. 57.

33. Anthony C. Yu, trans. and ed., *The Journey to the West,* 4 vols. (Chicago and London: Chicago University Press, 1977–86).

34. Anthony C. Yu, "Two Literary Examples of Religious Pilgrimage: The *Commedia* and *The Journey to the West,*" in *History of Religions* 22 (1983), pp. 215–16.

35. See Francisca Cho Bantly, "Buddhist Allegory in the *Journey to the West,*" in *The Journal of Asian Studies* 48 (1989), pp. 512–24.

Chapter 7. From Furor to Spiritual Vision

1. See my *Psychanodia I,* and a set of articles cited in my *Expériences de l'extase,* p. 173. Among the discussions of this book I would

especially like to mention the review by Jacques Flamant (in *Revue des Études Latines,* 1986) and a note by Philippe Gignoux, "Apocalypses et voyages extra-terrestres dans l'Iran mazdéen," in Claude Kappler, ed., *Apocalypses et voyages dans l'au-delá* (Paris: Cerf, 1987), pp. 370–71. Gignoux, one of the greatest specialists in Iranian apocalypses, totally agrees with my rejection of the theory of the Iranian background of Greek, Jewish, and Christian apocalyptic traditions.

2. H. S. Nyberg, *Die Religionen des Alten Iran,* trans. into German by H. H. Schaeder (Leipzig: J. C. Hinrichs, 1938).

3. See chapter 6, above.

4. See Gnoli "Ashavan," p. 438; see also my "Ascension," in L. E. Sullivan, ed., *Death, Afterlife, and the Soul* (New York: Macmillan, 1989), p. 113.

5. Herodotus, 4:73–75; see Karl Meuli, "Scythica," In *Hermes* 70 (1935), pp. 121–76.

6. Ginzburg, *Storia notturna,* p. 188.

7. Gherardo Gnoli, "Lo stato di 'maga,' " in AION 15 (1965), pp. 105–17.

8. Gnoli, "Ashavan."

9. Philippe Gignoux, "Corps osseux et âme osseuse: essai sur le chamanisme dans l'Iran ancien," in *Journal Asiatique* 277 (1979), pp. 41–79.

10. Philippe Gignoux, "Apocalypses," pp. 368–70.

11. Ibid., pp. 366–67. Gignoux has recently translated the *Book of Arda Viraz* into French: *Le Livre d'Ardâ Virâz* (Paris: ADPF, 1984). We will rely here on the most recent English translation, which is Fereydun Vahman, trans., *Ardâ Wirâz Nâmag: The Iranian Divina Commedia* (London and Malmo: Curzon Press, 1986).

12. Gnoli, "Ashavan," pp. 437–38.

13. Gignoux, "Apocalypses," p. 366.

14. *Dênkart* 7.4.75, in Marijan Molé "Le jugement des morts dans l'Iran préislamique," in *Sources orientales: le jugement des morts* (Paris: Seuil, 1961), p. 151.

15. Ibid., pp. 152–55.

16. The latest historical name occurring in the narrative belongs to the priest (*mobâd*) Wehshâpûhr, who lived under Xosrau I (531–79). Some scholars see this as an interpolation in an otherwise

more ancient text, yet there is no evidence for the existence of an earlier apocalypse. The story of Virâz was probably composed some time during the late Sassanian period, before the Muslim conquest of Persia in the seventh century.

17. Vahman, *Ardâ Wirâz*, pp. 227–28.
18. Ibid., p. 228, citing the *Persian Rivayat*.
19. Ibid., pp. 246–48.
20. Molé, "Jugement des morts," pp. 158–60.
21. These texts are found in Molé, pp. 162ff.
22. Vahman, *Ardâ Wirâz*, p. 199.
23. Ibid.
24. Ibid., p. 201.
25. Ibid., p. 202.
26. Ibid., pp. 208–9.
27. Ibid., p. 210.
28. Ibid., p. 212.

Chapter 8. Greek Medicine Men

1. Reference is made here to the prose translation of *The Odyssey* by S. H. Butcher and Andrew Lang (New York: Macmillan, 1888).
2. M. A. Gimbutas, *The Goddesses and Gods of Old Europe, 6500–3500 B.C. Myths and Cult Images*, 2d ed. (Berkeley and Los Angeles: University of California Press, 1982), p. 9.
3. Elémire Zolla, "Circe, la donna," in *Verità segrete esposte in evidenza: Sincretismo e fantasia, contemplazione ed esotericità* (Padua: Marsilio, 1990), pp. 131–52.
4. In actuality the autobiography is an eighteenth-century biography by the crazy saint Taksham; see note 5.
5. Keith Dowman, *Sky Dancer: The Secret Life and Songs of the Lady Yeshe Tsogyel* (London and Boston: Routledge & Kegan Paul, 1984). Western examples of attitudes of religious women toward rapists can be found in my "A Corpus for the Body," in *The Journal for Modern History*, March, 1991.
6. Trans. in Dowman, *Sky Dancer*, p. 16.
7. Ibid.
8. Ibid.

9. Ibid., p. 78.

10. Zolla, "Circe," p. 133.

11. Butcher and Lang, *Odyssey* 10:514–15, p. 169.

12. W. F. Jackson Knight, *Elysion: On Ancient Greek and Roman Beliefs Concerning a Life after Death* (London: Rider & Co., 1970).

13. Ibid., p. 101, the *Iliad* (18:535–7).

14. Ibid., p. 111.

15. "To sacrifice" is *thyein* to the gods, but *enagizein* to the dead; see ibid., p. 59.

16. Ibid., p. 61.

17. See Pierre Boyancé, *Le culte des Muses chez les philosophes grecs: Étude d'histoire et de psychologie religieuses* (1936; reprint Paris: De Boccard, 1972), pp. 244–46.

18. Boyancé, *Culte des Muses,* p. 69.

19. See W. R. Halliday, *Greek Divination: A Study of Its Methods and Principles* (London: Macmillan, 1913), p. 239.

20. Ibid., p. 241.

21. Ibid., p. 245.

22. Boyancé, *le Culte des Muses,* pp. 142–43.

23. See Jean Yoyotte, "Le jugement des morts en Égypte ancienne," in *Sources orientales,* vol. 5: *Le jugement des morts* (Paris: Seuil, 1961), pp. 41–50.

24. P. Raingeard, *Hermès Psychagogue: Essai sur les origines du culte d'Hermès* (Paris: Belles Lettres, 1935).

25. See John Pollard, *Seers, Shrines and Sirens: The Greek Religious Revolution of the 6th century* B.C. (London: Allen & Unwin, 1965), pp. 130ff.

26. See E. J. Edelstein and L. Edelstein, trans., *Asclepius: A Collection and Interpretation of the Testimonies,* 2 vols. (Baltimore: Johns Hopkins Press, 1945), vol. 1, pp. 1ff.; *Pythiae* 3:1–58.

27. Diodorus, *Bibliotheca Historica* 4:71, in ibid., vol. 1, p. 10.

28. Ibid., vol. 1, pp. 108ff.

29. Aelius Aristides, *Oratio* 48.31–35, in ibid., vol. 1, pp. 210–11.

30. See especially Rudolf Herzog, *Die Wunderheilungen von Epidauros: Ein Beitrag zur Geschichte der Medizin und der Religion* (Leipzig: Dieterich, 1931).

31. Sometimes the vision was very vivid like the one reported by

Aelius Aristides, *Oratio* 48.31–35, in Edelstein and Edelstein, *Asclepius,* vol. 1, p. 210.

32. Edelstein and Edelstein, *Asclepius,* vol. 1, pp. 204ff.

33. Inscription 14 in ibid., vol. 1, p. 232.

34. Inscription 23 in ibid., vol. 1, p. 234.

35. Inscription 42 in ibid., vol. 1, p. 237.

36. Ibid., vol. 2, p. 149.

37. For a larger description of these incubation rites, see my *Psychanodia,* vol. 1, pp. 43ff.; *Expériences de l'extase,* pp. 104ff; and *Iter in silvis,* vol. 1, pp. 53ff., with comprehensive bibliography.

38. See my *Expériences de l'extase,* p. 106.

39. Ibid., pp. 106–7.

40. Hans Dieter Betz, "The Problem of Apocalyptic Genre in Greek and Hellenistic Literature: The Case of the Oracle of Trophonius," in David Hellholm, ed., *Apocalypticism in the Mediterranean World and the Near East: Proceedings of the International Colloquium on Apocalypticism, Uppsala, August 12–17, 1979* (Tübingen: Mohr [Siebeck], 1983), p. 579.

41. Ibid., p. 583.

42. Gimbutas, *Goddesses,* pp. 195ff.

43. Bennett Simon, *Mind and Madness in Ancient Greece: The Classical Roots of Modern Psychiatry* (Ithaca and London: Cornell University Press, 1978), p. 251.

44. See sources in my "Iatroi kai manteis: Sulle strutture dell'estatismo greco," in *Studi Storico-Religiosi* 4 (1980) pp. 287–303; and in my *Psychanodia,* pp. 35ff. and *Expériences de l'extase,* pp. 25ff.

45. See Pollard, *Seers,* p. 108.

46. See my "Iatroi Kei manteis," 287–303.

47. Ibid.

48. See Halliday, *Divination,* p. 91.

49. Porphyry, *Life of Pythagoras,* ch. 17.

50. All references are contained in my works mentioned in note 44 above.

51. The people of the Uttarakuru mentioned in the Indian epics (*Râmâyana* 4.43; *Mahâbhârata* 6.7) are similar to the Hyperboreans. The Indian material was known in Greece and Rome. Pliny

speaks of the Attacori (*Natural History* 4.90; 6.55) and Ptolemy
mentions the Ottorokorrai (*Geographica* 6.16.5).

52. E. R. Dodds, *The Greeks and the Irrational*, (Berkeley and Los
Angeles: California University Press, 1951); and F. M. Cornford,
Principium Sapientiae (Cambridge: Cambridge University Press,
1952).

53. W. Burkert, *Lore and Science in Ancient Pythagoreanism* (Cambridge,
Mass.: Harvard University Press, 1972).

54. On ancient Greek apocalypses, see Walter Burkert, "Apocalyptik
im fruhen Griechentum: Impulse und Transformationen," in
Hellholm, *Apocalypticism*, pp. 235ff.

55. See my *Psychoanodia*, pp. 26ff. and *Expériences de l'extase*, pp. 46ff.,
based on my "Démonisation du cosmos et dualisme gnostique,"
in *Revue de l'histoire des religions* 3 (1979).

56. His observations are summarized in my *Expériences de l'extase*,
pp. 37–38.

57. F. R. Wehrli, *Die Schule des Aristoteles*, vol. 7 (Basel: Schwabe,
1957).

58. J. D. P. Bolton, *Aristeas of Proconnesus* (Oxford: Clarendon Press,
1962).

59. All extant evidence is analyzed in my *Psychanodia*, pp. 40ff. and
in *Expériences de l'extase*, pp. 50ff.

60. See the discussion in my *Psychanodia*, pp. 41ff., and in my
Expériences de l'extase, pp. 37–38.

61. Labeo, fragment 11, translated in my *Expériences de l'extase*, p. 37.

62. Plutarch, *De genio Socratis* 591a, in Ph. H. de Lacy and B.
Einarson, eds. and trans., *Moralia*, vol. 7 (London and Cambridge: Loeb Classical Library, 1959).

63. Ibid., 591c.

64. *De facie in orbe lunae* 943d, in H. H. Cherniss and W. C.
Helmbold, eds. and trans., *Moralia*, vol. 12 (London and Cambridge: Loeb Classical Library, 1957).

65. Ibid., 944c.

66. On this myth, see especially my *Psychanodia*, pp. 43ff.; *Expériences
de l'extase*, pp. 111ff., based on my essay "Inter lunam terrasque.
. . . Incubazione, catalessi ed estasi in Plutarco," in *Iter in silvis*,
pp. 53ff.

67. *De sera* 563d, our translation.

68. Ibid., 563e.
69. See Emily B. Lyle, "Dumézil's Three Functions and Indo-European Cosmic Structure," in *History of Religions* 22 (1982), pp. 25–44.
70. See my *Psychanodia*, pp. 46–47; *Expériences de l'extase*, p. 114.
71. See the fragment of *de anima*, in Stobaeus, *Florilegium* 1089h.
72. New light has been shed on this episode by an excellent article by Michel Tardieu, "Comme à travers un tuyau. . . .," in *Colloque international sur les textes de Nag Hammadi* (Toronto and Louvain: Laval University Press–Peeters, 1981), pp. 151–77.
73. The terms "subjectification" and "interiorization" have been applied by Hans Jonas to Plotinus's mysticism, in comparison with "objective" types of experience such as those featured in Gnosticism. See my *Gnosticismo e pensiero contemporaneo: Hans Jonas* (Rome: L'Erma di Brettschneider, 1985).

Chapter 9. The Seven Palaces and the Chariot of God

1. John J. Collins, ed., *Apocalypse: The Morphology of a Genre,* in *Semeia: An Experimental Journal for Biblical Criticism* 14 (1979). The issue contains papers by J. J. Collins (introduction, Jewish apocalypses, Persian apocalypses), Adela Yarbro Collins (early Christian apocalypses), F. T. Fallon (Gnostic apocalypses), A. J. Saldarini (rabbinical literature and Jewish mysticism). Much has been published lately on apocalypticism, yet notwithstanding rapidly shifting perspectives, the volume edited by Collins still retains all its value. Judaic, Christian and other texts related to heavenly ascent are also discussed in Alan F. Segal, "Heavenly Ascent in Hellenistic Judaism, Early Christianity and their Environment," in *Aufstieg und Niedergang der römischen Welt* (Berlin: De Gruyter, 1980), vol. 2, 23.2, pp. 1222–94.
2. Collins, introduction to *Apocalypse: Morphology,* p. 9.
3. On the *Ascension of Isaiah* (or his vision), see my "La Visione di Isaia e la tematica della 'Himmelsreise,' " in M. Pesce, ed., *Isaia, il diletto e la Chiesa,* Bologna, 1983, pp. 95–116.
4. See my *Psychanodia,* pp. 6–7.

5. Collections of the Jewish apocalypses in translation are: J. H. Charlesworth, ed., *The Old Testament Pseudepigrapha,* vol. 1: *Apocalyptic Literature and Testaments* (Garden City, Doubleday, 1983) and the older translation, in R. H. Charles, ed., *The Apocrypha and Pseudepigrapha of the Old Testament,* vol. 2: *Pseudepigrapha* (Oxford: Clarendon Press, 1913). See J. H. Charlesworth, *The Pseudepigrapha and Modern Study with a Supplement* (Chico, Calif.: Scholars Press, 1981) and J. J. Collins, *The Apocalyptic Imagination: An Introduction to the Jewish Matrix of Christianity* (New York: Crossroads, 1984).

6. The text is *Paralipomena Jeremiae (3 Baruch)* 3.3–5, in J. R. Harris, "The Rest of the Words of Baruch," in *Haverford College Studies* 2 (1989). Jeremiah sent Abimelech to Agrippa's vineyard to gather figs. He lay to rest under a tree and slept soundly for sixty-six years; see my *Psychanodia,* p. 63, n. 16.

7. Mary Dean-Otting, *Heavenly Journeys: A Study of the Motif in Hellenistic Jewish Literature* (Frankfurt, Bern, and New York: Peter Lang, 1984).

8. *De vita Mosis* 2.28ff.

9. Josephus, *Jewish Antiquities* 4.326; Dean-Otting, *Heavenly Journeys,* p. 5.

10. See Michael A. Knibb, *The Ethiopic Book of Enoch: A New Edition in the Light of the Aramaic Dead Sea Fragments,* 2 vols. (Oxford: Clarendon Press, 1970). The author bases his text on thirty-three Ethiopic manuscripts, the oldest of which was written in the fifteenth century. Fragments of eleven manuscripts of Enoch were found at Qumran, containing 196 lines out of the total of 1,062 lines of the Ethiopic version. A few Aramaic fragments differ largely from the Ethiopic text. The Greek version of *1 Enoch* derives from four sources; see the texts in Matthew Black, *Apocalypsis Henochi Graece* (Leiden: Brill, 1970). The three most important Greek manuscripts have been dated back to the fourth to sixth centuries C.E. The book of Enoch was canonical in the Ethiopic church. It was translated from Greek into Ethiopic between the fourth and the sixth centuries C.E.

11. J. T. Milik, *The Books of Enoch: Aramaic Fragments of Qumran Cave 4* (Oxford: Clarendon Press, 1976).

12. Dean-Otting, *Heavenly Journeys,* p. 41.

13. Johann Maier, "Das Gefährdungsmotiv bei der Himmelsreise in der jüdischen Apokalyptik und 'Gnosis,'" in *Kairos* 5 (1963), pp. 18–40.

14. Collins speaks of an "Enoch movement" that composed the different parts of *1 Enoch* (*Apocalyptic Imagination*, pp. 56–63).

15. Collins, *Apocalyptic Imagination*, p. 196.

16. Text in M. de Jonge, *Testamenta XII Patriarchorum* (Leiden: Brill, 1964); commentary in H. W. Hollander and M. de Jonge, *The Testaments of the Twelve Patriarchs: A Commentary* (Leiden: Brill, 1985). The earliest extant Greek manuscript of this writing is dated to the tenth century C.E., yet the earliest mention of the *Testaments* comes from Origen of Alexandria (d. 254 C.E.). In its present form, the writing may be Christian, yet it is undeniably based on an ancient Jewish tradition. Fragments of an Aramaic *Testament of Levi* have been known for quite a while, and a scroll of Levi has been dug up in Qumran (cave 4), whereas other fragments were found in cave 1. It is not clear in what language the present version of the *Testaments* was first composed. Scholars like de Jonge believe it was directly written in Greek; others prefer Hebrew, or even Aramaic, as the original language.

17. See Dean-Otting, *Heavenly Journeys,* pp. 80–81.

18. *Testament of Levi* 3.3, trans. in Hollander and de Jonge, *Patriarchs,* p. 136.

19. Text in J.-C. Picard, *Apocalypsis Baruchi Graece* (Leiden: Brill, 1967); A.-M. Denis, *Concordance de l'Apocalypse grecque de Baruch* (Louvain: Institut Orientaliste, 1970).

20. See Dean-Otting, *Heavenly Journeys,* pp. 98–152.

21. Text edited by Matthias Delcor, *Le Testament d'Abraham* (Leiden: Brill, 1973); text and translation in Michael E. Stone, *The Testament of Abraham* (Missoula: Scholars Press, 1972). Discussion in George W. E. Nickelsburg Jr., ed., *Studies on the Testament of Abraham* (Missoula: Scholars Press, 1976). Two Greek recensions are extant: a *longior* and a *brevior,* together with versions in several other languages. Most scholars favor the dating of the *Testament of Abraham* to the first century C.E.

22. Martha Himmelfarb, *Tours of Hell: An Apocalyptic Form in Jewish and Christian Literature* (Philadelphia: Fortress, 1985).

23. See especially my *Expériences de l'extase,* p. 20.

24. For sources and secondary literature see my "Visione di Isaia," pp. 95–111.

25. See my "Visione di Isaia," p. 104.

26. This hypothesis is not accepted, however, by the latest editors of the extant versions of the *Ascension of Isaiah,* in *Corpus Christianorum: Series Apocryphorum* (Belgium: Brepols, forthcoming).

27. Joseph Dan, *Gershom Scholem and the Mystical Dimension of Jewish History* (New York and London: New York University Press, 1987), p. 39.

28. Ithamar Gruenwald is the author of two fundamental works on early Jewish mysticism: *Apocalyptic and Merkavah Mysticism* (Leiden and Cologne: Brill, 1980) and *From Apocalypticism to Gnosticism: Studies in Apocalypticism, Merkavah Mysticism and Gnosticism* (Frankfurt, Bern, New York, and Paris: Peter Lang, 1988).

29. Michael A. Morgan, trans., *Sefer ha-razim: The Book of Mysteries* (Chico: Scholars Press, 1983).

30. The collected texts are found in Peter Schaeffer, *Synopse zur Hekhalot-Literatur* (Tubingen: Mohr, 1981).

31. See P. Alexander, "3 (Hebrew Apocalypse of) Enoch," in Charlesworth, *Pseudepigrapha,* vol. 1, pp. 223–315.

32. Ira Chernus, "The Pilgrimage to the Merkavah: An Interpretation of Early Jewish Mysticism," in *Early Jewish Mysticism: Proceedings of the First International Conference on the History of Jewish Mysticism* (Jerusalem: The Hebrew University of Jerusalem, 1987).

33. See Gruenwald, *Apocalypticism to Gnosticism,* p. 63.

34. Translated in David J. Halperin, *The Merkabah in Rabbinic Literature* (New Haven: American Oriental Society, 1980), p. 3.

35. See my *Expériences de l'extase,* p. 157.

36. Ibid., p. 154.

37. The text is found in Schaefer, *Synopse,* trans. in Naomi Janowitz, *The Poetics of Ascent: Theories of Language in a Rabbinic Ascent Text* (New York: SUNY Press, 1989), pp. 31–66.

38. *Maaseh Merkabah,* v. 714–18, in Janowitz, *Poetics,* p. 51.

39. *Pirkei Hekhaloth* 15:2, in David R. Blumenthal, *Understanding Jewish Mysticism: A Source Reader; The Merkabah Tradition and the Zoharic Tradition* (New York: Ktav, 1978), p. 57; Hebrew text based on ch. 15–29 of *Hekhaloth Rabbati,* from S. A. Wertheimer, *Batei*

Midrashot, trans. Lauren Grodner, ed. D. R. Blumenthal (Jerusalem: Mossad Harav Kook, 1968), vol. 1, pp. 90–114.

40. *Pirkei Hekhaloth* 22:3, Blumenthal, *Understanding,* p. 73.
41. Ibid., 16:4, p. 60.
42. *Hekhaloth Rabbati,* 17:2–7, Blumenthal, *Understanding.*
43. Ibid., 20:4, p. 67.
44. Ibid., 23:5, p. 76.
45. Ibid., 24:2.
46. *Tosefta Hagigah,* 113; *Jerushalmi Hagigah,* 2.1.77b; *Babli Hagigah,* 14b; see Maier, "Gefährdungsmotiv," p. 28.
47. *Babli Hagigah,* 15b; see Gruenwald, *Apocalyptic and Merkabah,* p. 87.
48. *Babli Sukkha,* 51b; *Babli Baba bathra,* 4a; see Maier, "Gefährdungsmotiv," p. 35.
49. See my *Expériences de l'extase,* pp. 72ff., with references.
50. Morgan, *Sefer ha-Razim,* 5, p. 17.
51. Ibid., 11–17 p. 18, with some changes in Morgan's translation.
52. On heavenly songs, see especially Gershom Scholem, *Jewish Gnosticism, Merkabah Mysticism and Talmudic Tradition* (New York: Jewish Theological Seminary, 1965).
53. See my "Ascension," p. 113.
54. See especially his *Jewish Gnosticism* (see note 52).
55. From Gruenwald, *Apocalypticism to Gnosticism,* p. 195.
56. Francis T. Fallon, "The Gnostic Apocalypses," in Collins, *Apocalypse: Morphology,* pp. 123–58; Madeleine Scopello, "Contes apocalyptiques et apocalypses philosophiques dans la bibliothèque de Nag Hammadi" in Claude Kappler, ed., *Apocalypses et voyages dans l'au de là,* pp. 321–50.
57. See my *Expériences de l'extase,* pp. 11–17; and Giovanni Casadio, "La visione in Marco il Mago e nella gnosi di tipo sethiano," in *Augustinianum* 29 (1989), pp. 123–46.
58. American scholars notoriously ignore European research in the field of Gnosticism and late antiquity. This ignorance works entirely to their disadvantage.
59. The fundamental text of Hippolytus, *Refutatio omnium haeresium* 5.19–22 has been recently translated and commented upon in an excellent article by Giovanni Casadio, "Anthropologia gnostica e antropologia orfica nella notizia di lppolito sui sethiani,"

in F. Vattioni, ed., *Sangue e antropologia nella teologia* (Rome: 1989), pp. 1295–1350. References are made to his translation.

60. We shall refrain here from engaging in the interminable and misconceived discussion concerning "Sethian Gnosticism," which is an invention of modern heresiologists. The label "Sethian" refers here exclusively to Hippolytus's system. For a clear statement of my position, see *Les Gnoses dualistes d'Occident* (Paris: Plon, 1990).

61. See my *Eros and Magic*.

62. After Casadio, "Antropologia," p. 1313.

63. See discussion in ibid., pp. 1329ff. Casadio believes that Sethian cosmogony derives from an ancient Orphic cosmogony.

64. Ibid., p. 1315.

65. See my *Expériences de l'extase*, pp. 13–14.

66. See Casadio, "Antropologia," p. 1322.

67. *Refutatio* 5.17; see my *Expériences de l'extase*, pp. 15–16.

68. Epiphanius, *Panarion*, 37, trans. by Frank Williams, *The Panarion of Epiphanus of Salamis*, book 1 (secs. 1–46) (Leiden: Brill, 1987), pp. 241ff.

69. Williams, *Panarion*, 4.4, p. 244.

70. Ibid., 5.6–7 p. 245.

71. See my *Expériences de l'extase*, pp. 128–29 for the description of such rituals.

72. But see Casadio, "Visione di Marco."

73. Alasdair Livingstone, *Mystical and Mythological Explanatory Works of Assyrian and Babylonian Scholars* (Oxford: Clarendon, 1986).

74. For other Gnostic reports of otherworldly journeys, see especially Casadio, "Visione di Marco."

75. Carl Schmidt and W. Till, eds., *Koptish-gnostische Schriften, Part 1: Die Pistis Sophia, Die beiden Bücher des Jeu, Unbekanntes altgnostisches Werk* (Berlin: Akademie 1954); same Coptic text, with English translation, in Violet MacDermont, trans., *The Books of Jeu and the Untitled Text in the Bruce Codex* (Leiden: Brill, 1978).

76. In Faulkner, *Egyptian Book of the Dead*, p. 145.

77. See my *Expériences de l'extase*, pp. 127–28.

78. Testimonies are gathered by Violet MacDermot, *The Cult of the Seer in the Ancient Middle East: A Contribution to Current Research on*

Hallucinations Drawn from Coptic and Other Texts (London: Wellcome Institute of the History of Medicine, 1971), pp. 538–74.
79. Ibid., pp. 541–42.
80. Ibid.
81. Ibid., pp. 551–53.
82. See especially Moshe Idel's books, *Studies in Ecstatic Kabbalah* (Albany: SUNY Press, 1988); *The Mystical Experience in Abraham Abulafia* (Albany: SUNY Press, 1988); and his synthesis, *Kabbalah: New Perspectives* (New Haven and London: Yale University Press, 1988).
83. See Nathaniel Deutsch, review of Idel's *Ecstatic Kabbalah,* in *Incognita* 1 (1990), pp. 91–93.
84. See Moshe Idel, "Métaphores et pratiques sexuelles dans la Cabale," offprint.
85. Idel, *Kabbalah,* pp. 75–88.
86. Ibid., pp. 78–96.
87. Ibid., pp. 97–103.
88. Ibid., pp. 103–11.
89. Ibid., p. 91.
90. Ibid., pp. 92–93.
91. Translated in Idel, *Kabbalah,* p. 94.
92. Louis Jacobs, trans., *On Ecstasy: A Tract by Dov Baer* (New York: Chappaqua, 1963).
93. From Jacobs's introduction in *On Ecstasy,* p. 15.
94. Jacobs, *On Ecstasy,* p. 68.
95. Ibid., p. 69.
96. Ibid., p. 165.

Chapter 10. Interplanetary Tours

1. Macrobius, *Commentary on the Dream of Scipio* 1.12.13–14, based on the English translation by William Harris Stahl (New York: Columbia University Press, 1952), pp. 136–37, slightly modified.
2. On Macrobius, see the excellent book by Jacques Flammant, *Macrobe et le néo-platonisme latin, à la fin du IVe siecle* (Leiden: Brill, 1977).
3. A complete survey of Gnostic sources and bibliography is provided in my *Gnoses dualistes.*

4. The *Apocryphon of John* (hereafter AJ) is quoted from Michel Tardieu, *Ecrits gnostiques: Codex de Berlin* (Paris: Cerf, 1984); the Berlin Codex (hereafter BC) is quoted from W. Till, trans. and ed., *Die gnostischen Schriften des koptischen Papyrus Berolinensis 8502* (Berlin: Akademie, 1955). If not otherwise stated, hereafter other Gnostic tractates are quoted from J. M. Robinson, ed., *The Gnostic Library* (San Francisco: Harper & Row, 1988).

5. Or: In our resemblance; AJ 2:15, Tardieu, *Ecrits,* pp. 1–4; BG, Till, *Gnostischen Scriften,* p. 137.

6. BC, Till, *Gnostischen Schriften,* p. 138.

7. Ibid., p. 139.

8. AJ 2 and 4, Tardieu, *Ecrits,* pp. 125–27.

9. See my *Expériences de l'extase,* pp. 122ff.

10. AJ 2 and 4, Tardieu, *Ecrits,* pp. 128ff.

11. Ibid., pp. 311–14.

12. BC, Till, *Gnostischen Schriften,* p. 142.

13. Ibid., p. 146.

14. AJ 2, Tardieu, *Ecrits,* p. 137.

15. Ibid., p. 157ff., and Till, *Gnostischen Schriften,* p. 184.

16. AJ 2, Tardieu, *Ecrits,* pp. 157ff.

17. BC, Till, *Gnostischen Schriften,* p. 174.

18. Ibid., p. 178, and Tardieu, *Ecrits,* pp. 33ff, p. 154.

19. See my *Psychanodia I,* and *Expériences de l'extase,* pp. 117–44.

20. *Pistis Sophia,* Schmidt and Till, *Koptish-gnostische Schriften,* p. 183, and MacDermot, *Book of Jeu,* pp. 283ff.

21. Schmidt and Till, *Koptish-gnostische Schriften,* ch. 113, p. 191.

22. Ibid., ch. 115, pp. 193ff.

23. Ibid., ch. 111, pp. 183–89.

24. *Pistis Sophia,* Schmidt and Till, *Koptish-gnostische Schriften,* pp. 217ff, and MacDermot, *Book of Jeu,* pp. 331–46.

25. *Enduma,* ch. 131, Schmidt and Till, *Koptish-gnostische Schriften,* p. 219.

26. Schmidt and Till, *Koptish-gnostische Schriften,* ch. 136ff., pp. 234ff.

27. Ibid., ch. 131, pp. 219ff.

28. Ibid., ch. 132, p. 223.

29. Ibid., ch. 132, pp. 224–26, and MacDermot, *Book of Jeu,* pp. 342–45.

30. See my "Astrology" in *The Encyclopedia of Religion* (New York: Macmillan, 1987).

31. See especially my *Psychanodia,* and *Expériences de l'extase.* Most of my articles prior to 1984 are mentioned in the latter, p. 173. Since then I have published the article on "Ascension" in the *Encyclopedia of Religion* and prepared an article on "Himmelsreise (heidnisch)" for *Reallexikon fur Antike und Christentum* (RAC); I understand it will now appear as "Jenseitsreise." I have also prepared an article entitled "Hypostasierung" for RAC.

32. See my *Psychanodia,* pp. 48–54, and *Expériences de l'extase,* pp. 119–52.

33. For analysis and bibliography, see my *Gnoses dualistes,* ch. 7.

34. For a full exposition of this myth in its context, see my *Gnoses dualistes,* ch. 9.

35. See especially my *Expériences de l'extase,* pp. 79ff., based on my "L'Ascension de l'âme dans les mystères et hors des mystères," in U. Bianchi and M. J. Vermaseren, eds., *La soteriologia dei culti orientali nell'Impero Romano* (Leiden: Brill, 1982), pp. 276–302; my *Expériences de l'extase,* pp. 93–101, based on my "Le vol magique dans l'Antiquité tardive," in *Revue de l'Histoire des Religions* 198 (1981), pp. 57–66; and my *Expériences de l'extase,* pp. 119–44, based on my "Ordine e disordine delle sfere," in *Aevum* 55 (1981), pp. 96–110.

36. *Metamorphoses* 11.23; my translation.

37. Origen, *Against Celsus* 6.22, edition M. Borret (Paris: Cerf, 1967), vol. 3, p. 233; my translation.

38. See my *Expériences de l'extase,* pp. 86ff.

39. For an ingenious interpretation of Mithraism, see David Ulansey, *The Origins of the Mithraic Mysteries: Cosmology and Salvation in the Ancient World* (New York and Oxford: Oxford University Press, 1989).

40. See Flamant's article in Bianchi and Vermaseren, *Soteriologia.*

41. See my *Expériences de l'extase,* p. 130.

42. Fragment 164, in Edouard des Places, *Oracles chaldaïques: Avec un choix de commentaires anciens* (Paris: Belles Lettres, 1971) p. 106; see also Hans Lewy, *Chaldaean Oracles and Theurgy* (Paris: Etudes Augustiniennes, 1978).

43. See des Places, *Oracles chaldaïques*, p. 169; this passage is my translation.
44. See my *Expériences de l'extase*, p. 129.
45. Ibid., p. 138.
46. Proclus, *Elements of Theology*, 209, ed. and trans. E. R. Dodds (Oxford: Clarendon, 1963), p. 182.
47. *I Quaestio* 89aI; see my *Eros and Magic*, p. 5.
48. Translated by Margaret Cook and myself in my *Eros and Magic*, p. 115.
49. Ficino, *De Amore* 6.4, translated in my *Eros and Magic*, pp. 42–44 by Margaret Cook, with minor revisions.

Chapter 11. The Apogee of Otherworldly Journeys

1. See Claude Kappler, "L'Apocalypse latine de Paul," in Claude Kappler, ed., *Apocalypses et voyages*, pp. 237–66. The most common long version is translated by E. Gardiner in *Visions of Heaven and Hell before Dante* (New York: Italica, 1989).
2. *Apocalypse of Paul*, translated by Gardiner in *Visions*, p. 18, with slight changes.
3. Colleen McDannell and Bernhard Lang, *Heaven: A History* (New Haven and London: Yale University Press, 1988), p. 100.
4. Himmelfarb, *Tours of Hell*. The texts analyzed by Himmelfarb include: *The Apocalypse of Peter* (mid-second century C.E.), the sixth chapter of the *Acts of Thomas* (first half third century), the Coptic *Apocalypse of Zephaniah* (fourth or fifth century), the *Apocalypse of Paul*, the Ethiopic *Apocalypse of Mary*, derived from the *Apocalypse of Paul*, the Ethiopic *Apocalypse of Baruch* (after 550 C.E., dependent on the *Apocalypse of Paul*), the Ethiopian Falasha *Apocalypse of Gorgorios*, the Greek *Apocalypse of Mary* (before ninth century), the *Ezra Apocalypses* (tenth century), the *Testament of Isaac* (extant in Coptic, Arabic, and Ethiopic versions, dependent on the *Testament of Abraham*), the Coptic Bohairic *Life of Pachomius*, the Hebrew *Darkhei Teshuvah* by Meir of Rothenburg (thirteenth century), the *Isaiah Fragment* (depending on the Babylonian Talmud), the Hebrew *Gedulat Moshe*, and the *Elijah Fragment*.

5. McDannell and Lang, *Heaven.*
6. Latin edition by Umberto Moricca, *Gregorii Magni Dialogi* (Rome: Tipografia del Senato, 1924); English version in Edmund G. Gardner, *The Dialogues of Saint Gregory* (London: Philip L. Warner, 1911).
7. From Gardiner, *Visions,* pp. 48–49.
8. Gardiner, *Visions,* pp. 49–50.
9. See Gregory of Tours, *History of the Franks,* 2 vols., trans. O. M. Dalton (Oxford: Clarendon, 1927). The passage is reported in Latin in my *Psychanodia,* p. 60.
10. This problem has been strongly emphasized by Gignoux, "Apocalypses."
11. From the Venerable Bede, *The Ecclesiastical History of England* (London: Dent, 1916), pp. 132–37; modernized translation in Gardiner, *Visions,* pp. 57ff.
12. Ibid., pp. 241–50, modernized in Gardiner, *Visions,* pp. 57ff.
13. Ibid., modernized in Gardiner, *Visions,* p. 59.
14. See my *Psychanodia I,* p. 45.
15. Ibid., p. 63.
16. Translation in Gardiner, *Visions,* pp. 65ff.
17. See J. Marchand, trans., *L'autre monde au Moyen Age: Voyages et visions; La Navigation de Saint Brandan; Le Purgatoire de Saint Patrice; La Vision d'Albéric* (Paris: 1940); see my "Pons subtilis," in *Iter in silvis,* pp. 127ff.
18. See my *Expériences de l'extase,* pp. 161ff. Sources and bibliography are indicated in the notes on pp. 210–11.
19. See Etienne Renaud, "Le recit du mi râj: une version arabe de l'ascension du Prophète dans le Tafsîr de Tabarî": in Kappler, *Apocalypses et Voyages,* pp. 267–92. I have analyzed other variants in *Expériences de l'extase,* p. 161. The story in Bukhârî and Muslim is translated in Miguel Asín Palacíos, *La Escatalogia musulmana en la Divina Commedia,* 2d ed. (Madrid and Granada: Editorial Cristianidad, 1943), pp. 430–31.
20. See Angelo M. Piemontese, "Le voyage de Mahomet au paradis et en enfer: une version persane du mi' râj," in Kappler, *Apocalypses et voyages,* pp. 293–320.
21. Editions cited in my *Expériences de l'extase,* pp. 164 and 201. The Latin text was edited by E. Cerulli in 1949, and the French text

by P. Wunderli in 1968. Both Cerulli and Wunderli analyzed and commented on these versions in other works.

22. See Farid al-Din Attar, *Muslim Saints and Mystics: Episodes from the Tadhkirat al-Auliya,* trans. A. J. Arberry (London: Routledge & Kegan Paul, 1966), pp. 104ff.

23. In R. C. Zaehner, *Hindu and Muslim Mystics* (New York: Schocken, 1969), pp. 198ff.

24. See Reynold A. Nicholson, *Studies in Islamic Mysticism* (Cambridge: Cambridge University Press, 1980), pp. 122ff.

25. David Shea and Anthony Troyer, trans., *The Religion of the Sufis: The Dabistan of Mohsin Fani* (London: Octagon Press, 1979), pp. 44ff.

26. See my *Expériences de l'extase.*

27. The classical edition and study of the Latin versions of the vision belongs to Theodore Silverstein, *Visio Sancti Pauli: The History of the Apocalypse in Latin Together with Nine Texts* (London and Toronto: Christophers, 1935).

28. See O. Wahl, ed., *Apocalypsis Esdrae: Apocalypsis Sedrach; Visio Beati Esdrae* (Leiden: E. J. Brill, 1977).

29. See my "Pons subtilis," p. 130, n.6.

30. Text edited and translated by Francesco Cancellieri, *Visione del Monaco Cassinese Alberico* (Rome: F. Bourlie, 1814). An excellent anthology of medieval visions has been recently published in German translation by Peter Dinzelbacher, *Mittelalterliche Visions-literatur* (Darmstadt: Wissenschaftliche Buchgesellschaft, 1989).

31. See my *Psychanodia,* pp. 61–62.

32. See my *Psychanodia,* p. 61.

33. Translation of this text in Gardiner, *Visions,* pp. 149ff.

34. Ibid., pp. 197ff.

35. The texts and historical tradition connected with St. Patrick's Purgatory at Lough Derg are now collected in Michael Haren and Yolande de Pontfarcy, *The Medieval Pilgrimage to St. Patrick's Purgatory and the European Tradition* (Enniskillen: Clogher Histor-ical Society, 1988). Carol Zaleski graciously brought this book to my attention.

36. Translation in Gardiner, *Visions,* p. 142.

37. Ibid., pp. 219ff.

38. McDannell and Lang, *Heaven,* pp. 73ff.
39. Ibid., pp. 76–77.
40. C. Vellekoop, in R. E. V. Stuip and C. Vellekoop, eds., *Visioenen* (Utrecht: Hes Uitgevers, 1986).

Indexes

SUBJECT INDEX

Metamorphosis, 38, 39, 42, 43, 171, 228
Metempsychosis, 77
Metensomatosis, 10, 77, 150, 184, 193,
    195. *See also* Reincarnation, Rebirth,
    Transmigration
Miasma, 130–131
Mind, ix, xi, 85, 93, 96, 101, 102, 153,
    159, 203, 233, 234; mind stuff, 100;
    nous. *See* Intelligence, 175; space,
    xii, 3, 4, 21; universal system of, xiii
Mirror image, 20, 23, 25, 28, 138
Monk, 76, 77, 98, 102, 217, 218, 224
Monkey, 79, 102–103
Monster, 53, 57, 116, 162, 202
Moon, 72, 75, 84, 85, 91, 96, 126, 141,
    146–149, 151, 152, 162, 188, 196,
    200, 202, 206–208, 211, 213, 218
Mortification, 39, 78, 80, 117
Mother, 56, 74, 77, 90, 97, 115, 120
Mountains, 34, 53, 83, 84, 122, 179,
    219, 230; cosmic, 54, 102
Mouse, 43
Mouth, 40, 112, 203, 213, 225; opening
    of, 60, 63, 95
Mushroom, 87, 104–105
Music, 206, 213; of the spheres, 125.
    See also Song
Mysteries, 151, 157, 159, 167, 175, 194,
    204, 205, 206
Mystic, mysticism, xi, 7, 10, 18, 21, 26,
    29, 89, 144, 152, 153, 156, 165–169,
    172, 176, 178–185, 214, 221, 222
Myth, viii, xiv, 32, 45, 59, 146, 150,
    160, 173, 191, 195, 196, 202, 203,
    221, 223, 224, 225
Mythology, 51, 199

Name, 66–68, 70, 81, 149, 159, 168–
    173, 178, 179, 182, 184, 226
Nazism, 15
Near-death experiences, 1, 12, 29, 41,
    76, 107, 128, 132, 140, 144, 145, 149,

152, 215, 217, 224, 225, 228, 231–
234
Neck, 149
Necromancy, 7, 79, 121, 126
Neoplatonism, 10, 192, 193, 199, 200,
    208–210
Net, 66, 67
New Age, 29, 235
Night, 54, 62, 75, 109, 137, 184, 205,
    217, 218
Nirvana, 92, 100
Nose, 83, 111, 112
Numerology, 177, 181, 182
Nymph, 115

Ocean, sea, 125, 147, 150, 183, 213,
    214; cosmic, 54; oceanic feeling, 89–
    90, 153
Oedipus complex, 98
Offering, 84, 119
One, the, 153
Oracles, 61, 62, 125, 129, 134, 149;
    corpse oracle, 121. *See also* Divina-
    tion, Soul raising
Ordeal, 36–37, 66, 108
Out-of-body experiences, 1, 7, 12, 27ff,
    132, 152, 216, 231, 234

Pagan religion, 188, 189
Pain, 39, 127, 137
Painting. *See* Image
Palace, 85, 166, 169, 170, 214; *hekhaloth,*
    166–170, 172, 181–183
Paradise, vii, xiv, 92, 95, 106, 107, 110,
    111, 135, 139, 140, 160, 163, 170,
    181, 186, 214, 219, 225, 226, 230. *See
    also* Heaven
Paradox, 23
Particle, 1, 12, 22
Patriarchy, 117
Pattern, xii, 8, 133, 153, 156, 174, 175,
    180, 225, 230, 233, 234
Perception, ix, x, xi, xiii, 1, 4, 5, 12,